G000068261

James Worrall has produced a classic l
attention on the MENA region and th
Arab core, it is surprising that no subst
the main structures of the regional syste.. ... ... institutions – has been
available in one volume. This substantial study addresses that short-
coming, I believe, bringing together the conceptual tools for decipher-
ing MENA regionalization as well as the rich empirical data for
understanding it. Dr Worrall shows that these institutions matter and
do have a role to play in shaping the region's fortunes. I will certainly
want a copy of this book by my side.

Anoush Ehteshami, *Durham University, UK*

In this clear, accessible and yet exhaustive volume the author does an
excellent job of highlighting the genesis, evolution and principal features of the major international organizations in the Arab speaking
world. He does so in a sympathetic and yet probing manner advancing
the literature on regionalism and regionalization. This book is a must
read for all students of international relations of the Middle East and
will prove very useful for everyone interested in international relations
more widely.

Matteo Legrenzi, *Associate Professor, Ca' Foscari University of
Venice, President of the Italian Association for Middle
Eastern Studies (SeSaMO) 2013–2016*

Worrall has produced a rigorous and scholarly work that adds to our
knowledge and understanding of the three institutions in focus - the
Gulf Cooperation Council, the Arab League and the Arab Maghreb
Union. More than that, he offers a valuable comparative examination
of some of the major institutions at the heart of the contemporary
Arab world. A timely and welcome study.

Rory Miller, *Professor of Government, Georgetown
University, Qatar*

This important and timely volume will provide immense practical
value to scholars and policymakers as a tool to contextualize and
analyze rapidly-changing regional developments across the Middle
East and North Africa in the aftermath of the Arab Spring.

Kristian Coates Ulrichsen, *Fellow for the Middle East, Rice
University's Baker Institute, USA*

International Institutions of the Middle East

This volume is a key text for understanding the major regional international organizations of the Middle East. Analyzing the Arab League, the Gulf Cooperation Council, and the Arab Maghreb Union in a concise and accessible format, it explores their successes and failures across their full range of activities (economic, social, and political), while contextualizing the reasons why many consider that these organizations have stalled.

The book:

- assesses the reasons why international organizations in the Middle East are underdeveloped relative to those organizations of neighboring regions;
- explores their history, evolution, and structure, while considering the successes and failures of each international organization;
- analyzes the reasons for the specific difficulties faced by each organization through the context of intra-regional relations;
- develops a new framework for analyzing the forces that have shaped these bodies, and challenges the existing narrative that largely ignores the achievements and prospects of the organizations; and
- considers the likely impact of the Arab Spring upon the future development of these frequently overlooked regional international organizations.

This book will be of great interest to students and scholars of Middle East studies, international organizations and global governance, as well as diplomats and policymakers.

James Worrall is Associate Professor in International Relations and Middle East Studies, in the School of Politics and International Studies (POLIS) at the University of Leeds, UK.

Global Institutions

Edited by Thomas G. Weiss
The CUNY Graduate Center, New York, USA
and Rorden Wilkinson
University of Sussex, Brighton, UK

About the series

The "Global Institutions Series" provides cutting-edge books about many aspects of what we know as "global governance." It emerges from our shared frustrations with the state of available knowledge—electronic and print-wise, for research and teaching—in the area. The series is designed as a resource for those interested in exploring issues of international organization and global governance. And since the first volumes appeared in 2005, we have taken significant strides toward filling conceptual gaps.

The series consists of three related "streams" distinguished by their blue, red, and green covers. The blue volumes, comprising the majority of the books in the series, provide user-friendly and short (usually no more than 50,000 words) but authoritative guides to major global and regional organizations, as well as key issues in the global governance of security, the environment, human rights, poverty, and humanitarian action among others. The books with red covers are designed to present original research and serve as extended and more specialized treatments of issues pertinent for advancing understanding about global governance. And the volumes with green covers—the most recent departure in the series—are comprehensive and accessible accounts of the major theoretical approaches to global governance and international organization.

The books in each of the streams are written by experts in the field, ranging from the most senior and respected authors to first-rate scholars at the beginning of their careers. In combination, the three components of the series—blue, red, and green—serve as key resources for faculty, students, and practitioners alike. The works in the blue and green streams have value as core and complementary readings in courses on, among other things, international organization, global governance, international law, international relations, and international political economy; the red volumes allow further reflection and investigation in these and related areas.

The books in the series also provide a segue to the foundation volume that offers the most comprehensive textbook treatment available dealing with all the major issues, approaches, institutions, and actors in contemporary global governance—our edited work *International Organization and Global Governance* (2014)—a volume to which many of the authors in the series have contributed essays.

Understanding global governance—past, present, and future—is far from a finished journey. The books in this series nonetheless represent significant steps toward a better way of conceiving contemporary problems and issues as well as, hopefully, doing something to improve world order. We value the feedback from our readers and their role in helping shape the on-going development of the series.

A complete list of titles can be viewed online here: https://www.routledge.com/Global-Institutions/book-series/GI .

The most recent titles in the series are:

The Politics of Expertise in International Organizations (2017)
edited by Annabelle Littoz-Monnet

Obstacles of Peacebuilding (2017)
by Graciana del Castillo

UN Peacekeeping Doctrine in a New Era (2017)
edited by Cedric de Coning, Chiyuki Aoi, and John Karlsrud

Global Environmental Institutions (2nd edition, 2017)
by Elizabeth R. DeSombre

Global Governance and Transnationalizing Capitalist Hegemony (2017)
by Ian Taylor

Human Rights and Humanitarian Intervention (2016)
edited by Elizabeth M. Bruch

The UN Peacebuilding Architecture (2016)
edited by Cedric de Coning and Eli Stamnes

International Institutions of the Middle East

The GCC, Arab League, and Arab Maghreb Union

James Worrall

LONDON AND NEW YORK

First published 2017
by Routledge
2 Park Square, Milton Park, Abingdon, Oxon OX14 4RN

and by Routledge
711 Third Avenue, New York, NY 10017

Routledge is an imprint of the Taylor & Francis Group, an informa business

British Library Cataloguing in Publication Data
A catalogue record for this book is available from the British Library

Library of Congress Cataloging in Publication Data
A catalog record for this book has been requested

ISBN: 978-0-415-81426-3 (hbk)
ISBN: 978-0-415-81427-0 (pbk)
ISBN: 978-1-315-20292-1 (ebk)

Typeset in Times New Roman
by Taylor & Francis Books

Contents

List of illustrations

Abbreviations

ACC	Arab Cooperation Council
ADF	Arab Deterrent Force
AIPU	Arab Inter-parliamentary Union
AISU	Arab Iron and Steel Union
ALESCO	Arab League Educational, Scientific and Cultural Organization
AMF	Arab Monetary Fund
AMU	Arab Maghreb Union
APSC	Arab Peace and Security Council
ARADO	Arab Administrative Development Organization
ASEAN	Association of Southeast Asian Nations
ATFP	Arab Trade Financing Program
AU	African Union
BADEA	Arab Bank for Economic Development in Africa
BCMA	*Banque de cooperation du Maghreb arabe*
COMELEC	*Comité Maghrébin de l'Electricité*
ECSC	European Coal and Steel Community
EEC	European Economic Community
ESC	Economic and Social Council (Arab League)
EU	European Union
FDI	foreign direct investment
GAFTA	Greater Arab Free Trade Area (Arab League)
GCC	Gulf Cooperation Council
GCCCAC	GCC Commercial Arbitration Center
GCCIA	Gulf Cooperation Council Interconnectivity Authority
GDP	gross domestic product
GIC	Gulf Investment Corporation
GOIC	Gulf Organization for Industrial Consulting
GSO	GCC Standardization Organization
IATIN	Intra-Arab Trade Information Network

IMC	Inter-Maghreb Commission
IMF	International Monetary Fund
IO	international organization
IR	international relations
LAS	League of Arab States
MAFTA	Mediterranean Arab Free Trade Area
MC	Ministerial Council (GCC)
NGO	nongovernmental organization
OAPEC	Organization of Arab Petroleum Exporting Countries
OAS	Organization of American States
OAU	Organization of African Unity
OCA	optimal currency area
OIC	Organisation of Islamic Cooperation
PLO	Palestine Liberation Organization
PS	Peninsula Shield (GCC)
SC	Supreme Council (GCC)
UAE	United Arab Emirates
UAR	United Arab Republic
UEA	Unified Economic Agreement (GCC)
UN	United Nations
UNDP	United Nations Development Programme
UNESCO	United Nations Educational, Scientific and Cultural Organization
WTO	World Trade Organization

Maps

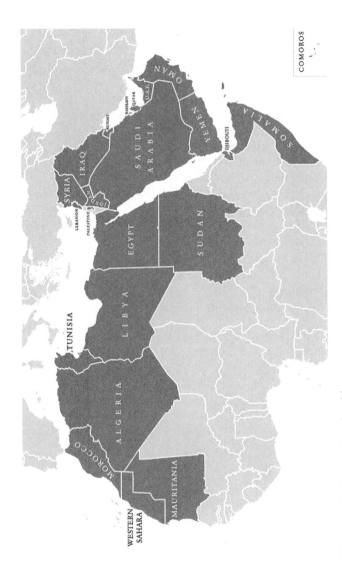

Map 1 Arab League Membership
Source: http://www.istockphoto.com/gb/vector/arab-world-political-map-gm589558350-101282575

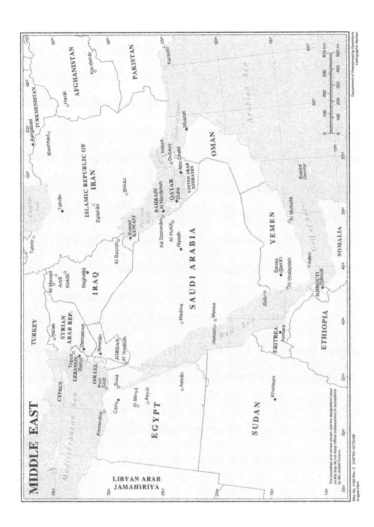

Map 2 The Middle East
Source: www.un.org/Depts/Cartographic/map/profile/mideastr.pdf

Acknowledgements

As ever, any major writing and research project demands the assistance, insight, support, and tolerance of a great many people. I would therefore like to thank Tom Weiss and Rorden Wilkinson, the series editors, who offered some useful advice on my initial proposal, including the widening to examine explicitly the role of the Arab League and the Gulf Cooperation Council during the Arab Spring. Thanks are also due to my editor Nicola Parkin, who supported the volume from the outset, and Lydia de Cruz, also at Routledge, for her encouragement, and for their tolerance and patience with the delays in me being able to finish this book.

Given the obscurity of much of the writing on the League and Arab Maghreb Union in particular, tracking down long-out-of-print volumes and single chapters hidden away in edited volumes has been a big challenge and thanks are due to the librarians at the British Library, the School of Oriental and African Studies Library, and the Brotherton Library at the University of Leeds. Many thanks to my friends and colleagues who have put up with me going on about the international organizations of the Middle East, and who have helped me to sharpen my thinking on a range of issues connected to these bodies and the regional environment in which they function. Special thanks also to my friend Dr Alam Saleh for his assistance with elements of translation from Arabic and for tracking down key bits of data when I was despairing of ever finding accurate information!

Thanks are due, as ever, to my family for their support roles in making any of this possible. Finally, I would like to dedicate this book to the memory of my Grandmother, who sadly did not see this volume published but whose curiosity about the world was inspirational, and whose support, love and encouragement I will always cherish.

Prologue

It was an overcast but warm spring morning in Beirut and the traffic was gridlocked in the mid-morning rush. Crawling along in a taxi heading towards the southern suburbs, hoping I might get to Sidon in time for lunch, a modernist building loomed alone to the right just before the main road plunged into an underpass. It appeared to be the kind of plate glass with polished concrete and steel of the offices of the headquarters of any international organization. As we slowly crept forward in the traffic, the front of the building gradually came into view. It looked like it was modeled on the Grand Arch of La Défense in Paris, albeit about a quarter of the size. It mimicked the structure uncannily, being essentially a concrete frame; the only difference was the vast expanse of plate glass that covered the central aperture of the building. I asked the driver if he knew what it was. He said it was just some Arab League offices and joked that the building was as hollow as the League itself. This simple exchange, many years ago now, sparked my interest—eventually resulting in this volume.

Introduction

The rapid transformation of popular protests in Tunisia in 2011 into the almost region-wide phenomenon of the Arab Spring has brought a great deal of attention to the Middle East in recent years. This renewed interest in the region as a whole, rather than as a series of specific issues such as the Israel–Palestine peace process or the Iraq war, has come from across the spectrum of those interested in international affairs—policymakers, think tanks, the news media, and even the wider community of international relations (IR) scholars, who had up until this point largely left the region to the area studies experts. This has at times led to rather shallow and circular debates which have often generated more heat than light. It is now painfully clear that the Arab uprisings and their consequences, which have dominated the global agenda since 2011, will take decades to play out, leaving the region negotiating the creation of a series of new or modified political orders at every level, and analysts scrambling to unravel the impact of the various protests, revolutions, and civil wars.

Amidst the upheavals facing the region in those early months of 2011, the role taken in the series of unfolding uprisings across the Middle East—from Yemen, to Syria, and to Libya—by the region's international organizations, principally the Arab League and the Gulf Cooperation Council (GCC), initially attracted a great deal of attention. The GCC's brokering of a deal to enable the Yemeni President Ali Abdullah Saleh to step down, and the deployment of Saudi and United Arab Emirates troops to Bahrain in March 2011 to support the ruling family under the auspices of the GCC's Peninsula Shield Force were high-profile moves of a sort rarely undertaken by the organization. Meanwhile, the Arab League suspended Syria's membership and then allowed the main opposition movement, the Syrian National Council, to take up the regime's seat. It was also clear that United Nations (UN) resolution 1973 authorizing the creation of a no-fly zone and offering a mandate for the protection of civilians in Libya from Col. Ghadaffi's regime would likely have been vetoed by Russia and China at the UN Security Council were it not for the calls from the GCC and the Arab League, and the unanimous support expressed for the measures in their councils. This flurry of activity and newly central role for the region's international organizations was soon to die down, but it reminded the world of the existence of these bodies and the potential for cooperation and the development of deeper institutional ties in the region. Indeed, in those early days of democratic revolution the prospects for revived institutions being able to create the conditions for newly democratic states to pool sovereignty in the greater good seemed almost tangible;[1] however, the initial hopes of the Arab Spring quickly became tarnished and were then largely forgotten as the forces of chaos asserted themselves, and with this and a rapid decline in the organizations' dynamism in the face of regional turmoil, principally in Syria, interest in the Middle East's international organizations and their potential promptly receded.

Despite this inevitable development, and a more general lack of scholarly interest in these organizations, their brief moment in the spotlight during the Arab Spring raises important questions about the region and its institutions. This is especially the case given the explosion in the number of international organizations around the world over the past few decades. Given this context, it is a perennial puzzle that the Middle East has lagged behind in both the number and the depth of its international institutions. Since the Arab World is one of the most homogeneous in terms of its language, religion, and culture one would naturally expect its international organizations to be well developed, especially when compared with neighboring regions, such as Europe and even Africa, yet clearly the Middle East lags far behind in both of these measures.

The reasons why the Middle East is seen to be an exception which is almost uniquely hostile to integration and the development of well-functioning mechanisms for cooperation under the auspices of its international organizations have long been explored in one form or another. While the present volume engages with this ongoing question it also takes the analysis further on a number of fronts, for while there is no denying that the Middle East's institutions are underdeveloped relative to those of neighboring regions, the frequent characterization of the Arab world's international organizations as being "frozen," "stalled" or even "dead letters"[2] is rather unfortunate because it closes down opportunities for analysis, forcing scholars into the funnel of analyzing why these organizations have "failed" rather than asking other questions that might open up scope for fresh examination. In this sense the volume seeks to qualify these existing approaches, both by highlighting alternative questions when examining the "success" or "failure" of the region's institutions and by exploring the potential that these bodies have for the future.

Any examination of the region's institutions brings with it the perennial problem of deciding where dividing lines lie between the specific organizations and the wider regional order. This is a difficult issue to tackle because of the interdependent nature of the two realities. This book, though, focuses more on the specifics of the organizations, moving regional politics and the "Arab order" into the background where they are used to explain developments surrounding the organizations themselves. In this sense then, while the constraints of regional politics are ever present, this is not a book about the Arab regional order, which then examines the region's international organizations as a mere expression of the vagaries of wider Arab politics. Instead, while acknowledging that the Middle East has been hostile territory for the establishment and growth of regional international organizations, the book takes a broad approach to understanding why this has been the case but also examines what has been achieved in spite of the obstacles facing the creation and development of international institutions in the Middle East.

The volume's core aim, then, is to introduce and explore the three key international organizations of the region, focusing on three key issue areas that form the bodies' main areas of operation—namely, economic integration, security concerns, and socio-cultural activities. An examination of the role of the region's international organizations through their successes and failures in these key issue areas allows for a fuller picture of their activities to be built up, comparisons to be made and analysis to be conducted.

A key question when exploring regional international organizations within the Middle East comes in terms of the choice of focus.[3] Here the book has compromised between depth and comprehensiveness. In order to create space for analysis only three organizations are chosen—they were chosen based on three criteria: geographic concentration, importance, and scope. The volume therefore excludes bodies such as the Organization of Arab Petroleum Exporting Countries (OAPEC), the Arab Cooperation Council (ACC),[4] and even the Organisation of Islamic Cooperation (OIC), as being respectively: too narrowly focused on a single issue area; essentially defunct after initially having been seen as a bloc between the two other sub-regional organizations examined here; and finally, despite being largely geographically concentrated in the Middle East the OIC has 57 member states and cannot therefore fully be described as being a Middle Eastern international organization.

The three organizations dealt with in this book are chosen for their adherence to these criteria, comprising as they do bodies that deal with a broad range of issues, are focused on either the entire Middle East or sub-regions thereof, and are active and significant in the region's politics. At this juncture it should be pointed out that there are, of course, no truly Middle East-wide institutions. All of the organizations discussed in this volume are restricted to the Arab States of the Middle East and thus exclude Iran, Israel, and Turkey. Indeed, many of these bodies were explicitly created, or came to be defined by their opposition to one or more of these three Middle Eastern neighbors. In addition, given the dominance of the Arab League and the Gulf Cooperation Council, the Arab Maghreb Union (AMU), being a younger, more limited and less active organization receives rather less attention in this book than the other two bodies. It is included here because of its future potential and as an aid to comparison and analysis.

The book's scope is thus wide enough to allow for comparison between the three different regional and sub-regional bodies in the Middle East, while also allowing sufficient space to explore the particular history, structure, potential, and areas of activity of each organization. In this way, the volume is designed to act as a general introduction to both the individual organizations themselves and the nature of Middle Eastern regionalism, while also offering scope for deeper comparison and analysis of the problems, prospects, and achievements of each organization, within both the context of regional politics and a theoretical framework that draws from area studies and international relations, thus providing new perspectives on Middle Eastern regionalism and the three international organizations themselves.

In order to engage with these issues and the trajectories of the three separate international organizations, the book is organized into five *parts* and 11 *chapters*. Part one contains Chapter 1, which provides context and analytical tools with which to better explore and engage with our three supranational bodies.

Part two focuses on the Arab League, as being the region's oldest and only universal body it is important to engage with its history and its achievements and failures. Chapter 2 begins this process by exploring the League's structures and evolution. Since the Arab League was expected to play a role in issues of peace and security, and is recognized under Chapter VIII of the UN Charter, Chapter 3 explores its role in conflict resolution and peacekeeping. Chapter 4 meanwhile explores the League's role in economic, social, and political cooperation, before part two is brought to a close in Chapter 5 with an analysis, using tools from Chapter 1, of the problems and prospects facing the Arab League.

Part three focuses on the Gulf Cooperation Council and follows a similar pattern. Thus Chapter 6 explores the GCC's structure and evolution, Chapter 7 its role in regional disputes, Chapter 8 its social and economic activities, which are the most advanced in the Arab world, before Chapter 9 again uses the tools of analysis to examine the GCC's prospects and the problems it faces.

Part four, meanwhile, comprises Chapter 10, which is a single-chapter examination of our third international organization of the region, the Arab Maghreb Union.

Part five is made up of Chapter 11, which explores the role of the Arab League and GCC in the Arab Spring, using this as an analytical springboard for the book's general Conclusion, which engages once more with the issues raised in this Introduction.

We begin, in the next chapter, by both establishing the analytical framework to be used in this volume and exploring the regional and international context in which the international institutions of the region operate.

Notes

1 Khalid Sekkat, "Inter-State Tensions and Regional Integration: Could the Arab Spring Initiate a Virtuous Circle?" *Contemporary Arab Affairs* 7, no. 3 (2014): 363–379. The International Institute for Democracy and Electoral Assistance, the United Nations University and the United Nations Economic Commission for Africa (UNECA) even held a conference in Brussels on 22–23 November 2012 on the theme of "The Role of Regional Organizations after the Arab Spring." www.idea.int/wana/the-role-of-regional-orga nizations-after-the-arab-spring.cfm.
2 Simon Murden, "The Secondary Institutions of the Middle Eastern Regional Interstate Society," in *International Society and the Middle East*, ed. Barry Buzan and Ana Gonzalez-Pelaez (Basingstoke: Palgrave, 2009), 117.
3 The book avoids engaging in debate on where the borders of the Middle East may lie.
4 Curtis R. Ryan, "Jordan and the Rise and Fall of the Arab Cooperation Council," *Middle East Journal* 52, no. 3 (1998): 386–401.

1 Context and framework

- **Context**
- **Themes**
- **Concepts**
- **Framework**
- **Conclusion**

Understanding the state system, politics, and international relations of the region is critical in appreciating the difficulties faced by the regional institutions of the Middle East. There have been a number of attempts to explain the perceived "failure" of the region's institutional mechanisms in enabling meaningful cooperation across a broad range of issue areas from trade and industry to war and peace, with these explanations often drawing upon the wider international relations literature, especially theories of international cooperation and conflict. In addition, there have been attempts to examine the obstacles facing these institutional mechanisms, which focus much more on the specific dynamics of Arab regional politics, drawing on the importance of ideological differences, clashes of personality, and the specific dynamics of the types of authoritarian regimes in question.

Perhaps the greatest issue here is the difficulty of effectively bringing together regional politics and area studies approaches to the region, with their nuanced historical understanding, and broader international relations approaches which attempt to explain how international organizations (IOs) generally form and how they subsequently develop over time. These theories by their very nature have to omit detailed and specific dynamics and were frequently designed to explore the specific nature of organizations that have followed a particular path driven by liberal democratic Western states.

This chapter begins by outlining the broad *context* within which the region's IOs were created and developed. This takes the form of a brief chronological survey of key periods in the shaping of a Middle Eastern order over the course of the twentieth century, which highlights key events and themes and provides the reader with the relevant background material against which the specific IOs were operating. The second part of the chapter consists of an exploration of the various tools that have been applied to the region's IOs to explain the difficulties the region has faced in creating genuinely cooperative and empowered shared institutions. It assesses the utility of these various *concepts* before going on to outline, in the final part of this chapter, its own hybrid *framework* for analysis, which subsequently guides discussion in later chapters.

Thus we begin by providing the necessary context and background for what follows with a brief examination of the emergence of the state system in the modern Middle East, alongside an exploration of key tensions and dynamics that have had an impact upon the process of institutionalization across the Arab world and its two key sub-regions. Subsequent chapters draw upon this context in their analysis to explore the specific ways in which regional events and dynamics accelerate or derail processes of institutionalization.

Context

Any understanding of the development of the international institutions of the Middle East must be grounded in an awareness of the nature of the Arab States system and the authoritarian structures of rule, which have predominated across the region since independence. These more structural factors must also be tempered by an understanding of the normative, popular, and intellectual discourses amongst the populations of Middle Eastern states for some kind of Arab unity. Here, using Michael Barnett's division of the region's recent history as a rough chronological structuring tool,[1] key events and themes are highlighted within each time period before some more general observations are made, both about changes to the regional order in general, and to the structure, ideology, and preoccupations of individual states and peoples, and what this means for IOs in the region.

The embryonic years, 1917–46

Beginning in the late nineteenth century as the ideas of nationalism and socialism spread to the Middle East, Arab consciousness began to grow as the Ottoman Empire gradually ceded control and European colonialism began to penetrate the region in a more comprehensive manner.[2] The combination of changing power dynamics in the region, and increasing exposure to Western ideas and technologies gradually brought about a revolution in Arab thought which spread rapidly from the intellectual classes into the wider popular consciousness often through cultural channels.[3] With the final dissolution of the Ottoman Empire upon the foundation of the Republic of Turkey in 1923 and with the promises made to the Arabs during the war in order to secure their support in the campaign against the Turks only being partially fulfilled, space was created for discussion around the future forms of Arab unity that might be achieved.[4] During this crucial period key themes emerged, which were to shape regional politics over the coming decades. The first of these, of course, was the Balfour Declaration of 1917 promising a "national homeland for the Jewish people in Palestine."[5] While the declaration was deliberately not promising a "Jewish state" the growing numbers of Jewish immigrants into the British-mandated territory of Palestine was to become a major issue during the 1930s, which gave the Arabs a common cause.[6] British and French control of League of Nations mandated territories, while clearly not the kind of colonialism practiced elsewhere, also contributed to the creation of a common enemy, which has traditionally been a necessary requirement of nationalism and forms the second major theme.[7] Even during the height of this colonial époque mandated territories were receiving their independence, albeit with strong residual colonial influence and often a continuing military presence.[8] Thus over this period Arab States, many of which were created from scratch through the mandate system, began to form links and to promote various schemes for greater Arab unity.[9] It is during this period that the map of the Middle East as it is today was formed, with the Al-Saud finally coalescing their territorial gains and formally establishing Saudi Arabia in 1932,[10] Iraq receiving its independence from Britain in the same year,[11] followed by the French retreat from Lebanon in 1943, Syria in 1946,[12] and Britain's formal handover of power in Jordan in the same year. These states, plus Egypt, which had received its nominal independence in 1922,[13] were to form the core of the Arab world and consistently tried to lead the growing Arab Nationalist movement and promote schemes for Arab unity.[14]

Consolidation, 1946–55

During the previous period the Middle East had been defined by the independence of many of its core states. This new period saw further decolonization with Libya gaining full independence in 1953 from French and British oversight, after having been an Italian colony before the war. More significant changes emerged as Arab Nationalism grew further in popularity and began to dominate domestic politics in the newly independent states of the region. One must also bear in mind that most of the countries in the region were monarchies during this period, the only exceptions being Syria and Lebanon, and these monarchies had close relationships with Britain and relied upon London for political, economic, and military assistance. This of course often brought the regimes into conflict with their Arab Nationalist populations who, as a core tenet of Arab Nationalism, were stridently anti-colonial and frequently explicitly anti-Western.[15] As the various different creeds of Arab Nationalism consolidated their influence they increasingly aligned themselves with stridently socialist rhetoric to go alongside their anti-Western ideology.[16]

During this period, and despite the clear similarities between the various strains of Arab Nationalism, dividing lines began to emerge between the expressly communist groupings and those that advocated other forms of Arab Nationalism, including Ba'athism.[17] These differences were later to entwine with other regional tensions and undermine moves towards Arab Unity. Arab Nationalism had by now gained deep roots in societies across the region with cells of the various strands of Arab Nationalism operating even at village level. These roots soon enabled the various movements to penetrate the structures of the state, including the security forces.[18] This would lead to a series of *coups d'état* across the region during the course of the 1950s and 1960s.[19] The most important of these coups came in 1952 with the colonels' plot in Egypt, which removed King Farouk, eventually replacing him with Col. Gamal Abdul Nasser.[20] As the region's largest state by population, and the most important in terms of its cultural influence, being the major Arab center for publishing and cinema, this meant that core soft power tools were now controlled by Arab Nationalists. Nasser set about spreading his beliefs and fomenting unrest elsewhere. Before that, though, he had to consolidate his rule and find a way of removing the British from their base in the Suez Canal Zone. This he achieved in 1954 after a subversive campaign and a skillful treaty renegotiation.[21]

The other crucial development during this period was of course Britain's withdrawal from its Palestine mandate, and the declaration in 1948 of the State of Israel after a UN partition plan for Palestine was rejected by the Arab States. The Arab–Israeli War which ensued led to the surprising defeat of the combined might of the Egyptian, Syrian, Jordanian, Iraqi, and Lebanese Armies, and was a humiliation for the Arabs who were faced with the exodus of hundreds of thousands of Palestinian refugees.[22] The episode became known as *an-nakhba*, or the catastrophe, and was to drive regional politics, Arab Nationalism, and the search for unity over the coming decades.

The peak of Arab Nationalism, 1956–66

With Arab Nationalism now consolidated amongst the populations of the core states of the Middle East, even the Saudi monarchy was aware of the power of the movement, and the idea of Arab unity, amongst large elements of its population. The Algerian war of independence against the French, which had been running since 1946, became especially violent during this period, attracting widespread Arab support that would eventually lead to Algeria's independence in 1962.[23] This was preceded by Tunisian, Moroccan, and Sudanese independence in 1956, and British protection over Kuwait ending in 1961. These years were pivotal for Arab Nationalism's power in the region and in terms of the political attempts at Arab unity, which were prosecuted through a number of different schemes. The period also saw the deposition of more of the region's monarchies in North Yemen in 1962 and Iraq in 1958, along with Arab Nationalists taking over in Syria.

Perhaps the most obvious development in this era was the Suez Crisis of 1956 in which Nasser nationalized the Suez Canal, which was swiftly followed by Britain and France intervening militarily in Egypt to protect the canal, in collusion with the Israelis who offered a pretext when they invaded the Sinai Peninsula.[24] The subsequent global condemnation, and withholding of US monetary and diplomatic support, led to the intervention failing politically rather than militarily. This handed a colossal propaganda victory to Nasser whose popularity across the region soared to unprecedented levels. The collusion between the colonial powers and the Israelis only confirmed Arab Nationalist conspiracy theories and was in hindsight the movement's apogee.[25]

What the series of coups, wars, and rhetoric concealed, though, were two other important themes that came to the fore during these years. The first of these was that Nasser's prominence drew a backlash from other Arab leaders as he attempted to meddle in their affairs. Other states and leaders wanted to lead the Arabs and other forms of Arab Nationalism other than Nasserism were further promoted, thus widening divisions in the movement, and the meddling came to be seen as a security threat, leading to Arab politics becoming increasingly securitized at elite level. The second major change was economic. The region saw a rapidly emerging split develop between those states that produced oil in large quantities and those that did not have the same oil resources.[26]

The other economic change was principally led by the new Arab Nationalist regimes whose socialist tendencies led them into large-scale nationalizations, of which the Suez Canal is the prime example. These nationalizations in Egypt led to Greek, Italian, and Armenian business owners fleeing the country and many businesses floundering under their new state owners. The implementation of large-scale industrialization (including the Aswan High Dam and Helwan City), often chaotic land reform, and import substitution programs caused significant economic and environmental damage without providing the benefits so loudly trumpeted by the regimes.[27] Despite these failures, these new regimes were often quite successful in providing minimum safety nets and basic health care, and the period also saw rapid declines in illiteracy and infant mortality levels; however, these programs were expensive and the tax base was eroded as many business owners left to find opportunities elsewhere. Growing populations also led to a constant need for the state to create new jobs, and many Egyptians, Syrians, and Iraqis left to find work in Saudi Arabia and Kuwait.

The period also saw a number of attempts to drive forward real forms of Arab unity, rather than through the creation of international organizations.[28] Thus in 1958 Egypt and Syria formed the United Arab Republic (UAR), a political union formed as a first step towards a larger pan-Arab State.[29] This new state was enfolded within a slightly wider grouping called the United Arab States in which the UAR was in a loose confederation with North Yemen.[30] At almost exactly the same time a rival form of Arab State, the so-called Arab Federation, known also as the Arab Union, was drawn up. This was to be a way of bringing together the two Hashemite Kingdoms in the Middle East— Iraq and Jordan. The new state lasted only six months, being dissolved when the Iraqi branch of the family was deposed in July 1958.[31] Although there was much rhetoric at the time, no other states seriously considered joining with either of these two concrete experiments in Arab unity. In fact the failure of these experiments was in the long run to weaken the project of Arab unity. Nasser's power was such that the UAR quickly became very one-sided and Syrian politicians were sidelined. The Union soon began to look more like Egyptian colonialism than a genuine Arab State, which led to formal Syrian withdrawal in 1963 after an earlier coup in 1961, in turn followed by a Ba'athist coup in 1963 leading Syria further away from Nasserism.[32] The civil war that engulfed North Yemen after its spiritual-temporal leader Imam al-Badr was overthrown by Arab Nationalists in 1962, drew Egypt into the conflict to support the new government, leading to around 70,000 Egyptian troops being deployed and Egyptian planes dropping poison gas on Arab villages, which supported the Yemeni royalists, who were in turn supported by the Saudis.[33] This war, which has been described as Egypt's Vietnam, was critical in demonstrating to monarchical leaders in particular that Nasser was not to be trusted.[34] Thus reinforcing a fault line that ran through the Arab world between the remaining monarchical regimes and the Arab Nationalist republican regimes who were already becoming fragmented amongst themselves, this "Arab Cold War," as it became known, was to be a major stumbling block to further experiments at Arab unity in the form of the creation of federative, confederative and united state structures, and would leave IOs as the only possible way of creating cooperation, which given the increasingly tense relations between Arab States was already extremely difficult.

The retreat to the state, 1967–90

With the seeds of decline already sown during the peak of the Arab Nationalist era it was inevitable that the successes of the 1950s could not be sustained. The decline of Arab Nationalism was not abrupt; indeed, as we shall see, it still retains a degree of emotional value and continues to play a role in Arab politics to this day. However, the possibility of Arab Nationalism achieving its final form in a formally constituted Arab State of whatever form had essentially disappeared even by the end of the 1960s.[35] Parallel to the rhetorical focus on Arab Nationalism, many states also, through their modernization processes, had been building up state nationalism, while the increasing focus on security and the constant threat of coup, counter-coup, and military intervention in politics more generally made many regimes in the region increasingly authoritarian and concerned with issues of both internal and external security.[36] Alongside this, rhetoric about the West and the Israelis continued to serve an important purpose. Indeed, in some cases rhetoric was the starting point. Nasser had, from the 1950s, been using his influence in North Yemen to undermine the British position in South Arabia, and by the 1960s was arming and training rebel groups fighting an insurgency against the British with the aim of driving Britain from its presence in the Gulf States. In 1967, when Britain rapidly abandoned its position in Aden, it appeared to be another victory for the Arab Nationalists against colonialism. What followed, however, was a brief but bloody civil war between Marxist and Nasserite rebel forces in which the Nasserists were soundly beaten.[37]

This defeat for Nasser was largely overshadowed by a much larger Egyptian defeat in the June 1967 War. After years of cross-border raids into Israel by Arab guerrilla forces backed by various Arab States, Israel was given the pretext for war when Nasser closed the Straits of Tiran to Israeli shipping, thus crossing a stated Israeli red line.[38] The ensuing conflict, which also involved Syria and, more reluctantly, Jordan, saw another catastrophic Arab defeat. Not only could the Arab forces only manage to put up a fight for six days but significant areas of Arab land were captured and occupied by the Israelis. Egypt lost its Sinai Peninsula, Syria the Golan Heights, and the Palestinians lost the Egyptian-administered Gaza Strip and the Jordanian-administered West Bank including East Jerusalem and the Haram al-Sharif, the third holiest site in Islam.[39] The high-flying rhetoric about the Arabs liberating the lands of their brothers in Palestine proved to be entirely hollow. Aside from a spirited but ultimately doomed attempt to defend East Jerusalem by the Jordanians, the Arab forces were routed and the Egyptian Air Force was destroyed on the ground.

Many have seen the defeat of 1967 as the death knell of Arab Nationalism as a force in the region,[40] yet in reality the ideas still carried much weight and still shaped the discourse and perceptions of the region's people and politicians. The underlying reality was now that experiments in formal Arab unity had clearly failed, meaning that further attempts were no longer engaged in it. Instead, Arab Nationalism focused even more on Israel, and in Khartoum at an Arab League Summit meeting the famous "three nos" were issued—*no* peace with Israel, *no* recognition of Israel, *no* negotiations with Israel. The summit also obliged the oil-rich Gulf States to help the front-line states rebuild. This rhetoric, though, overshadowed the reality that without recognizing and respecting each other's sovereignty there was no chance of defeating Israel—this was essentially a formal abandonment of the idea of creating one (or more) Arab States and was thus a significant milestone for Arab Nationalism. Nasser's death on 28 September 1970 was perhaps a clearer marker, meaning the end of Nasserism as a regional force and spurring competition for the leadership of the Arab world, which was still an attractive prize for many leaders.[41]

The region saw further turmoil with the deposition of King Idris in Libya by Col. Muammar Ghadaffi in 1969, and in 1970 during "Black September" when Palestinian forces in Jordan controlled by the Palestine Liberation Organization (PLO) and supported by the Ba'athist government in Syria, which had come to power in a 1966 coup, attempted to topple King Hussein and take over the state. King Hussein survived and held on to power but the attempt further reinforced the split in the region between monarchical and republican regimes.[42] It was also a clear example of Palestinian frustration with the inability of the Arab States to bring about any improvement in their situation by defeating Israel, leading them to exercise their own agency in the struggle rather than relying on others.[43]

Nasser's successor Anwar Sadat faced competition for leadership of the Arab world from Ghadaffi and the new Syrian President Hafiz al-Asad, who came to power in a "correctionist" coup within the Syrian Ba'ath in November 1970. Meanwhile, Sadat led moves back in the direction of the Western powers and away from the communist states, expelling Soviet military advisors and Air Force personnel on 18 July 1972. He was also determined to regain Egyptian land lost in 1967 and to demonstrate that the Israelis were not invincible. The October 1973 Arab–Israeli War, which occurred after a careful Egyptian build-up, managed to restore an element of Arab pride, while still not delivering a real victory for the Arab forces.[44] The deployment of the much-touted Arab oil weapon against states supporting Israel worked much better than it had in 1967, and while the rapid hike in oil prices had considerable effects, in reality it had little impact on policy towards Israel, instead promoting energy efficiency drives and the diversification of oil supplies.[45] On the economic front too Sadat realized that socialism was not helping the Egyptian economy to perform well and launched a series of political and economic reforms, promoting greater political freedom and a less interventionist and more pro-market set of economic policies, which became known as *Infitah*, or opening up. In effect, Egypt ended up with a hybrid economy, which was unable to embrace the free market effectively while still retaining many elements of Nasser's socialist command-style economy.[46]

Sadat's other significant move came as Egypt signed a series of disengagement agreements with Israel over Sinai in 1974 and 1975, and then made his momentous visit to Jerusalem in 1977, which was to lead to the US-brokered and financed Camp David Accords of September 1978 and the March 1979 Egypt–Israel Peace Treaty.[47] Thus, in less than a decade from taking office Sadat had essentially abandoned three core elements of Arab Nationalism—socialism, anti-Westernism, and absolute hostility to Israel. The signing of the peace treaty between Israel and Egypt was clearly more of a cold peace, but it led to the most populous and influential Arab State being suspended from the Arab League, a brief border war with Ghadaffi's Libya, the seat of the Arab League being moved to Tunis, and a further widening in the vacuum of Arab leadership.

In 1979 Saddam Hussein cemented his grip on power in Iraq and in the wake of the Iranian Revolution, which had overthrown the Shah, he invaded Iran in a fabricated dispute over the *Shatt al-Arab* waterway and a claim to protect Arab populations inside Iran. The Iran–Iraq War, which was to define the 1980s in the region, offered a chance for the Arabs to unite in the face of their traditional Persian enemy, but in reality, aside from rhetorical and some financial support, the Arab States evinced little real commitment to the fight and continued to consolidate their own state structures and nationalisms.[48] The insecurity in the Gulf as a result of the conflict and the so-called "Tanker War" was a major spur for the Gulf States to come together to form the Gulf Cooperation Council in what was essentially an admission that the Arab League was ineffective and any dream of an Arab State was certainly over. This development also cemented further inter-Arab division—that between monarchies and republics and, perhaps more importantly, between rich and poor in the region.

A further signal that the Arab Nationalism of the mid-twentieth century was dead came in 1989 when Egypt was readmitted as a member of the Arab League and its headquarters returned to Cairo.[49] This was effectively a tacit, Arab-wide recognition that Israel was not going anywhere and that all Arab efforts to extinguish the state and ensure the return of Palestinians to the whole of the land of mandate Palestine had failed.

The new Arab system? 1990–

By the end of the 1980s it was abundantly clear to most observers that Arab Nationalism had failed. The 1990s only emphasized that viewpoint's validity, and yet the idea of pan-Arab solidarity remained strong despite the rise of one-state nationalism across the region.[50] This meant that Arab Nationalist rhetoric remained strong and there was still clear public and, at times, political desire for greater cooperation and integration between the Arab States. The older forms of Arab Nationalism were still not dead however; explicitly Arab Nationalist regimes still retained power in Iraq and Syria, and Arab Nationalism still formed a substantial part of the ideological framework that legitimized authoritarian rule in many other states, including Yemen, Algeria, and Egypt.[51]

Saddam Hussein's invasion of Kuwait in 1990 was a further serious blow to sympathy for the political goals of the old forms of Arab Nationalism. With Iraq exhausted after the Iran–Iraq War and the Gulf Arabs unwilling to extend further lines of credit or grants, Saddam reactivated Iraq's claim to Kuwait and invaded.[52] This blatant erasure of Kuwaiti sovereignty brought a form of Arab unity as all Arab States bar the newly united Yemen and the PLO joined together to condemn the invasion, with the Saudis, Bahrainis, Qataris, Moroccans, Omanis, the United Arab Emirates, the Egyptians, and the Syrians all contributing forces to Operations Desert Shield/Storm. Saddam's invasion, which he attempted to cloak in Arab Nationalist rhetoric, therefore saw republican and monarchical regimes coming together (along with the West) to defeat him.[53] For Kuwait, which had long been a vocal supporter and financial contributor to Arab Nationalist causes, the episode further demonstrated the importance of having external relationships with the United States and Britain, as well as strong sub-regional ties with its fellow Gulf States.

The way in which many Arab States united under US auspices to remove Saddam from Kuwait on the surface looked like the ultimate humiliation of Arab Nationalism. Inviting Western powers in to defend the Gulf States from a fellow Arab State was an indictment of the failures of the Arab unity project and to a large extent of the Arab League and the GCC, which could not deal effectively alone with the threat of Saddam. On the other hand, though, the way in which the Arab countries had largely united to defend a fellow Arab State did show that the seeds of potential common interests (even if only at the base level of state survival) did exist and offered the opportunity to abandon the most high-flying dreams of Arab unity and replace them with more prosaic and low-key initiatives through IOs and other initiatives. The first clue of the potential for a new approach came in March 1991 with the Damascus Declaration in which the GCC states agreed to mutual security cooperation with the Egyptians and the Syrians, which was designed to protect the Gulf from future threats from Saddam, meaning that the West would not have to be called upon again. In reality the mutual mistrust and fear of the Gulf States of having Egyptian and Syrian troops on their soil meant that the Declaration was never implemented.[54]

The 1990s also saw further changes in the relationship with Israel. With the signing of the Oslo Accords in 1993 and the clear prospect of a two-state solution on the cards, the transformation of the conflict and the PLO's recognition of Israel removed the Israeli card from the Arab Nationalists even further than Egypt's recognition had. This change was followed by the signing of the Israeli–Jordanian Peace Treaty in 1994[55] and a series of secret negotiations with the Syrians, which came close to fruition in the late 1990s.[56] The transformation in the conflict was so remarkable that in 2002 the Arab Peace Initiative was launched under Arab League auspices, which offered Israel full recognition by all 22 member states in return for the full implementation of a fair two-state solution with the remaining issues being satisfied.[57]

On the economic front, this period saw economic reforms being enacted as population growth soared, job creation stalled and many states struggled to grow their economies. Syria and Yemen were also greatly impacted by the end of the Cold War and the collapse of the Soviet Union, which meant that subsidies and other support dried up almost overnight.[58] These economic struggles, which afflicted most states outside the Gulf, further added to the focus on the state, with regimes further consolidating and not wanting to enter into engagements with other states that had financial implications.

Essentially the 1990s and 2000s represented a strange twilight zone for Arab Nationalism. Even the US invasion of Iraq in 2003 brought little real condemnation or obvious spur to Arab unity, although moves were made in the economic sphere that were actually partially sponsored by the United States itself. With colonialism over, US hegemony seeming hardly worth challenging, especially given most countries' close relations with Washington, and the Israel issue on the back burner given peace treaties and widespread agreement on the desirability of the two-state solution, major driving forces behind Arab Nationalist sentiment had been considerably diminished. The strength and resilience of Middle Eastern states, the need to focus on internal problems to preserve and legitimize authoritarian structures and the obvious failure of many high-profile Arab unity schemes meant that there was little appetite to do much more than pay lip service to Arab Nationalism, which left the Arab League, GCC, and AMU as the only real vehicles with which to make any steps towards lesser forms of intergovernmental and functionalist forms of inter-Arab progress.[59]

Themes

In his *Dialogues in Arab Politics*, Michael Barnett highlights three key themes that run through the Arab Nationalism that so dominated Middle Eastern politics during the twentieth century. He uses these within his chronology to demonstrate how the changing nature of debates on these issues shaped the direction of Arabism and how this in turn shaped the region's politics. It is clear that anti-colonialism/ anti-Westernism, anti-Zionism, and Arab unity schemes were vital in driving discourses of Arab politics. However, as the discussions above demonstrate, there are further key factors that contributed to regional dynamics and disrupted attempts at regional unity.

The first of these is economic. The split between the oil-producing states with small populations and the non-producing (or in reality limited production) states with much larger populations was a key dynamic. Dreams of Arab unity came up hard against the reality of costs and sharing of resources. This reality was also further exacerbated by the failure of the socialism embedded at the heart of all forms of Arab Nationalism to fulfill its promise and create more than a basic form of social provision and technological progress. This gradually ossifying economic and political structure could never keep up with the pace set by the rentier economies of the Gulf States,[60] thus further exacerbating existing divisions.

The political division between monarchical and republican regimes across the Middle East was another key fault line, and while states such as Jordan and Kuwait attempted to straddle this divide, it was never an especially comfortable place to be. The tensions between the different regimes could only ever be temporarily papered over because at their heart was a serious security challenge between states whose mistrust only grew over time. This divided both republican and monarchical regimes, and even those republican regimes that espoused supposedly the same Ba'athist Arab Nationalist doctrine, namely Iraq and Syria. Even the Gulf States could never bring themselves fully to trust Saudi Arabia, whose expansionist tendencies pre-dated the arrival of serious pan-Arab sentiment in the sub-region. These tensions and security concerns were consistently to undermine attempts at cooperation and unity, and many came about as a direct result of competition to lead the Arab world, as well as the fact that Arab Nationalism was often used as a cloak for state nationalism.

Equally, internal security was a further issue that helped to undermine both the doctrine and the attempts at bringing Arab Nationalist dreams to fruition. As the Arab Nationalist states became ever more authoritarian and were able to fulfill fewer and fewer of the high-flown promises made to their ever-expanding populations, so they became more and more concerned with their own survival from coups and popular revolts.[61] Especially given the already tense regional situation, internal fears merged with perceptions of external threats further reducing the idea of Arab Nationalism to rhetoric and gesture politics.[62] Given this complex mix of factors it is little surprise that grand Arab unity schemes failed and Arab Nationalism was gradually hollowed out. This reality did, however, leave IOs as the main carriers of the potential for cooperation, but given the regional environment it should be no surprise that the rhetoric surrounding these organizations could never match the reality.

Concepts

Any study of the international institutions of the Middle East must grapple with a wide range of concepts and approaches, coming from a variety of different disciplinary and theoretical traditions, that have been applied to the region. Understanding the different prisms and perspectives through which the region, and its progress towards greater cooperation, has been viewed is but one aspect of this book; actually using and combining these concepts to explore the current level of institutionalization and the obstacles in the path of greater cooperation is another. Perhaps the most striking thing when examining the literatures of any of these traditions, is the pessimism that pervades accounts of Arab regionalism and the formation of IOs within the Middle East. While there are clearly good reasons to err on the side of pessimism, as best exemplified in the section above, it can, however, frequently feel as if the prospects for regional cooperation, let alone integration, are overwhelmingly bleak, and that points of light are very few and far between. While much of the evidence may seemingly confirm this pessimism, it also appears that the conceptual frameworks applied to the region, understandings of the Middle East's regional and domestic politics, and the comparisons made with other regions merely serve to exacerbate the negative perceptions of the region's level of institutionalization and the perception of the "failure" of its three main IOs. This is problematic on a number of levels and raises a series of questions about existing studies of the Middle East's IOs, especially their measurement of "success."

At this juncture it is useful briefly to examine some of the key concepts that underpin the regional system present in the Middle East. These "primary institutions" provide the foundation stones upon which cooperation and integration attempts rest and are often key obstacles to those processes. This is very much the case for the Middle East as a region, and while many of its primary institutions are the same as those of other regions, it is instead their rigidity and reification that form the stumbling blocks to deeper and more consistent cooperation through the region's IOs.

Using Barry Buzan's definition of primary institutions, which "are durable and recognised patterns of shared practices rooted in values held commonly by the members of interstate societies, and embodying a mix of norms, rules and principles,"[63] we can highlight the key norms that have provided a basis for cooperation while also highlighting where primary regional institutions also impede cooperation. Ana Gonzalez-Pelaez highlights eight of these primary institutions and compares the ways in which these are similar to and different from the same primary institutions at the global level as they have been developed and applied in the Middle East. She concludes that "the Middle East is a sub-global interstate society on the basis of regional differences collected both in the interpretation of the global master institutions, and in the specific presence or absence at the regional level of some derivative institutions."[64]

The eight key primary institutions are: sovereignty, diplomacy, territoriality, great power management, nationalism, equality of people, market, and environmental stewardship. Clearly elements of all these are present in the Middle East. Given that they are highlighted and compared with the core Western states in the wider international society, which has managed to make moves towards deeper forms of society supported through IOs, it is clear that there is at least some common basis upon which to build IOs within the Middle East. The problem lies in the fact that these primary institutions in the region often work in different ways and are ranked differently by the governments of Middle Eastern states.[65]

This provides what Buzan terms a "basic, coexistence" level of regional society which is less-than-fertile soil for the development of IOs, known as "secondary institutions." It is also evident that measuring the different understandings of these primary institutions across the region and between regions is highly problematic. Thus while sovereignty can be weak in some states in the region, in others it is stronger in the *de facto* sense, while all states are highly protective of their *de jure* sovereignty. The presence of a regional system shaped by authoritarian, dictatorial or monarchical regimes is also often assigned as being a primary factor in the prioritization of some primary institutions over others, and in the differing interpretations of those norms compared to the same norms in other regions. Thus for example, the strength of the protection of the sovereignty norm, rather than the flexibility of the sovereignty norm if absolute gains can be assured, appears to be a classic difference of the Middle East region's interpretation of a seemingly globally shared norm. While there is a great deal of truth in this observation, it is easy to forget that authoritarian regimes are not immune to other regional norms, which are less prevalent elsewhere in the world or which are unique to the region, especially when these norms prove popular with the general public. This means that various regimes must take into account these demands in order to assure their own survival in power, as well as preventing ideological visions such as Arab Nationalism or pan-Arabism from potentially undermining other key primary institutions. This can make comparing primary regional institutions with those at the global level difficult and obscures dynamics that shape primary institutions in the Middle East, which in turn have impacts upon the levels and quality of secondary institutions, i.e. international organizations. Essentially Middle Eastern states may wish to uphold some of these norms, which both facilitate and inhibit integration, while also being subject to different norms, which promote integration and cooperation. This dynamic is important to understanding the forms cooperation through IOs takes over time.

In terms of the final destination of integration and cooperation, clearly grandiose schemes of integration were always unlikely to succeed, which leaves IOs as the only realistic path towards greater cooperation and unity. It is, however, important to be clear on some key items of nomenclature used in this book. While the core focus of the volume is on the region's IOs, as explored above, this takes place against a wider backdrop. As Beth Simmons and Lisa Martin explain, the use of the term "international institution" refers to a broad range of phenomena from IOs themselves, the norms that underpin interaction, the range of informal structures like sovereignty which structure interactions, alongside bureaucratic elements, the wider idea of regimes and a whole range of other factors that shape the interactions of states in both conflict and cooperation.[66] This phrasing, rather than a regime approach,[67] which would be inappropriate in a work covering many issue areas, or the approach of an explicit study of the internal dynamics of the IOs (whether structural/bureaucratic,[68] behavioral or normative) allows us to avoid explicitly choosing a particular theoretical perspective and to study internal and external impacts upon the organizations, thus giving us greater flexibility.

A further contested definitional problem in the literature is the debate about processes of regionalization, regionalism, and what defines a region.[69] To avoid needlessly becoming sidetracked in these debates, we can agree simply that since a) the Middle East is widely used as a unit of analysis in the media, public discourse, policymaking and academia, and b) the Arabs have made multiple efforts to create regional IOs, which are clearly underpinned by the existence of cultural, linguistic, and political instructions of all kinds, then the Middle East can safely be considered a region and that regionalization processes have occurred.[70] While clearly the process of regionalism in the Middle East has been somewhat imperfect, the idea of regionalism as an "evolutionary and cumulative process" within wider structures of global governance is useful when thinking about the Middle East's attempts to create IOs and to move towards deeper, more systematic forms of cooperation.[71]

In order to gain a clear picture of the conceptual challenges when studying the Middle East's IOs as an expression of regionalism, it is important to explore the existing approaches taken, not just to understand these organizations, but also to understand the regional environment, while also posing a number of key questions that go on to inform the study undertaken in this book.[72]

Referring back to the goals outlined in the Introduction to this volume and with an awareness of the approaches taken in existing studies of the region's institutions and organizations, it is possible to highlight four key areas that raise important questions about the region but which also offer conceptual tools with which to engage in analysis of the region's organizations and levels of achievement when it comes to the building of institutions of all kinds both across the region and in its two key sub-regions, the Gulf and the Maghreb.

Perhaps the greatest problem when exploring these issues is the divide between IR scholars who have taken broad conceptions of IR theory and used the Middle East as a case study, and area studies experts who have rooted their analyses in specific regional dynamics and in the nature of authoritarian regimes.[73] Clearly, the study of IOs has mostly focused on a small number of "usual suspects," which is problematic for understanding non-Western, non-technical and, particularly, regional organizations in the Third World. Meanwhile, the existing examinations of the Middle East's IOs tend to be theoretically underpowered and rely instead on detailed political analysis of regional politics rather than necessarily an understanding of the IOs themselves. While both of these approaches have added to our understanding of the state of regional institutions of the Middle East, there are other approaches and questions, which tend to be excluded by these existing approaches. Thus, if we conceive of four key areas that can enhance our conceptual understanding of the institutions of the Middle East and then examine their constituent parts, it will be possible to assemble a conceptual toolkit, which will assist our analysis throughout this volume.

These four core areas from which analysis might proceed can be labeled thus: the "regional environment," "IR theoretic approaches to the study of IOs," "organizational goals and achievements," and "theories of IOs." While clearly there is some crossover between these areas, they also form discrete areas of study within IR and have associated theories and conceptual frameworks, which have been used to shed much light on a range of phenomena relevant to a range of IOs and to regional and international politics as well.

Much of the derivation of this toolkit arises from the development of a series of key questions about the topic and an awareness of the content of the existing literature on the region:

- To what extent are Arab IOs connected to, and independent from, the regional environment?

- How has this hindered their genesis, design, and agency?
- What are the main similarities and differences between the region's IOs?
- What have been the main achievements of the region's IOs?
- To what extent have the region's IOs evolved and changed over time?

Thus we can say that this work is a study of the IOs of the Middle East, within the context of the wider regional institutions of the Arab State system, and the economic, security, and political environment of the Middle East.

Framework

In the interests of brevity and not overcomplicating an already complex picture, it should be noted that the framework used here is not an attempt to construct a theory of Middle Eastern IOs but is merely a structure, which draws together some existing tools that have been applied to both the understanding of the Middle East and to the study of the IOs of the region, in order to frame some of the analytical discussions in this volume. By applying a range of theoretical prisms and questions we can open up different perspectives and examine processes in different ways. Some of these ideas have already been discussed in this chapter, thus this section serves to bring them together in one place, to add new dimensions, and to order and structure ideas, so that they can be used consistently to frame the analysis, which takes place both within, but more especially at the end of the examination of each of the three IOs of the region, and in the Conclusion to this volume.

Regional environment

This chapter has already attempted to frame the regional backdrop against which the IOs of the Middle East were created and which formed some of the key constraints on their operation. Thus the rich literatures on Arab authoritarianism, identity politics from both above and below (especially Arab Nationalism), and the regional political and security tensions have already been introduced. Clearly both the domestic politics of Arab States and the regional order created by these states, have had a major impact on the perceptions, fears and hopes of the peoples and governments of the region, and have in turn affected the formation and development of the region's IOs that have emerged from this regional environment. It is important here to add some further perspectives that have been used to frame this environment and the attempts at Arab unity that have been made.

Three broad perspectives will be highlighted here, which draw upon (in various measures) three levels of analysis: the international, the regional, and the domestic, all of which combine to shape the regional environment as a whole. The three perspectives can be briefly summarized as: the realist, the constructivist, and the specific, all of which recognize in their various ways the interconnectedness of issues that shape the region.

The first of these draws directly upon IR approaches to understand the political interactions of Arab States but also their interactions with Israel, the United States, and other powers. Thus for example, realist studies by John Mearsheimer on conventional deterrence and Stephen Walt on alliances[74] have been attempts to test theory on Middle East cases. Realism itself has long been a useful and popular tool with which to understand the actions of states in the region, and since the region's states often appear to be statist, survival focused, and prioritizing self-help (although often willing to accept help from non-regional actors), it is natural to turn to this theory to understand interactions and state behavior.[75]

The second, constructivist approach highlights instead the importance of ideology, namely of the transnational Arab Nationalist kind. Barnett's combination of the sovereignty norm and Arabism, and the way in which he explores the dialogues between these two norms and the way in which the symbolic and strategic interactions of Arab States changed the very meaning of Arabism over time, remains a seminal work in the study of the region's politics.[76] Realism, as Barnett shows, cannot explain the region's experiments in unity but he perhaps at times overstates the impact of Arabism in explaining regional shifts, neglecting to bring in insights from realism, which better explain power shifts in the region.[77]

The third, specific approach comprises two attempts to bridge the divide between regional realities and IR theory. The first of these is Mohammed Ayoob's work on the way in which conflict and security in the Third World are driven by the early stage of state building, which these states are living through. This explains the region's reification of the sovereignty norm and the lack of democratic structures, both of which make it difficult for states to cooperate. It also explains the way in which security narratives impact upon all areas of policy, thus making functional cooperation more difficult than elsewhere.[78] The second is Fred Halliday's work, which attempts to draw together IR, ideology, and the realities of politics to theorize the region.[79] His nuanced attempt to bridge these divides, especially between IR theory and area studies, through the use of a complex form of historical sociology, enables an exploration of key components of social and political life, and how the institutions (in all senses) that constitute these two realms are established, maintained, and evolve. Thus while the broader historical context matters, it remains vital to go beyond existing explanations "to one within historical sociology in terms of the political and social character of the countries involved, the nature of their Janus-like states, the priorities of their rulers, and the broader domestic context in which foreign, and military, decisions are made."[80]

We must therefore remember that domestic politics of different Arab States has also played a powerful role in shaping regional order. The drive for survival by authoritarian regimes, especially in the post-Nasser era, has also impacted upon the regional environment. The backdrop against which attempts to cooperate through the region's IOs have been made are thus a complex mix of three different levels and three broad approaches, which explain the behaviors of the range of actors.[81]

IR theoretic approaches to the study of IOs or cooperation

IR scholars have long puzzled over the existence and growth of IOs. This is, of course, a much bigger arena and is linked strongly to the regional (and global) environment. Martin Koch and Stephan Stetter deploy the useful tool of metaphors in order to explore the ways in which different IR theories conceptualize the reasons for the existence of IOs and cooperation in the world.[82] Thus one key way of viewing IOs is as the *instruments* of states: they exist to serve states' purposes and are controlled and guided by states. This is very much the realist and neo-realist perspective. In the Middle Eastern context this viewpoint rings very true and is often used to explain the weaknesses of the region's IOs. States either have too little need of these bodies or there are so many regional tensions that proper cooperation is impossible. A further explanation is that the lack of an overwhelmingly powerful state to dominate ensures that the region's IOs are simply arenas of competition between similarly powerful states.[83]

Conversely when viewed as *arenas* these bodies provide an institutional structure which assists states in reaching agreements and enables them to coordinate national strategies and engage in cooperation. By providing a physical infrastructure, calendar, information processing and sharing facilities, and by setting the agenda, and perhaps offering adjudication or legitimacy, IOs are essential facilitators and trust builders and encourage states to cooperate by reducing risks and enhancing outcomes. This is very much in the vein of neoliberal institutionalist theories and goes back to the earliest days of this literature led by Robert Keohane and Joseph Nye.[84] In this sense IOs are actors but have limited but essential power in assisting states' cooperation. In the Middle Eastern sense clearly the IOs do play some of these roles but it is the extent of their role, the resources to support essential functions such as monitoring and information sharing, which are constraining factors, alongside legitimacy and perception deficits.

The third broad approach views IOs as real actors in their own right, rather than as facilitatory agents, combining roles as both an arena and a manager of complexity, which also has a place in shaping norms. This is much more of a constructivist perspective and links into literature on global governance, as overlapping institutions and networks increasingly work together.[85] In this view states become less important units of analysis as study shifts to the IOs themselves. In the Middle Eastern sense this appears not to have happened and IOs have been kept on a tight lead. Yet at the same time, as the main expression of Arab unity the Arab League does have elements of a distinct authority and in some fields may have more agency than it is necessarily given credit for. These approaches then at the very least help us to see areas in which the region's IOs may be able to act in their own right.[86]

Organizational goals and achievements

This is an important area of analysis for this volume given the frequent tendency towards pessimism in the literature in terms of the success of the region's IOs. Naturally, this category within the framework is influenced by the other categories and particularly by the specific shape of the region's IOs, which acts to constrain agency. Despite the regional and structural factors involved, expectations of the success of organizations like the Arab League have frequently been wildly unrealistic, in part fueled by the rhetoric and grandiose gestures and initiatives made by the organization's member states at frequent intervals. Given these expectations it is natural that the IOs of the region have consistently fallen short. This raises the vital question of how the success of these bodies should be measured, something which has surprisingly not been properly explored before. One way of doing this is to explore the foundational treaties of the bodies and compare them with the institutional realities. Initially this seems to be an eminently sensible way of proceeding but given the regional environment these aims were always too ambitious, as indeed they are for most IOs. As Dag Hammarskjöld famously once said: "The UN was not created to take mankind to heaven, but to save humanity from hell."[87] It seems all IOs are constantly held to impossibly high standards. It is therefore important to be more realistic about what success for the Middle East's IOs might look like.

Many studies of regionalism inevitably either explicitly or implicitly use the European Union (EU) as the blueprint or the gold standard against which the success of other regional projects is judged. Leaving aside the EU's current woes and contradictions, which were perhaps less apparent when those comparisons were made, was it ever likely that, even if those bodies had the express aim of following the same path, they could imitate the level of integration seen in Europe, especially given the absence of the experience of catastrophic warfare and the presence of liberal trading economies and democratic institutions? A better way of assessing success would seemingly be to examine what has been achieved against the backdrop of both internal structural restraints and regional politics and insecurities. This volume does not create a formalized system of measuring the success of the region's IOs, but instead begins from the position that there must have been *some* successes driven by, or through, these bodies in terms of regional cooperation, standardization, understanding or in terms of practical outcomes such as increased trade. Lowering our expectations of what was/is achievable thus enables us to appreciate smaller-scale and practical achievements, stepping stones on the road to greater cooperation and possibly integration in the future. As the study of IOs reminds us, the engine room of international cooperation lies in the functional needs of individual states.[88] The Middle East is not immune to this need but positive spillover effects are clearly harder to generate in a region where politics are driven by suspicion, fear, and the defense of sovereignty.[89] The book therefore assumes that the states were willing to cooperate on functional matters, which were not (or could not) be framed as security concerns and which offered personal, regime or national benefits, and that the IOs (i.e. as corporate bodies) and the people working within them sought to maximize inter-Arab cooperation wherever possible.

Theories of IOs

There is a rich literature that theorizes and explores the functions, institutional design, sociology, and agency of IOs—far too much for any summary to cover adequately. Rather than delving too far directly into the theories on offer within this literature here, it is instead important to highlight some key themes and questions that arise within this literature and which have resonance for the IOs of the Middle East.[90]

The first of these is the importance of the formal structures and frameworks within the bodies' functions. This leads into an extensive sub-field, which examines institutional variation. This is useful for us in terms of comparing similarities across the three regional IOs in question here, but also because the states' design of these organizations was focused on maintaining a high degree of control over their development and competences in order to protect the primary institution of sovereignty.[91] This in turn leads into the study of the levels of independence[92] and agency within IOs, both of which are important questions, since the existing literature has broadly assumed that these are both essentially non-existent in the Middle East's IOs. While independence and agency are always likely to be difficult to trace properly within the region's IOs, it is clearly important to be aware that it is likely to be present in some form. Indeed, as this volume shows, there have been occasions when the IOs have been able to exercise their own agency over many matters, inevitably in less contentious and more functionalist arenas but still with important results.

The very existence of these IOs, in however circumscribed a form, clearly has had impacts of varying kinds upon the region and upon inter-Arab politics. The concept of sociological institutionalism, which explores the way in which institutions create meaning for individuals, is evidently useful,[93] as is the idea of constructivist institutionalism[94] in a region in which Arab Nationalism has been such an important emotional and political force. While both of these connected ideas originate within the so-called new-institutionalist tradition, which has been criticized as being too much of a top-down approach to the study of organizations, we are less interested here in the detail of this approach, which is not necessarily appropriate for the region, than in the fact that these concepts force one to think outside realist and liberal conceptions of cooperation. The ideas themselves are extremely useful in two broader senses: first, that the only way in which schemes of greater Arab unity and cooperation are now discussed is through these organizations; and second, that these schemes are in fact discussed and the organizations themselves and the wider Arab population have some (limited) inputs into them.

Another useful question that emerges from the literature on IOs is how they change and evolve over time. Ernst Haas provided three models of change in IOs. He argues that the redefinition of problems goes through two separate processes: adaptation and learning. The first is a process of technical-incremental change. The second is one where original assumptions are challenged and reinterpreted, and new ends devised based on new knowledge and the development of consensus. He further subdivides the adaptation model into "incremental growth" and "turbulent non-growth," and suggests that organizations can switch between the three models. On the surface the "turbulent non-growth" model seems best to fit the region with its self-effacing reactive leadership, unstable revenue sources and relatively weak status of experts, but elements of the model such as simple majority voting do not always seem to fit too well.

In order to build his typology, Haas assumes that: "all international organizations are deliberately designed by their founders to 'solve problems' that require collaborative action for a solution. No collaboration is conceivable except on the basis of explicit articulated interests."[95] Given that his book focuses on organizations such as the World Bank, which tend to have a much narrower remit than regional organizations, his book's focus on explaining "the change in the definition of the problem to be solved by a given organization"[96] is much more difficult to pin down since the range of issue areas covered is much larger in scope.

Identifying the problems designed to be solved by the IOs of the Middle East can be something of a challenge both because of the wider scope, and because of a real lack of clarity on the purpose of these bodies. Are they most concerned with issues of security, economy, culture or society? Indeed, what if the organizations actually have no functionalist purpose or specific problem set to solve in the sense that other IOs do? One could conclude that the real purpose of the region's intergovernmental bodies is performative: they simply provide a platform for Arab leaders to perform to their own and other Arab populations. It may be that the Arab bodies are simply a façade to protect the primary institution of sovereignty by absorbing attention and creating the impression of greater moves towards Arab cooperation or unity. Add this to a realist prism, awareness of the popularity of Arab Nationalism and an understanding of the ways in which ideology is used by authoritarian regimes in the region, and it is easy to see why these organizations are so readily written off.

This, then, highlights the difficulties of studying the region's IOs. What are they for? Do they have the same goals and intentions as other similar organizations? A persuasive case can be made along the lines above, but this is probably far too cynical an approach. Is the region, and its institutions, really quite that different from other regions? Clearly the states have in fact used these bodies as instruments to advance their interests and they have also become arenas in which business does get done. Likewise, these bodies clearly do have some agency, have evolved over time in various ways, and have the potential for further change.

Through a combination of these different approaches to the study of the region and to IOs we have a range of tools at our disposal to examine the Arab League, GCC, and AMU, highlighting the range of different processes and inputs that shape the bodies both internally and externally.

Conclusion

This chapter has provided the essential historical background, established some key themes and questions, and provided, through a brief examination of four key areas, some awareness of useful theories and ideas which can guide and support analysis and investigation throughout this volume. By declining to take a fixed theoretical perspective it is hoped that the volume will be able to draw insights from a number of traditions to understand the IOs of the region in the round.

In establishing the history and ideas here, the reader is aware of both the background context and the theoretical tools used in this book from the outset, allowing greater focus within the chapters on the thematic issues, and upon the structures, agency, successes, and failures of the IOs themselves, which is the main purpose of this volume. We now turn to the region's oldest and most inclusive international organization, the Arab League, to begin our investigations.

Notes

1 Michael Barnett, *Dialogues in Arab Politics: Negotiations in Regional Order* (New York: Columbia University Press, 1998).
2 Rashid Khalidi *et al.* (eds), *The Origins of Arab Nationalism* (New York: Columbia University Press, 1991).
3 Albert Hourani, *Arabic Thought in the Liberal Age, 1798–1939* (Cambridge: Cambridge University Press, 1983).
4 James Barr, *A Line in the Sand: Britain, France and the Struggle that Shaped the Middle East* (London: Simon & Schuster, 2012).
5 Jonathan Schneer, *The Balfour Declaration: The Origins of the Arab-Israeli Conflict* (London: Bloomsbury, 2011).
6 Tom Segev, *One Palestine, Complete: Jews and Arabs Under the British Mandate* (London: Abacus, 2001).
7 Elie Kedourie, *In the Anglo-Arab Labyrinth: The McMahon-Husayn Correspondence and its Interpretations 1914–1939* (Cambridge: Cambridge University Press, 1976). Also Philippe Prévost, *La France et la tragédie palestinienne: Retour sur les accords Sykes-Picot* (Paris: Erick Bonnier, 2012).

8 On Iraq see: Ali Allawi, *Faisal I of Iraq* (New Haven, Conn.: Yale University Press, 2014).

9 For interesting insight into the complex interactions between different groups and the colonial regimes that contributed to the rise of Arab Nationalism see: Keith Watenpaugh, *Being Modern in the Middle East: Revolution, Nationalism, Colonialism, and the Arab Middle Class* (Princeton, N.J.: Princeton University Press, 2012).

10 See: Madawi al-Rasheed, *A History of Saudi Arabia* (Cambridge: Cambridge University Press, 2010).

11 Peter Sluglett, *Britain in Iraq: Contriving King and Country* (London: I.B. Tauris, 2007).

12 Philip Khoury, *Syria and the French Mandate: Politics of Arab Nationalism, 1920–45* (London: I.B. Tauris, 1986).

13 John Darwin, *Britain, Egypt and the Middle East: Imperial Policy in the Aftermath of War 1918–1922* (London: Palgrave, 2014).

14 For an interesting (and somewhat controversial) discourse on the historical roots of Arab Nationalism and its popular appeal see: Raphael Patai, *The Arab Mind* (New York: Charles Scribner, 1973).

15 Youssef Choueiri, *Arab Nationalism: A History* (Oxford: Blackwells, 2000).

16 Ali Kadri, *The Unmaking of Arab Socialism* (London: Anthem Press, 2016).

17 Bassam Tibi, *Arab Nationalism: A Critical Enquiry* (Basingstoke: Palgrave Macmillan, 1990).

18 Wm. Roger Louis, *The British Empire in the Middle East 1945–51* (Oxford: Oxford University Press, 1984).

19 For an interesting discussion of why this period of coups ended abruptly in the late 1970s see: Eliezer Be'eri, "The Waning of the Military Coup in Arab Politics," *Middle Eastern Studies* 18, no. 1 (1982): 69–128.

20 Said Aburish, *Nasser: The Last Arab* (London: Gerald Duckworth & Co, 2005).

21 John Kent, "The Egyptian Base and the Middle East, 1945–54," in *Emergencies and Disorder in European Empires after 1945*, ed. Matthew Holland (London: Frank Cass, 1994).

22 Benny Morris, *1948: A History of the First Arab-Israeli War* (New Haven, Conn.: Yale University Press, 2009).

23 Alistair Horne, *A Savage War of Peace: Algeria 1954–1962* (London: Macmillan, 1977).

24 Keith Kyle, *Suez: Britain's End of Empire in the Middle East* (London: I.B. Tauris, 2011).

25 Laura James, *Nasser at War: Arab Images of the Enemy* (Basingstoke: Palgrave, 2006).

26 Malcolm Kerr, *The Arab Cold War, 1958–1970: A Study of Gamel 'Abd Al-Nasir and his Rivals* (Oxford: Oxford University Press, 1972).

27 Anthony McDermott, *Egypt from Nasser to Mubarak: A Flawed Revolution* (London: Routledge, 1988).

28 Derek Hopwood (ed.), *Arab Nation, Arab Nationalism* (Basingstoke: Palgrave, 2000).

29 James Jankowski, *Nasser's Egypt, Arab Nationalism and the United Arab Republic* (Boulder, Col.: Lynne Rienner, 2001).

30 Elie Podeh, *Decline of Arab Unity: The Rise and Fall of the United Arab Republic* (Brighton: Sussex Academic Press, 1999).

31 Gerald de Gaury, *Three Kings in Baghdad: The Tragedy of Iraq's Monarchy* (London: I.B. Tauris, 2007).

32 Nikolaos Van Dam, *The Struggle for Power in Syria: Politics and Society Under Asad and the Ba'th Party* (London: I.B. Tauris, 2011).

33 Clive Jones, *Britain and the Yemen Civil War, 1962–1965: Ministers, Mercenaries and Mandarins* (Brighton: Sussex Academic Press, 2004).

34 Jesse Ferris, *Nasser's Gamble: How Intervention in Yemen Caused the Six-Day War and the Decline of Egyptian Power* (Princeton, N.J.: Princeton University Press, 2015).

35 Adeed Dawish, *Arab Nationalism in the Twentieth Century: From Triumph to Despair* (Princeton, N.J.: Princeton University Press, 2002).

36 Joseph Sassoon, *Anatomy of Authoritarianism in the Arab Republics* (Cambridge: Cambridge University Press, 2016).

37 Peter Hinchcliffe, Maria Holt and John Drucker, *Without Glory in Arabia: The British Retreat from Aden* (London: I.B. Tauris, 2006).

38 Michael Oren, *Six Days of War: 1967 and the Making of the Modern Middle East* (Oxford: Oxford University Press, 2002).

39 Tom Segev, *1967: Israel, the War and the Year that Transformed the Middle East* (London: Abacus, 2008).

40 Rashid Khalidi, "The 1967 War and the Demise of Arab Nationalism: Chronicle of a Death Foretold," in *The 1967 Arab-Israeli War: Origins and Consequences*, ed. Wm. Roger Louis (Cambridge: Cambridge University Press, 2012), 264–284.

41 Fouad Ajami, *The Arab Predicament: Arab Political Thought and Practice Since 1967* (Cambridge: Cambridge University Press, 1992).

42 Nigel Ashton, *King Hussein of Jordan: A Political Life* (New Haven, Conn.: Yale University Press, 2010), 136–158.

43 Paul Chamberlin, *The Global Offensive: The United States, The Palestine Liberation Organization, and the Making of the Post-Cold War Order* (Oxford: Oxford University Press, 2015).

44 Asaf Sinever (ed.), *The October 1973 War: Politics, Diplomacy, Legacy* (London: Hurst & Co., 2013).

45 Daniel Yergin, *The Prize: The Epic Quest for Oil Money and Power* (London: Simon & Schuster, 2009), 570–594.

46 John Waterbury, *The Egypt of Nasser and Sadat: The Political Economy of Two Regimes* (Princeton, N.J.: Princeton University Press, 2009).

47 Lawrence Wright, *Thirteen Days in September: Carter, Begin, and Sadat at Camp David* (London: OneWorld, 2014).

48 Williamson Murray, *The Iran-Iraq War: A Military and Strategic History* (Cambridge: Cambridge University Press, 2014); and Shahram Chubin and Charles Tripp, *Iran and Iraq at War* (London: I.B. Tauris, 1988).

49 Gregory Aftandilian, *Egypt's Bid for Arab Leadership: Implications for U.S. Policy* (New York: Council on Foreign Relations Press, 1993).

50 This process took place in even the most ardently Arab Nationalist states. See for example: Youssef Chaitani, *Post-colonial Syria and Lebanon: The Decline of Arab Nationalism and the Triumph of the State* (London: I.B. Tauris, 2007).

51 See for example: Lisa Weeden, *Ambiguities of Domination: Politics, Rhetoric, and Symbols in Contemporary Syria* (Chicago, Ill.: University of Chicago Press, 2015).

52 Jeremy Long, *Saddam's War of Words: Politics, Religion, and the Iraqi Invasion of Kuwait* (Austin, Tex.: University of Texas Press, 2004).

53 Alastair Finlan, *The Gulf War 1991* (Oxford: Osprey, 2003).

54 Bruce Maddy-Weitzman and Joseph Kostiner, "The Damascus Declaration: An Arab Attempt at Regional Security," in *Regional Security Regimes: Israel and its Neighbors*, ed. Efraim Inbar (Albany, NY: State University of New York Press, 1995).

55 Stephen Zunes, "The Israeli-Jordanian Agreement: Peace or *Pax Americana*?" *Middle East Policy* 3, no. 4 (1995): 57–68.

56 Ahron Bregman, "The Deal That Never Was: Israel's Clandestine Negotiations with Syria, 1991–2000," in *Israel's Clandestine Diplomacies*, ed. Clive Jones and Tore Petersen (London: Hurst & Co., 2013), 225–240.

57 Joshua Teitelbaum, *The Arab Peace Initiative: A Primer and Future Prospects* (Jerusalem: Jerusalem Center for Public Affairs, 2009).

58 For demographics especially, see: Melani Cammett *et al.*, *A Political Economy of the Middle East* (Boulder, Col.: Westview Press, 2015).

59 On authoritarian consolidation see: Roger Owen, *Rise and Fall of Arab Presidents for Life* (Cambridge, Mass.: Harvard University Press, 2012).

60 On rentierism see: Hazem Beblawi and Giacomo Luciani (eds), *The Rentier State* (London: Croom Helm, 1987).

61 Mohammed Ayoob, "Review: The Security Problematic of the Third World," *World Politics* 43, no. 2 (1991): 257–283.

62 For an excellent examination of the merging of internal and external security concerns, alongside regime survival strategies, see: Mohammed Ayoob, *The Third World Security Predicament* (Boulder, Col.: Lynne Rienner, 1995).

63 Barry Buzan, *From International to World Society: English School Theory and the Social Structure of Globalization* (Cambridge: Cambridge University Press, 2004), 181.

64 Ana Gonzalez-Pelaez, "Primary Institutions of the Middle Eastern Regional Interstate Society," in *International Society and the Middle East: English School Theory at the Regional Level*, ed. Barry Buzan and Ana Gonzalez-Pelaez (London: Palgrave, 2009), 114.

65 Michael Barnett highlights this issue well when he explores the inherent tensions between sovereignty and pan-Arabism. Michael Barnett, "Institutions, Roles, and Disorder: The Case of the Arab States System," *International Studies Quarterly* 37, no. 3 (1993): 271–296.

66 For greater discussion of these terms see: Beth Simmons and Lisa Martin, "International Organizations and Institutions," in *Handbook of International Relations*, ed. Walter Carlsnaes, Thomas Risse and Beth Simmons (London: Sage, 2012), 192–211.

67 In the sense of regime theory, see Stephen Krasner (ed.), *International Regimes* (Ithaca, NY: Cornell University Press, 1983), and Andreas Haschenclaver *et al.* (eds), *Theories of International Regimes* (Cambridge: Cambridge University Press, 2008).

68 See for example Barnett and Finnemore's groundbreaking work on the bureaucratic power of IOs: Michael Barnett and Martha Finnemore, *Rules for the World: International Organizations in World Politics* (Ithaca, NY: Cornell University Press, 2004).

69 While Joseph Nye and others have proposed simple definitions of a region and regionalism, Ernst Haas and others have pointed out the need to distinguish between nomenclature. Ernst Haas, "The Study of Regional Integration: Reflections on the Joy and Anguish of Pretheorizing," *International Organization* 24, no. 4 (1970): 606–646.

70 See for example: Fredrik Söderbaum and Timothy Shaw, *Theories of New Regionalism* (Basingstoke: Palgrave, 2003).

71 Louise Fawcett, "Exploring Regional Domains: A Comparative History of Regionalism," *International Affairs* 80, no. 3 (2004): 429–446.

72 There is some good literature on the so-called "Arab States System" which is essentially a shorthand for understanding the regional interactions of the Arab Middle East. This system pre-dates the arrival of the Arab League and has fundamentally shaped the region and its primary institutions. See: Elie Podeh, "The Emergence of the Arab State System Reconsidered," *Diplomacy & Statecraft* 9, no. 3 (1998): 50–82; on the role of conflict in shaping regions see: Raimo Väyrynen, "Regional Conflict Formations: An Intractable Problem of International Relations," *Journal of Peace Research* 21, no. 4 (1984): 337–359.

73 Leonard Binder, "The Middle East as a Subordinate International System," *World Politics* 10, no. 3 (1958): 408–429.

74 John Mearsheimer, *Conventional Deterrence* (Ithaca, NY: Cornell University Press, 1983); Stephen M. Walt, *The Origins of Alliances* (Ithaca, NY: Cornell University Press, 1987).

75 For a modified version of realism applied to the region, by regional specialists see: Raymond Hinnebusch and Anoushiravan Ehteshami (eds), *The Foreign Policies of Middle East States* (Boulder, Col.: Lynne Rienner, 2002).

76 Barnett, *Dialogues in Arab Politics*.

77 For greater detail on both realist and constructivist approaches to the region see: F. Gregory Gause III, "Systemic Approaches to Middle East International Relations," *International Studies Review* 1, no. 1 (1999): 11–31.

78 Ayoob, *The Third World Security Predicament*.

79 Fred Halliday, *The Middle East in International Relations: Power, Politics and Ideology* (Cambridge: Cambridge University Press, 2005).

80 Halliday, *The Middle East in International Relations*, 191.

81 For a volume that tries to bring these themes together see: Emily Landau, Tamar Malz and Zeev Maoz (eds), *Building Regional Security in the Middle East: Domestic, Regional and International Influences* (London: Frank Cass, 2004).

82 Martin Koch and Stephan Stetter, "Sociological Perspectives on International Organizations and the Construction of Global Political Order—An Introduction," *Journal of International Organizations Studies* 4 (2013): 1–10.

83 John Mearsheimer, *The Tragedy of Great Power Politics* (New York: W.W. Norton & Company, 2001).

84 Robert Keohane and Joseph Nye, "Transnational Relations and World Politics: An Introduction," in *Transnational Relations and World Politics*, ed. Robert Keohane and Joseph Nye (Cambridge, Mass.: Harvard University Press, 1972).

85 Ian Hurd, "Theorizing International Organizations: Choices and Methods in the Study of International Organizations," *Journal of International Organizations Studies* 2, no. 2 (2011): 7–22.

86 For a more region-specific examination of these three perspectives plus the role of domestic politics see: Etel Solingen, "The Genesis, Design and Effects of Regional Institutions: Lessons from East Asia and the Middle East," *International Studies Quarterly* 52, no. 2 (2008): 261–294.

87 Cited in Thomas Weiss, *Thinking about Global Governance: Why People and Ideas Matter* (London: Routledge, 2011), 2.

88 David Mitrany, *The Functional Theory of Politics* (New York: St Martin's Press, 1975).

89 Ernst Haas, *Beyond the Nation-State: Functionalism and International Organization* (Stanford, Calif.: Stanford University Press, 1964).

90 An interesting study on the evolution of theoretical approaches to understanding the regional integration of the EU is useful for understanding broader structures and theories: James Caporaso, "Regional Integration Theory: Understanding Our Past and Anticipating Our Future," *Journal of European Public Policy* 5, no. 1 (1998): 1–16.

91 This leads to path dependence which often in the region critical junctures even find hard to disrupt: Orfeo Fioretos, "Historical Institutionalism in International Relations," *International Organization* 65, no. 2 (2011): 367–399.

92 This has traditionally been a somewhat understudied field, see: Yoram Z. Haftel and Alexander Thompson, "The Independence of International Organizations: Concept and Applications," *Journal of Conflict Resolution* 50, no. 2 (2006): 253–275.

93 Martha Finnemore, "Norms, Culture and World Politics: Insights from Sociology's Institutionalism," *International Organization* 50, no. 2 (1996): 325–347.

94 Vivien Schmidt, "Discursive Institutionalism: The Explanatory Power of Ideas and Discourse," *Annual Review of Political Science* 11 (2008): 303–326.

95 Ernst Haas, *When Knowledge is Power: Three Models of Change in International Organizations* (Berkeley: University of California Press, 1990), 2.

96 Haas, *When Knowledge is Power*, 3.

2 The Arab League

Structure and evolution

- **Founding the Arab League**
- **Role and purpose**
- **Structures**
- **Conclusion**

The Arab League is the longest-established international organization of the region with the largest membership, comprising 22 member states (see Table 2.1 for the list of member states with their dates of accession). It is also the region's historically most pre-eminent institution, has the closest to universal membership of any international organization of the Middle East, and probably does have universal membership (if one excludes Western Sahara) by the terms of its own pact, which states that membership is open to "every independent Arab State."[1]

This chapter begins by briefly exploring the early history of the organization, its formation and initial developments, with particular focus on the 1948 war with Israel, which was to define the League, as well as drawing upon some of the key colonial, political, and intellectual contexts, as discussed in the previous chapter, that drove its early years. With this as a backdrop, the second part of the chapter proceeds to outline the structures of the League and how they have been added to down the decades. This is designed not only to lay out the institutional framework within which the League functions but also to assess the aims, functions, and scope of the organization. Linking together the way in which the organization began and its structures and framework will enable an examination of the evolution of the role of the Arab League and the frameworks within which it operates. This will also allow for an analysis of the impediments and opportunities presented by the origins, structures and influences on the organization, as well as providing an understanding of the League's institutional framework, which will inform the discussion in the following three chapters.

Table 2.1 Arab League members and observers

Country	Date of accession
Egypt	22.03.1945
Iraq	22.03.1945
Jordan	22.03.1945
Lebanon	22.03.1945
Saudi Arabia	22.03.1945
Syria	22.03.1945
Yemen	05.05.1945
Libya	28.03.1953
Sudan	19.01.1956
Morocco	01.10.1958
Tunisia	01.10.1958
Kuwait	20.07.1961
Algeria	16.08.1962
Bahrain	11.09.1971
Qatar	11.09.1971
Oman	29.09.1971
United Arab Emirates	06.12.1971
Mauritania	26.11.1973
Somalia	14.02.1974
Palestine	09.09.1976
Djibouti	04.09.1977
Comoros	20.11.1993
Observer status:	
Eritrea	January 2003
Brazil	2003
Venezuela	September 2006
India	April 2007

Founding the Arab League

The League of Arab States (LAS) was founded at a rather odd time and by following many of the discussions that were underway during that period one almost gets the impression that World War II was somehow bypassing the Middle East. This of course was not the case; the League's birth was influenced by a range of factors affecting the region, including the war—from the rise of Arab Nationalism and the spread of anti-colonialism to the desire of Arab leaders to find ways of protecting and even enhancing the sovereignty of their state, and in many cases their own personal hold over that sovereignty. The discussions that were to lead to the formal establishment of the LAS in May 1945, making it the first regional organization founded in the post-war era, were also of course caught up in the wider discussions about the likely shape of a post-war order more generally, and the foundation of the United Nations in particular. Indeed, as Barnett and Solingen note, the Arab League "was in keeping with the times, especially given that the role model was the Council of the League of Nations and the UN Security Council."[2]

The original discussions around the possibility of the formation of an organization for the Arab States are usually dated back to the 1941 suggestion of then British Foreign Secretary Anthony Eden, who had studied Arabic and Persian at Christ Church College Oxford, and who stated in a Mansion House speech: "many Arab thinkers desire for the Arab peoples a greater degree of unity than they now enjoy [and] ... they hope for our support. No such appeal from our friends should go unanswered."[3] Up until this point the focus of most Arabs had been on ridding themselves of the colonial powers but there had also been, particularly over the previous decade, a growth of Arab Nationalism and alongside it a desire for formal union of the Arab States, although there was still much debate over what precise form this should actually take. As discussed in the previous chapter, the foundation of a regional international organization represented a compromise between the status quo of minimal cooperation and maximum suspicion on the one hand, and full-blown attempts at the federation or the confederation of the Arab States on the other. Thus much of the early discussions around what form this unity might actually take were rather grandiose schemes for unions of states, which tended to focus on a core group that were more open to these kinds of schemes, with Egypt, Yemen,[4] and Saudi Arabia resistant to this vision. Naturally these speculations about the future form that greater Arab unity would take were also an intensely political game for many states, all of which wished to be linked to the idea, with some wanting to be seen as the regional leader while, of course, at the same time, most wished to preserve the maximum amount of sovereignty and room for movement. This consistent tension would, almost inevitably, lead to some kind of compromise agreement that would in reality satisfy the protection of sovereignty while creating the mirage of unity.

By 1943, with discussions over the future of Arab unity having progressed very little, Egyptian Prime Minister Mustafa Nahas suggested that a preparatory conference on Arab unity should be held in Cairo.

The outcome of these discussions led to the realization that any form of formal union of the Arab States was far too fraught with difficulty to be worth pursuing, and that some more practical and limited form of association, which protected state sovereignty, was the outcome most likely to be achievable.[5] Having finally converged around a more realistic notion of what "Arab unity" might actually mean, discussions became more fruitful and led to the seven Arab States with some degree of practical independence (Egypt, Iraq, Jordan, Lebanon, Saudi Arabia, Syria, and North Yemen) coming together in Alexandria between 25 September and 6 October 1944 for the first formal negotiations. This was clearly a successful meeting and led to the announcement of what became known as the Alexandria Protocols.[6] This document became the basis of further discussions which, after a further six months of negotiations, would lead to the signature of the Charter of the League of Arab States in Cairo on 22 March 1945, with the League formally coming into existence on 10 May 1945.[7] The Protocols laid out the broad outlines of the future of the Arab regional order on the basis of the creation of a regional body that could make decisions that would be binding upon its members, arbitrate and peacefully assist in the settlement of disputes, and which would guide the creation of formal structures to foster inter-Arab cooperation. It also decided that the League would focus in particular upon social, cultural, and economic matters. In addition to these core roles for the future organization, the Alexandria conference also issued two resolutions, which were not concerned directly with the role and purpose of the League but which would have implications for the nascent organization, and which tell us a great deal about the preoccupations of the states that were to found the League. The first of these resolutions recognized Lebanese independence and sovereignty and was, in effect, the region's recognition of the immutability of the colonially imposed boundaries, much like the recognition by the Organization of African Unity (OAU) of the *uti possidetis* principle. Although only referred to obliquely in its charter, in article 3, it was later stated explicitly in the African Union Charter in article 4. This has become one of the strongest norms of international relations on the African continent, and is equally import (if less explicitly stated) for the League.

Despite all the schemes that were to come later, designed to produce political unions of various Arab States, all of which ultimately failed (or failed even to get off the drawing board)—and which fell outside the auspices of the LAS—the explicit recognition of Lebanese sovereignty and independence showed not only the (legitimate) fears of smaller states in the face of their more powerful neighbors but also exposed the concern of all the states taking part in the negotiations in Alexandria: that the maintenance of their sovereignty was the bottom line. The second of these resolutions issued at Alexandria, not focused on the proposed new regional organization itself, was one which emphasized the need to protect the Palestinian Arabs. The issue of Palestine was, and would remain, one of the most important unifying factors for the Arab States, and one which would give the League purpose while also being used as a source of legitimacy and distraction by many of the states of the region from public demands for greater Arab unity.

While the Protocols essentially formally acknowledged that the direction of travel was no longer towards formal unity of Arab States, or groupings of Arab States, in the Middle East, it was also clear that the kind of organization envisaged at Alexandria was intended to be rather stronger and more activist than that which was given life in May 1945. During the course of the further negotiations leading up to the formal signature of the League's founding pact, the tendency was to dilute the vision at Alexandria rather than to strengthen it. What emerged over the course of the extended negotiations was more of a body that could *potentially* foster cooperation rather than one in which the project towards greater Arab unity could be pursued through binding resolutions, the harmonization of foreign policies, the potential for defense and security cooperation, and a functional regional form of collective security. In effect, the new organization was to become one which was designed to protect rather than pool sovereignty as Saudi Arabia, Egypt, Lebanon, and to a lesser degree Yemen rowed back even from the more limited vision expressed in Alexandria.

While the previous chapter examined the issue of the Israel–Palestine conflict and the following chapter also partly builds upon this theme, it is important here briefly to explore the role and implications of the 1948 Arab–Israeli war and the Palestine issue for the very earliest years of the League's existence.[8] Jewish settlement of Palestine, which began in the late nineteenth century and grew slowly during the 1920s, began to accelerate rapidly during the 1930s leading to a rise in tensions and the Arab riots of 1936, which forced Britain as mandate power to agree to impose restrictions on Jewish migration into Palestine. These tensions meshed with the anti-colonialism of the time and became one of the key fulcrums of Arab Nationalism, galvanizing popular opinion and mobilizing Arabs to become more interested in politics. The League's rejection of the UN's 1947 partition plan for Palestine resulted in the 1948 first Arab–Israeli war, the traumatic defeat of the combined forces of Egypt, Syria, Jordan, Iraq, and Lebanon, along with smaller contingents from Saudi Arabia and Yemen, and the foundation of the

State of Israel. This trauma, which led to many thousands of Arabs fleeing their homes in the new state, became known as *an-nakhba*, or the catastrophe, and placed the issue of Palestine at the forefront of Arab minds for decades to come. In many ways it can be argued that in terms of Arab unity and the League itself the Palestine issue represented a double-edged sword. On the one hand, the issue consistently[9] gave the Arabs something to agree on, created a shared enemy, and gave the new body an extra purpose. Yet on the other, the issue often dominated, distracted, and was used as a smokescreen by many of the member states both to enhance their own leadership or Arab Nationalist credentials while obstructing concrete moves towards reform of the League or new initiatives that might undermine the sovereignty of the member states, and by extension, in most cases, the survival of the political structures and regimes that ran those states. The League in many senses became a forum for rhetoric, display, one-upmanship, and veiled *realpolitik*, where grandiose ambitions could be agreed upon but which were rarely followed up, and all the organization itself and those who worked for it could do was to test the limits of cooperation, use their own limited power and resources to push forward on the more innocuous functionalist programs, while awaiting meaningful consensus that might allow for deeper forms of cooperation.

Having explored the genesis and early years of the League, the remainder of this chapter goes on to examine the envisaged role and purpose of the body in more detail and to explore the Arab League as a polity by focusing on the formal constitution of the new body in terms of both the founding pact of the LAS and the institutional structures it created, and how these have developed from birth down to the Arab Spring.

Role and purpose

Aside from the purpose of the League as a means to protect the sovereignty of its member states and going some way towards "satisficing" the demands of the Arab public for unity at the time of its establishment (and since), the role and purpose of the new regional organization as laid out in the pact of the League has continuing implications for its work. The preamble to the pact uses the usual lofty language but at the same time has the important role of setting the direction and aspirations of the new body:

> With a view to strengthen[ing] the close relations and numerous ties that bind the Arab States, and out of concern for the

cementing and reinforcing of these bonds on the basis of respect for the independence and sovereignty of them, stated, and in order to direct their efforts toward the goal of the welfare of all the Arab States, their common weal, the guarantee of their future and the realization of their aspirations, and in response to Arab public opinion in all the Arab countries, have agreed to conclude a pact to this effect.[10]

These aspirations are expressed slightly more clearly in article 2 of the pact, which, while reiterating what for the member states was the fundamental underpinning principle of "safeguard[ing] their independence and sovereignty," also laid out the general principles and thematic scope of the new organization:

> The purpose of the League is to draw closer the relations between member states and coordinate their political activities with the aim of realizing a close collaboration between them, to safeguard their independence and sovereignty, and to consider in a general way the affairs and interests of the Arab countries.

It also has among its purposes a close cooperation of the member states with due regard to the structure of each of these states and the conditions prevailing therein, in the following matters:

- economic and financial matters, including trade, customs, currency, agriculture, and industry;
- communications, including railways, roads, aviation, navigation, and post and telegraphs;
- cultural matters;
- matters connected with nationality, passports, visas, execution of judgments, and extradition;
- social welfare matters; and
- health matters.

In many ways, then, we can see that the League's remit is potentially extraordinarily wide, especially for an organization founded in the 1940s, and that it treads on areas that even outside the Middle East may be considered to be crucial for state sovereignty such as issues of nationality. Even seemingly innocuous areas of cooperation, such as in communications, can be far more political in the region than elsewhere. Thus on paper the purpose of the League is somewhat contradictory, protecting sovereignty while offering up a vision of greater cooperation and pooled sovereignty. Yet the procedures and structures contained in the pact weigh more heavily in favor of the former rather than the latter, as Michael Barnett and Etel Solingen put it. The institution was "specifically designed to fail at producing the kind of greater collaboration and integration that might have weakened political leaders at home."[11] There is much merit in this argument. Internal and regional politics were critical in circumscribing the League's abilities to fulfill the lofty ambitions that pervaded the rhetoric of the region's political leaders, as indeed were the provisions in the pact that set the cooperative bar so high. One could also make the argument that the very fact that the League was designed to fail makes its achievements all the more remarkable, for while they are more limited than those of other regional organizations, they are still real. While these achievements may indeed be outweighed by the failure of various initiatives and the problem of "big talk, little action" there is a strong tendency to judge the League in comparison to other organizations and against the ambitions laid out at the level of regional high politics. It is easy to forget that the list articulated above offers a sound basis for functional cooperation and that over the years, despite numerous lofty projects having stalled, there have been a number of smaller initiatives that have got going and have produced results. The League, over the years, has developed an extensive infrastructure across the region (and beyond), and its staff have been able to use their agency to push for greater cooperation, especially in technocratic and functional arenas, despite the restrictive nature of the pact and the organizational structures of the League.

Structures

International organizations tend to display a high level of continuity when it comes to their structures. Whether this is down to there only being one logical way of organizing such bodies or whether there is a natural level of imitation and conscious modeling on other bodies, in terms of their institutional design, is open for debate. What is clear, though, is that these similarities mask much more significant differences when it comes to the power, agency, and resources not only of the constituent parts of an organization but also of the organization as a whole. Thus, while the framing of the role and purpose of a body is critical, so too is the way in which that body is constituted in practice. This is not to deny the continuing agency of member states to shape the organization, either through acting as constraint or encouragement to the modification of its purpose or structures; or indeed, on the other hand, to deny the ability of an international organization itself to exercise agency in relation to its institutional frameworks and member states. Rather it is to suggest that the initial design of the charters, covenants, and founding treaties of all international organizations have lasting legacies for that organization which, depending on its exact institutional makeup (especially in this case), tend to make it all the harder for the employees of that organization to exercise their agency. This can be seen all too clearly when examining both the constitution of the League's institutional structures and the wider Pact of the League of Arab States within which these structures operate.

The League is nowadays structured more around the classic quasi-mimicry of the state itself, which with various adaptations is the pattern for all international organizations.[12] Although, one might say that in the case of the League it naturally looks rather more like the structure of your typical Arab State itself.[13] Today, after decades of slow evolution the League comprises multiple bodies and agencies, of which the key elements are: a secretariat (the bureaucracy); a parliamentary body (the Arab Parliament); an executive of sorts in the form of the Council of the League, where all members are represented; as well as separate councils dealing with matters such as economic and social affairs. At its establishment in 1945, however, the structure of the League as laid out in the Pact of the League of Arab States, was much simpler and more obviously reflected the concerns of (most) of its founder members that decisions that they had not agreed to should not be imposed upon them.

The pact laid out two main structures of the League: those of the Council and the secretariat. In its balancing act between appearing to be moving in the direction of Arab unity while actually enhancing and preserving the sovereignty of its members, the pact left many doors open in terms of the future structures of the League while also more explicitly offering protections for its member states. Over the longer term this lack of specificity regarding structure enabled member states to use their agency to add to the organizational framework, and for the League itself to agitate for the creation of new bodies and powers. In effect this led to the League (as represented by the secretariat) participating more fully than had been initially intended in the politics of both the organization itself and its member states. This, though, does not mean to say that the member states did not ultimately remain in control, protected as they were by the clarity of the articles in the pact that sanctified their sovereignty and their right to veto initiatives with which they disagreed.

In its institutional design from the outset, then, the odds were stacked against the League developing the levels of agency that would be seen in other international organizations. There were at least 12 key provisions in the pact, which were there to sanctify the sovereignty of the member states. These were, and continue to be, the provisions that have the most impact upon the League in terms of its abilities, ambitions, and activities. While the fact that the purposes of the League as laid out in article 2 of the pact made it clear that upholding member states' sovereignty was a core function of the new organization, this was not enough on its own; the states went further to cement their control of the League. This is evident from the way in which, in article 3, authority is vested in the Council, giving it power to: "realize the purpose of the League and of supervising the execution of agreements concluded by member states." Article 3 also gives the Council the right to determine "the means whereby the League will collaborate with the international organizations that may be created in the future to guarantee peace and security and organize economic and social relations." These two provisions give the member states, through the Council, the right to interfere in how agreements made are executed, thereby acting as a brake on the secretariat's agency, while arrogating the right to control the League's relations with other international organizations further curtails any power that the secretariat may develop. Clearly this provision was written in the awareness of the imminent arrival of the UN. The use of the words "will collaborate" rather than "may collaborate" implies strongly that the founders did not view the League as a competitor to the UN or other bodies; indeed, ensuring collaboration with other bodies gave an extra layer of control. This is also seen in the provision of article 4, which specifies that initiatives deriving from the League's special committees have to be "submitted to the Council for its consideration."

Two further articles provide fundamental guarantees to the member states. First, in conjunction with the provisions of article 3, in particular, article 7 provides two crucial brakes on the League: all decisions (except for minor procedural matters covered in article 16, agreed on a still high-threshold two-thirds majority vote, and issues to do with expulsion of a member or acts of aggression where the party subject to a resolution has no vote) were to be taken unanimously, thereby ensuring that all states had a veto. In addition, article 7 provides explicit reassurance that any decision passed by a majority will not be binding upon those that did not vote in favor. Furthermore, the same article also arrogates to the states themselves the right to execute the decision "in accordance with the fundamental structure of that state." There is also no proper oversight of how decisions are implemented and no court to which matters concerning non-implementation can be referred.[14] Further reassurance is also given in article 9, which effectively rules out a role for the League in harmonizing the foreign policies of member states. It allows League members to conclude treaties amongst themselves to further their unity, while at the same time making them non-binding on other states, and allowing states to keep existing treaties and agreements with other states while ensuring that other League members are not bound by them. This enabled those states that saw more potential, or which had more Arab Nationalist populations, to make their own deals and enabled states to keep their own arrangements made with the great powers. In addition, under the provisions of articles 18 and 19, a mechanism was built in that enabled withdrawal from the League. Finally, and somewhat strangely, the provisions of article 8 explicitly stated that: "Every member state of the League shall respect the form of government obtaining in the other States of the League, and shall recognize the form of government obtaining as one of the rights of those States, and shall pledge itself not to take action tending to change that form." This article, similar to some extent to article 2(4) of the UN Charter, was clearly designed to protect the sovereignty of members, as well as to prevent any potential field of competition opening up that would enable the League to be used as a tool in regional disputes. It further highlights the suspicions the states had of each other, and of the League as a new mechanism.

With these key provisions embedded in the pact and stated so explicitly, the member states, collectively and individually, were in control of the organization and had the ability to rein-in the ability of other member states to use the new body to enhance their interests at the expense of others. Seemingly then, the League was totally hobbled from the start. Although while it is true that these provisions in the pact were extremely powerful, they could not account for the agency of the states themselves, of the secretariat, or the fact that the pact itself left open much space, either implicitly or explicitly for further development. Often these developments were ones from which the member states could not afford to be seen to be openly dissenting.

While the provisions for withdrawal were clear in the pact, the League itself, essentially overnight, became the expression of much of the politics and aspirations of the Arab world. It would have been a brave leader indeed to have exercised their rights under articles 18 or 19. This fact, combined with the scope left to the League in terms of its function of promoting cooperation in such a wide range of areas meant that dynamics, which advanced greater integration from both key states and the League itself, forced states that were reluctant to surrender sovereignty to move further down the road to integration than perhaps they had ever intended. When the express provisions in article 9 allowing for groups of states to pursue their own arrangements for closer integration outside the auspices of the League are added, the scope for their use as a rhetorical tool, creating a degree of competitive bidding among the states of the Arab system, is significant. In addition to this, the pact also (in article 19) provided for amendments to be made by a two-thirds majority and not by unanimity, allowing any state that disagreed to leave the League. Indeed, much of the thrust of the pact is implicitly acknowledging the need for the development of further institutions to assist with its project of drawing "closer the relations between member States ... with the aim of realizing a close collaboration between them."[15]

As the League expanded its membership, and began its formal program, while at the same time creating and bedding-in internal rules and procedures, it became increasingly able to make more progress than the terms of the pact would suggest. While the pact itself contained contradictions between the protection of sovereignty and the desire to create greater regularity in state practices, which prevented anything like the kind of integration and cooperation desired by Arab populations, it did provide a framework and an arena that contained and constrained some hostilities, while at the same time allowing for some degree of collaboration on a number of issues. There would, however, always be a gulf between the rhetoric about the League and what was attainable in terms of Arab unity. After all, the League was a compromise arrangement from the outset since federation or confederation had already been proven an unreachable goal.

This tension, between what is written and spoken about the League, and what it is able to achieve in reality, has been present from the very foundation of the organization in 1945 and continues to shape it to this day. In comparison to the Charter of the United Nations, which runs to 111 articles spread over 19 chapters, the pact of the Arab League has no chapters and consists of just 20 articles and three brief annexes, dealing with Palestine, cooperation with Arab States that are not members of the League, and with the appointment of the first secretary-general.

The initial institutional structures laid down by the pact were extremely simple and are outlined in articles 3, 4, and 12. Article 3 states: "The League shall have a Council composed of the representatives of the member states. Each state shall have one vote, regardless of the number of its representatives." Article 4 meanwhile established special committees for each of the main purposes of the League; these contain representatives from all the member states, plus other Arab States that were not full members of the League, at the discretion of the Council.

These special committees had the initial purpose of preparing agreements which, subject to Council approval, would set out the basis and
scope of their work. As such, in terms of their construction they
represent a series of issue-specific mini-councils rather than the broader
nature of similar-sounding bodies at the UN or the EU, which often
give formal roles to civil society actors. Finally, article 12 states: "The
League shall have a permanent General Secretariat, composed of a
Secretary-General, Assistant Secretaries and an adequate number of
officials." These foundational structures of the League remain in place
today. The pact of the League has not been altered since its inception
in 1945, although other organs have since been added.

The Council

The Council of the League is the most important and without doubt
the most powerful organ, and often meets at foreign minister level
rather than heads of government level. It meets at least biannually, in
March and September, at the League's seat in Cairo.[16] Each member
has one vote and its presidency rotates between the members. The
Council also appoints the secretary-general by a two-thirds majority,
along with a series of other League officials in consultation with the
secretary-general. The League's budget, internal organization, and the
termination of each session are agreed in the same manner. All other
decisions are made by unanimity, although there is of course scope for
those who agree to implement further cooperation, thus there are some
specialized agencies of the League which operate in its name but in
which only half of the League's members participate. This rule has been
useful in enabling the League to push forward where there is sufficient
enthusiasm for initiatives emanating from groups of states.

In addition to the formal Council, a series of sub-councils have been
established in which the relevant ministers meet. These include:

- Council of Arab Housing and Construction Ministers
- Council of Arab Information Ministers
- Council of Arab Interior Ministers
- Council of Arab Justice Ministers
- Council of Arab Ministers for Communications
- Council of Arab Ministers for Electricity
- Council of Arab Ministers for Environmental Issues
- Council of Arab Ministers for Health
- Council of Arab Ministers for Social Affairs
- Council of Arab Ministers for Tourism

- Council of Arab Ministers for Youth and Sports
- Council of Arab Transportation Ministers

The general secretariat

The League is not a large organization in terms of its bureaucracy, with a total staff of perhaps 1,000 split between headquarters in Cairo, field offices, and diplomatic offices in major foreign capitals, and attached to other international organizations such as the UN and the OIC. The secretariat is arranged around a series of functional departments, each headed by a deputy secretary-general and in turn made up of a series of offices. The secretariat has experienced a high degree of change in its organizational structures since inception, with a number of internal reorganizations and changes necessitated by wider decisions taken either at various summits or by the League Council. The relatively small nature of the League's secretariat may in part be designed to restrict its agency on the part of the member states, yet it has managed to do quite a lot with a relative paucity of resources.[17]

Appointed on a five-year term, which can be renewed without term limit, the League has only had seven secretaries-general in its 70 years of existence. The office is less clearly defined than that of the UN secretary-general, and the founding pact of the League is vague on what the role entails; however, this, combined with often long terms of office, has given a number of incumbents who are often very well connected a degree of flexibility and agency. As the public face of the Arabs to the wider world, a number of secretaries-general have used the platform to push forward with specific projects and have, especially in more recent years under Amr Moussa and Nabil Elaraby, publicly called for reform of the League's structures and a renewal of its focus on regional cooperation and integration.[18]

The special committees

The pact of the League, under article 4, envisaged a special committee being established for each of the areas of cooperation outlined in article 2. As the League expanded, these committees were replaced by the Ministerial Councils outlined above, supplemented by specialized agencies and other forums. This has left a rump of special committees dealing with internal League business, which were not suitable for this treatment; thus the committees on legal affairs, information affairs, and financial and administrative affairs are still in existence. These have been supplemented by newer bodies, designed to complete the internal

Table 2.2 Arab League secretaries-general

Secretary-general	Term began	Term ended	Nationality
Abdul Rahman Azzam	22 March 1945	September 1952	Egyptian
Abdul Khalek Hassouna	September 1952	1 June 1972	Egyptian
Mahmoud Riad	1 June 1972	March 1979	Egyptian
Chedli Klibi	March 1979	September 1990	Tunisian
Ahmed Asmat Abdel-Meguid	15 May 1991	15 May 2001	Egyptian
Amr Moussa	15 May 2001	1 July 2011	Egyptian
Nabil Elaraby	1 July 2011	1 July 2016	Egyptian
Ahmed Aboul Gheit	1 July 2016	Incumbent	Egyptian

governance structures of the body, including: an administrative court dealing with cases concerning procedures and structures of the secretariat and its staff; the Higher Auditing Board, which is made up of representatives from seven states chosen every three years, which audits the accounts of the secretariat and oversees some administrative procedures; and finally the Investment Arbitration Board, which oversees the implementation of the unified Agreement on Arab Capital Investments in member states, which became operational in 2003.

Other offices that are more closely tied to the central organs of the League, such as the Special Bureau on the Boycott of Israel and the Political Committee, were formed over time and their status appears to be somewhat informal compared to both the core structures of the League established by the pact and innovations arising from other treaties and agreements that have been signed since the pact.

Thus, in addition to these core bodies envisaged by the pact, the League has expanded its institutional structures still further. Many of these have been somewhat symbolic in nature, while others began with more promise. The Treaty of Joint Defense and Economic Cooperation of the League of Arab States, which is discussed in the next chapter, for example, created a number of new bodies that became core structures of the League. These include the Joint Defense Council, the Permanent Military Commission, and (in theory) the Arab Unified Military Command, as well as the Economic Council, which was renamed the Economic and Social Council in 1980 (this body is further discussed in Chapter 4). In more recent institutional innovations there has also been the establishment of the Arab Peace and Security Council (discussed in the next chapter).

Arab League summits

In 1964, perhaps seeking a new stage, President Nasser began the practice of Arab League summit meetings for heads of state and government. These proved to be headline grabbing and were an organizational innovation for the League. Taking place on average biannually, they have become an annual fixture since 2000, having seemingly fallen out of fashion in the 1990s (see Table 2.3). Whilst offering a new forum for policy coordination, they also had the effect of marginalizing the role of the main institutional bodies of the League, although it could equally be said that the often poor turnout by the actual heads of state at many of these meetings does not always assist in their ability to take the initiative. The summits are perceived to have been quite successful and have led to the holding of specific economic and social summits, and three joint Arab–African summits in 1977, 2010, and 2013, as well as Arab–South American summits in 2005, 2009, and 2012.

Arab Parliament

The Arab Parliament was proposed in 2001 at the League's summit in Amman and has existed for a number of years as an Arab Transitional Parliament, based in Damascus until 2012. The idea of an Arab Parliament had been discussed during the 1950s but could never come into being because many believed it would require a change in the pact and also because most member states were extremely wary of direct popular representation and how it might change balances within the League itself. The lack of progress on this issue led to the creation of the Arab Inter-parliamentary Union (AIPU) in 1974, which was an extra-League body.[19] During the 1980s the League secretariat and the AIPU began to work on closer cooperation and discussed the potential for an Arab Parliament under League auspices. The League's Council has still not taken a final decision on the Parliament's status and at present it exists in a form of limbo with no real power, despite a key amendment being ratified by most member states in 2007. There are no plans for it to be directly elected at present, and it is made up of four seconded members from each of the diverse range of parliaments and advisory councils across the Arab world. The Parliament sits twice yearly in sessions that each last for two months and mirrors the March/September structure of the League's Council.[20]

Table 2.3 Arab League summit meetings

Date	Location
13–17 January 1964	Cairo
5–11 September 1964	Alexandria
13–17 September 1965	Casablanca
29 August 1967	Khartoum
21–23 December 1969	Rabat
21–27 September 1970*	Cairo
26–28 November 1973	Algiers
29 October 1974	Rabat
17–28 October 1976*	Riyadh
25–26 October 1976	Cairo
2–5 November 1978	Baghdad
20–22 November 1979	Tunis
21–22 November 1980	Amman
6–9 September 1982	Fez
7–9 September 1985*	Casablanca
8–12 November 1987*	Amman
7–9 June 1988*	Algiers
23–26 June 1989*	Casablanca
28–30 March 1990*	Baghdad
9–10 August 1990*	Cairo
22–23 June 1996*	Cairo
21–22 October 2000*	Cairo
27–28 March 2001	Amman
27–28 March 2002	Beirut
1 March 2003	Sharm el-Sheikh
22–23 May 2004	Tunis
22–23 March 2005	Algiers
28–30 March 2006	Khartoum
27–28 March 2007	Riyadh
29–30 March 2008	Damascus
28–30 March 2009	Doha
27–28 March 2010	Sirte
10–11 May 2011	Baghdad (cancelled)
27–29 March 2012	Baghdad
21–27 March 2013	Doha
25–26 March 2014	Kuwait City

Date	Location
28–29 March 2015	Sharm el-Sheikh
7 January 2016*	Riyadh
7 April 2016	Marrakesh[21]
March 2017	Manama

* Emergency summit

Conclusion

Thus from this overview of the initial history and analysis of the aims, scope, and structures of the League we get a picture of an organization that is wide in scope and ambition, attempts to bring together security functions and more functionalist economic, political, and social concerns, and, despite a series of innovations over its history, is still bound by the restrictive nature of its founding pact. These multiple contradictions and restrictions have not made the League's existence easy and have led many to label it a failure, usually based solely on its role in the domain of peace and security.[22] This seems an unnecessarily harsh judgment given the environment and structural factors under which the League operates. Certainly the League has been unable to live up to the expectations vested in it by many Arabs, and the rhetoric placed upon it by Arab politicians and leaders, but this is something true of most, if not all, international organizations and while the League often suffers when compared to other bodies this often serves to obscure the areas where and occasions when the League has been able to make a contribution to greater Arab unity, harmony, and prosperity.

The next three chapters build on the structures, dynamics, and constraints explored here by studying the specific structures, provisions, and evolution of the League's activities in terms of its involvement in issues of regional peace and security, and with regard to its economic, social, and cultural activities, thus beginning an assessment of the League's achievements and difficulties in these various areas.

Notes

1 Pact of the League of Arab States, article 1.
2 Michael Barnett and Etel Solingen, "Designed to Fail or Failure of Design? The Origins and Legacy of the Arab League," in *Crafting Cooperation: Regional International Institutions in Comparative Perspective*, ed. Amitav Acharya and Alistair Johnston (Cambridge: Cambridge University Press, 2007), 192.

3 George Kirk, *Middle East in the War* (Oxford: Oxford University Press, 1952), 334.
4 Both Yemen and Egypt later became much more enthusiastic about these experiments, of course.
5 For extensive discussion of this history see: Robert Macdonald, *The League of Arab States: A Study in the Dynamics of Regional Organization* (Princeton, N.J.: Princeton University Press, 1965); and A. Burdett, *The Arab League: British Documentary Sources, 1943–1963* (Cambridge: Cambridge University Press, 1995).
6 Ahmed Gomaa, *The Foundation of the League of Arab States: Wartime Diplomacy and Inter-Arab Politics 1941 to 1945* (London: Longman, 1977).
7 The entry into force of the ratification of some states came a little later than 10 May. Lebanon's ratification entered into force on 1 June 1945, Syria's on 4 June 1945 and (North) Yemen, while still considered a founder League member, actually only signed the Pact itself on 5 May 1945, its ratification too occurred much later than the other members on 6 February 1946, entering into force on 26 February 1946.
8 So important is the Palestine issue to the League that the original Pact contains a special annexe on Palestine which provided for a representative of Palestine to be present and stated that: "Her [Palestine's] existence and her independence among the nations can, therefore, no more be questioned *de jure* than the independence of any of the other Arab States."
9 Consistently is used somewhat advisedly here because while boycotts and rhetoric are one thing the essential annexation of the Gaza Strip by Egypt and the actual (if "temporary") annexation of the West Bank by Jordan in April 1950, resulted in a vote on Jordan's expulsion from the League which was defeated with support from Yemen and Iraq forcing the League to declare the annexation a temporary measure and that Jordan was the trustee of the West Bank for the Palestinians. That the League did not admit the State of Palestine as a member until 1976, instead having the Palestine Liberation Organization as a member speaks to some of the intra-Arab tensions on the Palestine issue which bubbled below the mask of unity on the surface.
10 Preamble to the Pact of the League of Arab States. For a discussion of the Pact see: Philip Ireland, "The Pact of the League of Arab States," *The American Journal of International Law* 39, no. 4 (1945): 797–800.
11 Barnett and Solingen, "Designed to Fail or Failure of Design?" 181.
12 For an interesting comparison of the League and the Economic Community of West African States (ECOWAS), see: Constanze Koitzsch, "Institutional Similarities Between Regional Organizations: An Analysis of ECOWAS and the Arab League," in *Roads to Regionalism: Genesis, Design, and Effects of Regional Organizations*, ed. Kai Striebinger, Lukas Goltermann, Mathis Lohaus and Tanja Börzel (Farnham: Ashgate, 2012), 117–140.
13 By this I mean that power is concentrated and controlled, structures are often confusing, duplicated, and hollow, and decision making is often slow, with implementation even slower.
14 Although the pact does state in article 19 that amendments to the pact include the creation of an "Arab Court of Justice," this court has still not come into being despite repeated discussions.

15 Pact of the League of Arab States, article 2.
16 From 1979 to 1989 the League's seat was in Tunis due to Egypt's suspension over its unilateral recognition of Israel.
17 For a detailed historical discussion of the secretariat see: Robert MacDonald, *The League of Arab States: A Study in Dynamics of Regional Organization* (Princeton, N.J.: Princeton University Press, 1965), 124–145. See also the Arab League's Website, www.lasportal.org/en/sectors/Pages/default.aspx.
18 Some of these initiatives are discussed in Chapter 4.
19 For more information on the Parliament see: www.europarl.europa.eu/meet docs/2009_2014/documents/dmed/dv/5b_arabparliame/5b_arabparliament.pdf. Also the Arab League website has a fuller than usual description: www.lasp ortal.org/en/arabparliament/Pages/default.aspx.
20 The website of the AIPU does relatively little to avoid giving the impression that it might be connected to the League. It is not until later on the page that the phrase "The AIPU maintains an ever developing relation with the League of Arab States" is to be found. www.arab-ipu.org/english/.
21 Morocco actually canceled this summit, a leaked communiqué from the Moroccan Foreign Ministry states: "Current conditions do not favour a successful Arab summit that can come out with decisions up to the level of the situation and the aspirations of the Arab peoples." See: "Morocco 'Cancels' Arab League Summit: Useless and Hypocritical," *The New Arab*, 20 February 2016, www.alaraby.co.uk/english/news/2016/2/20/morocco-ca ncels-arab-league-summit-useless-and-hypocritical.
22 See for example: H. McCoubrey and J. Morris, *Regional Peacekeeping in the Post Cold War Era* (The Hague: Kluwer, 2000), 189.

3   The Arab League
Peace and security

- **Architecture and role**
- **Record**
- **Assessment**

This chapter examines the successes and failures of the Arab League in the fields of peace and security. As the only pan-Arab body it is theoretically perfectly placed to act under Chapter VIII of the UN Charter[1] and has, on a number of occasions, been involved in intra-Arab mediation efforts, both between member states and with internal conflicts in Arab States, even occasionally deploying its own peacekeeping forces either independently or in conjunction with the UN. The first part of this chapter examines both the frameworks within which the League operates and the regional environment that constrains and enables the League's role in these issues. The second part of the chapter takes a closer look at the record of the League in mediating disputes between members and in promoting peace and security in the Middle East, with particular emphasis on the position of the League regarding intra-Arab peace and security issues. While Arab–Israeli tensions were explored in both of the previous chapters, in various contexts, this chapter concludes by briefly exploring the Arab League's role in the peace process from the mid-1990s.

Architecture and role

The League was clearly seen from the outset as having a role to play in the maintenance of regional peace and security. This makes its efforts in this sphere of critical importance in judging the limitations and constraints facing the organization, while also offering opportunities for examining when and where the League can have an impact. That the Middle East as a region is known worldwide as one of oil and conflict is not in doubt, but what is interesting is that if one excludes the Arab–Israeli wars and the Iran–Iraq War of the 1980s there have actually been very few conflicts between Arab States. Tensions between Arab States are legion but they are often expressed more through rhetoric, posturing or by covert participation in proxy wars than by invasion or direct conflict. Of course, the role of the Arab League in the creation of this seemingly anomalous situation is unclear but in one sense perhaps this fact makes its job somewhat easier. On the other hand, however, in those (relatively) rare instances when one League member does invade another, as with Iraq in Kuwait in 1990, and the response of the League is confined to rhetorical and symbolic action followed by many of its members calling for Western support to remove Saddam's forces, the natural reaction is to describe the League as toothless, pathetic or worse.

This urge, while overwhelmingly tempting, is neither a fair nor an accurate portrayal of the League's abilities and purpose, and reflects more upon the wishful thinking of Arabs about what they think the League *should* be doing or on the limitations of any regional body when faced with a breach of international law on this scale, let alone the realities of global politics and the distribution of military cap-abilities. The League is often not helped by the desire of its members to make it appear to be more than it is, and indeed can be, given the constraints it faces. Thus, when on 3 August, in the aftermath of Sad-dam's invasion, the League passed a resolution that called for a solu-tion to the crisis from within the League itself and opposed any foreign intervention, it was clearly both late, coming after the UN Security Council had passed resolution 660 some 24 hours earlier, and unrea-listic. It was only natural in this instance of extreme aggression that the UN became the key forum in this crisis and that it should lead the collective security efforts, for while it should also be remembered that many Arab States outside the Gulf contributed troops to both Opera-tions Desert Shield and Desert Storm, with Egypt, Syria, and Morocco each contributing in excess of 10,000 troops, even with the force con-tribution of the GCC states of around 100,000 troops this Arab ele-ment of the wider coalition lacked the ability to tackle Saddam's forces effectively alone. What also hampered the League on this occasion was the lack of unanimity of its members on the issue, with both Libya and the PLO opposing a resolution demanding that Iraq withdraw from Kuwait. Sudan then appeared to side directly with Iraq while both Yemen and Jordan were reluctant to support foreign intervention to remove Iraq from Kuwait.[2] Given the need for unanimity at the League, as outlined in the previous chapter, these divisions would effectively have paralyzed the League anyway and prevented it from being able to deliver collective security for Kuwait, thus leaving the vast majority of League members who wished to see Iraq removed no option to use the League for this purpose, even without the reality of their military inability and unwillingness to do the job.

That this kind of invasion and occupation is infrequent does not lessen the need for the League, in many ways, in managing the range of tensions within the region, which can and have spilled over into lesser forms of conflict such as border skirmishes. The League, though, faces many obstacles in this field despite the fact that since the signature of the pact in 1945, provisions in the area of peace and security were strengthened in 1950 with the signature of the Joint Defense and Economic Cooperation Treaty,[3] and in 2006 with the innovation of the Arab Peace and Security Council. At first glance the pact, which in article 5 allows for the peaceful settlement of disputes and outlaws the use of force in their settlement, also allows for the decisions of the Council of the League to be binding upon member states; however, rather like the International Court of Justice the states in question have to ask the Council to review the case for this provision to come into effect. In essence then, this makes settling disputes even less likely as the League's Council is a political body and not a court and no state would agree to submit its case unless it thought it had an advantage.

Article 6 of the pact, which allows for self-defense if invaded, also enables the victim of aggression, by either a League member or a third party, to call an emergency meeting of the League, which must then unanimously agree on the measures to be taken to end the aggression, although unanimity does not apply if the aggressor state is a League member.[4] This means that the League has a mixture of both collective defense and collective security in its DNA. Despite being unable to take action in the event of aggression without unanimity the League Council can, however, "initiate mediatory or arbitral missions by a majority vote (excluding the parties to a dispute),"[5] which is similar to those measures under Chapter VI of the UN Charter, which is the basis upon which most League actions have proceeded. A further complication means that even if unanimity were present in the case of aggression, any actions decided upon by the Council would be considered not binding if they trod directly upon the independence, sovereignty or territorial integrity of the states involved. Clearly this is open to an extremely restrictive reading and also represents an escape clause that enables rhetorical and symbolic action in the League's chambers but places no obligation for enforcement of decisions taken. The League has therefore struggled to get over these obstacles ever since its founding.

After the Arab defeat at the hands of Israel in the 1948 war there appeared to be more desire to strengthen mechanisms against Israel and also to try to ensure that the League would qualify under Chapter VIII as a regional organization that was capable of dealing with any disputes between its members before they were referred to the UN. This resulted in the Joint Defense and Economic Cooperation Treaty being signed in 1950 but there was little interest in changing the insurance policies, which were built into the pact by its founding states. This meant that while the new treaty did lead to members agreeing that an act of aggression against one member would be regarded as an act of aggression against all members and spelled out the fact that immediate measures should be taken, which included "all steps available, including the use of armed force, to repel the aggression and restore peace," little changed in reality.[6] The treaty did bring into being two new bodies—the Joint Defense Council and the Permanent Military Commission (and envisioned an Arab Unified Military Command)—but rather like the provision for a similar body at the UN, these new structures have hardly been transformatory for the League, especially since any decisions made in the Joint Defense Council are still subject to final approval in the League Council, thus negating the move made away from the unanimity principle to a two-thirds majority needed to pass plans in the new body. Given the politics of the time, this could have been a useful structure that might have worked in the face of Israeli aggression but clearly was not going to be of much use in the event of intra-Arab tensions.[7]

Whether or not the League is a Chapter VIII regional organization is also subject to some debate. The UN General Assembly associated itself with the League in 1947 but relations between the League and the UN soured over the League's rejection of the UN's plan for the formal partition of Palestine into two states. The League was then granted formal Observer Status in the General Assembly in 1950, yet the League's pact of course makes no reference to Chapter VIII, having been signed before the UN Charter, although resolutions have been passed in the League's Council which state that the League believes it is a Chapter VIII organization. The ambiguity and lack of criteria surrounding qualification for Chapter VIII status helps the League, though, and in 1995 UN Secretary-General Boutros Boutros-Ghali stated that this ambiguity was actually helpful, allowing the UN to work with a range of organizations in the maintenance of peace and security,[8] meaning that while some legal ambiguity and political dispute over the League's status in this regard remains, its normative and *de facto* status means that it can be considered a Chapter VIII body.

Record

Despite the League having much of the architecture, and on the surface the will, to deal with regional tensions and conflicts of all kinds, it has more often sidestepped involvement. As Barnett and Solingen estimated in 2007, of 77 conflicts in the region between 1945 and 1981 the League had only successfully intervened in six,[9] largely owing to the fact that conflicts are only referred to the League when its member states see the prospect of a resolution of some kind being in their interests, either due to ripeness, face-saving or indeed a lack of real interest in the conflict from the more powerful states in the region. It is striking that the League's involvement in conflict management or resolution (let alone its successes in this area) have largely been in what can be perceived to be proxy wars or civil conflicts in weak and/or peripheral states of the region, such as Lebanon, Yemen, Sudan, and Mauritania.

The League has only taken forms of military action in two conflicts in its history, deploying peacekeeping forces on both occasions. The first of these was upon Kuwait's independence from Britain on 19 June 1961 when its protectorate treaty was revoked and the Arab Nationalist regime of Abd al-Karim Qasim who had taken power in a *coup d'état* in Iraq in 1958 immediately mobilized his forces and seemed to be on the verge of invading Kuwait. The newly independent state, which had signed a defense pact with Britain, immediately requested British assistance, which rapidly deployed troops and warships that headed off the immediate invasion threat. At this stage Kuwait was not yet a member of the League but was admitted on 5 July on the condition that British forces would be asked to leave and would be replaced by an Arab League force, which would guarantee Kuwait's sovereignty and effectively act as a peacekeeping force between the two states.[10] The League force, funded directly by Kuwait, consisting of Saudi, Egyptian, Sudanese, and Jordanian forces,[11] did some good work, laying down a temporary border, which became known as the "Arab League Line," and were gradually withdrawn leaving only a few Sudanese observers by the end of 1962.[12] This compromise was achieved despite the fact that Iraq never formally agreed to any of these actions and can be seen as a real success for the League.

On the second occasion the League intervened in Lebanon after the collapse of its government and its descent in civil war and can be seen to have initially played a rather positive role in the conflict. In the initial phases before the Israeli intervention in 1978 the League managed to get an agreement for the creation of a peacekeeping force, which would later be transformed into the "Arab Deterrent Force" (ADF) in October 1976, which essentially consisted of Syrian troops. Although the fact that these troops ended up being an occupying force until 2005 in spite of the end of the civil war with the signature of the Tai'f accords in 1990 rather exposes the power politics and the nature of Lebanon as something of a playing field for proxy conflicts, the role of the League and the performance of the force was actually quite creditable. Naturally enough, the peacekeepers fell short of achieving their objective of (in their initial guise) only 2,500 troops, the ADF, however, can be said to have "made a genuine contribution to the restoration of peace and security in the Lebanon."[13] This was, however, short-lived and the League's preference for summits between Arab leaders, which excluded the various factions actually fighting, a tendency to focus on symptoms rather than causes, and the sheer complexity of the fighting and the hatreds that had been unleashed left the League scrambling to catch up and the civil war to descend to new depths throughout the 1980s. It was not until the sides were exhausted internally and their external sponsors had realized the existence of a stalemate that diplomacy could begin again and the League could play a role in facilitating the agreement at Tai'f. The League's role was also not helped by their reliance on Syrian peacekeepers who made up 80 percent of the force and who were clearly less than neutral, and who as the fighting intensified after 1978, became more brutal and less objective.[14]

These two examples of the deployment of peacekeeping forces under the banner of the League often tend to dominate considerations of the League's effectiveness in this sphere and obscure attempts at League intervention in terms of mediation in other disputes. The most significant of these are listed (in Table 3.1) and then briefly discussed here in order to demonstrate their diversity both geographically and in the types of conflict concerned.

As can be seen from the list below, the League has been rather less inactive, and has contributed, at least in part, to a number of successfully resolved crises. While a number of these efforts were perhaps contingent and temporary, and came due to a combination of factors, often with work by the OAU/African Union (AU), the League has had a role to play in internal conflict resolution and management. Interestingly, the League has also attempted mediation and good offices missions in conflicts outside its borders and even geographic region[15] (having, for example, played a role in negotiations over the Moro conflict in the Philippines), and appears to be increasingly willing to involve itself in the internal crises of some member states in the past decade or so, perhaps in the light of the Tunis Declaration of 2004.

Table 3.1 Intra-Arab crises, 1945–2008

Conflict	Dates	League response
Syria–Iraq crisis	1949	No action
Jordanian internal crisis and Syrian threat	1957	No action
Lebanese internal crisis with Egyptian/Syrian threat	1958	Arab League Council debate/good offices
Kuwait–Iraq	1961*	Arab League peacekeepers
North Yemen civil war with Egyptian and Saudi intervention	1962–67	Arab League recommendation/judgment
Algerian invasion of Morocco (the Sand War)	1963*	OAU-brokered ceasefire after three weeks, League mediation led to a peace agreement and a demilitarized zone
Jordanian internal crisis and Syrian threat	1966	No action
Black Friday Palestinian uprising in Jordan and Syrian/Iraqi threat	1970	No action
Kuwait–Iraq	1973	Mediation mission
Syria–Iraq dispute over the Euphrates waters	1975	
South Yemeni internal crisis and Saudi and North Yemeni intervention	1969–72	No action
Omani internal war	1971–76	Arab League Council debate/attempt at conciliation
North Yemen–South Yemen War	1972*	Arab League Council debate/mediation
Moroccan internal crisis and Algerian threat	1976–77	No action
Mauritanian internal crisis and Algerian threat	1976–77	No action
Western Sahara conflict	1976–present	No action
Libyan–Egyptian border war	1977	No action
North–South Yemen tensions	1979*	League mediation prevented escalation
Lebanese civil war	1975–90*	Arab League peacekeepers 1976–82/involvement in the 1990 Tai'f Accords
Sudanese civil war	1983–2009	Mediation

Conflict	Dates	League response
Somali civil war and state collapse	1988–present	Mediation efforts since 2005 and an Arab League Committee on Somalia exists
Kuwait invasion	1990–91	Arab League Council debate
Yemeni civil war	1994	Arab League mediation
Comoros crisis	1997	No action
Darfur crisis	2003–present	Mediation and a series of peace initiatives
Mauritanian coup crises	2005, 2008*	Mediation
Lebanese presidential crisis	2008*	Arab League mediation

(List compiled from a range of sources including: Mark Zacher, *International Conflicts and Collective Security, 1946–1977* (New York: Praeger, 1979), 194; and Marco Pinfari, "Nothing but Failure? The Arab League and the Gulf Cooperation Council as Mediators in Middle Eastern Conflicts," *LSE Working Papers*, no. 45 (2009))

* League success or significant contribution. Note that the list does not include Arab–Israeli conflicts or external interventions into the region.

Mauritania has also been an important but largely hidden site of League action in recent years. In 2005, when a military coup deposed the long-term leader Maaouya Taya who had held power since 1984, the coup leaders held a widely recognized referendum on a new constitution, with presidential term limits enshrined in 2006. Presidential elections were held in March the following year and Sidi Abedllahi was elected in the second round. Then on 6 August 2008 another coup took place, after the president had sacked some senior Army figures and some members of his own party had turned against him. The League was quick to respond, sending a delegation to attempt a mediation between the two sides just two days later.[16] The League was the principal actor, along with the EU and AU, in the subsequent Dakar Agreement, which paved the way for new presidential elections in 2009 which returned the coup leader, Mohamed Abdel Aziz, as president, whose dismissal as chief of staff and head of the Presidential Guard had in part sparked the coup.[17] The crisis had largely been resolved by these actions and the outcome of the new elections was widely recognized internationally, although protests during the Arab Spring demonstrated that the solution arrived at in Dakar was not universally popular in Mauritania.

It should also be stated that in recent years the League has begun monitoring elections, first deploying election observers to the Algerian presidential elections in 1995 and in every subsequent presidential election there, as well as, by 2010, having monitored elections in the Comoros, Djibouti, Iraq, Lebanon, Mauritania, Sudan, and Tunisia. Clearly it is debatable quite how "free and fair" some of these elections may have been—this area of activity is carried out only on the invitation of the state concerned and it is clearly not a core activity of the League—but it does demonstrate a greater commitment by the League to increasing democratization in the region, although it was conspicuous by its absence from the first post-Arab Spring elections in Tunisia in 2011. Interestingly, the League has worked with monitors from other organizations during this process, including the Arab Maghreb Union, the OIC, the AU, and *La Francophonie*.[18]

Assessment

Given the clear limitations placed upon the League by its member states in the fields of peace and security, it would be unfair to judge the League too harshly because it has either not been asked or has refrained from involving itself in certain regional disputes. Being so constrained by its member states in this area means that it should really be directly judged only on its record in those conflicts in which it has played a direct role and should instead be seen as a useful, and largely legitimate, tool in dealing with a specific sub-set of crises and conflicts in the region. Having been a belligerent in the Arab–Israeli situation for most of its history, the League cannot have a claim to uphold regional peace and security across the Middle East anyway; it simply does not have legitimacy with non-Arab States in the region.

Perhaps one of the most interesting recent developments has been in regard to Israel and the Palestine question. While the League has not lost its focus on this issue, which remains at the heart of much League business and one of the key areas of consensus, in 2002 the League was the forum at which a major change was announced. The Arab Peace Initiative[19] unveiled at the Beirut summit of the Arab League's heads of state and government in March 2002 built on an earlier resolution at the extraordinary Arab League summit in Cairo of June 1996, which had affirmed that a fair, final, and comprehensive settlement of the Arab–Israeli conflict was the strategic goal of the Arab States. The Arab Peace Initiative sponsored by Saudi Arabia would recognize a two-state solution with East Jerusalem as the capital of a Palestinian state within the pre-1967 borders, and would in turn lead to a full peace agreement between Israel and the Arab States with recognition and normalized relations, even referring to "good neighborliness." This seemingly extraordinary offer ended the historic "three nos"—one of the driving forces behind much of the League's diplomatic activity and at times seemingly the only real point of solidarity between its members—and it did so right in the middle of the second intifada. While the initiative failed to reignite the momentum behind the peace process, which had been lost at Camp David in 2000, the fact that it received unanimous approval at the Beirut summit (when so many other peace and security issues never got close) is quite remarkable. The initiative is extremely vague on the so-called "right of return" of Palestinian refugees but is clearly not designed to be a part of a final settlement between Israel and the Palestinians, which is for them to negotiate.[20] The initiative was subsequently readopted, again unanimously, at the 2007 Riyadh Arab League summit.[21] While the Arab Peace Initiative was not designed or promoted directly by the League—this was clearly a Saudi, Egyptian, and Jordanian proposal[22]—the very fact that they used the auspices of the League and were able to achieve the elusive unanimity of its 22 states is not only highly symbolic but is clearly part of the renaissance of the League that has been witnessed in recent years.[23]

Since the turn of the millennium greater focus has been placed on strengthening the tools at the League's disposal for dealing with conflict. In March 2000 at the League's Council meeting its foreign ministers agreed to explore means of better conflict prevention, management, and resolution between Arab States. This was to result in the adoption of the Statutes of the Arab Peace and Security Council in Khartoum six years later. Importantly, the new structures and this document makes the League the formal first resort for the settlement of disputes and improves its ability to intervene in disputes that involve sovereignty. The new structures, which began to come into existence from 2008, include the Arab Peace and Security Council (APSC), which meets twice a year before the League's Council meetings and can hold additional sessions at the request of either the secretary-general or any member. The APSC is composed of five rotating members determined by when they held (or will hold) chairmanship of the League Council. It was envisioned that the new APSC will deal with a range of disputes, humanitarian crises, and post-conflict reconstruction. So far the APSC has been activated outside its usual schedule by Djibouti in reference to a border issue with Eritrea, and has made headlines in condemning the International Criminal Court's indictment of Sudanese President Omar al-Bashir and in failing to reach agreement over how to tackle Somali piracy.[24] The APSC also proved useful in enabling a response to the 2008 crisis in Lebanon which resulted in the successful brokering of the Doha Accords, in which the League played a part,[25] resulting in a de-escalation of internal tensions and a framework for a form of power-sharing and elections, which at least gave some stability.[26]

The APSC is currently a rather reactive body but is designed to be complemented by a series of early-warning and intervention mechanisms, which could make it a more useful body. However, we should bear in mind that its decisions are still subject to full Council approval, which of course requires unanimity, and in addition by 2012 only 12 League members had actually signed up to the new structures. The mechanisms, namely a data bank, an early-warning system based in the League's secretariat, which will be able to table reports, and the so-called Board of Wise Personalities which will be available to act as envoys, mediators, and conciliators between parties to a dispute or a conflict,[27] are still not currently in place. All this means that despite some important moves forward on the surface, the League's abilities are still shackled by the unwillingness of its members to make major changes, which would amend their protections in the League's pact. Having said this though, disputes over sovereignty are far less prevalent in the region than before,[28] and the very fact that moves towards reform are being made suggests on the one hand the diminishment of one form of conflict and a greater willingness to give the League a role. As an example of the latter, at its 2015 summit in Sharm el-Sheikh in March 2015, under the slogan "70 years of joint Arab action," the member states once more spoke about the creation of a Joint Arab Force which, according to the final declaration of the summit, would be available for "rapid intervention in any Arab State whose national security and sovereignty are threatened or faces the threat of terrorism, at the request of the concerned state."[29] This force, which is of course voluntary for member states, seems like potentially a big step but is likely to be small and will of course not be deployable without unanimity in the Council. Any forward steps taken by the League in recent years, however good on paper, remain tethered to the pact and subject to the vagaries of regional power dynamics, meaning that while the League has a role in regional peace and security it will always be limited and contingent but can, given the right circumstances, still be of value.

Notes

1 Israel contested this role in the first UN debate on the status of the Arab League. See W. Hummer and M. Schweitzer, "Chapter VIII Regional Arrangements," in *The Charter of the UN. A Commentary*, ed. Bruno Simma *et al.* (Oxford: Oxford University Press, 2002).

2 This lack of solidarity with the Gulf States by the Palestinians, Yemenis and Sudanese in particular was punished by the expulsion of hundreds of thousands of their citizens from their jobs in the Gulf States, see: Hisham Foad, "The Effects of the Gulf War on Migration and Remittances," *SSRN Working Paper* (2009), http://dx.doi.org/10.2139/ssrn.1551539; see also: Ziad Swaidan and Mihai Nica, "The 1991 Gulf War and Jordan's Economy," *Middle East Review of International Affairs* 6, no. 2 (2002), www.rubincenter.org/2002/06/swaidan-and-nica-2002-06-07/.

3 Also known as the Arab Collective Security Pact (ACSP).

4 See: Dace Winther, *The Regional Maintenance of Peace and Security Under International Law* (London: Routledge, 2014), 126–143.

5 Mark Zacher, *International Conflicts and Collective Security, 1946–1977* (New York: Praeger, 1979), 165.

6 Zacher, *International Conflicts and Collective Security*, 166.

7 Pinar Bilgin, *Regional Security in the Middle East: A Critical Perspective* (London: Routledge, 2004), 102.

8 Christine Gray, *International Law and the Use of Force*, 3rd edition (Oxford: Oxford University Press, 2008), 383.

9 Michael Barnett and Etel Solingen, "Designed to Fail or Failure of Design? The Origins and Legacy of the Arab League," in *Crafting Co-operation*, ed. A. Acharya and I. Johnstone (Cambridge: Cambridge University Press, 2007), 214. This seems to be based largely on Zacher's prior work.

10 E. Lauterpacht, C.J. Greenwood, Marc Weller and Daniel Bethlehem (eds), *The Kuwait Crisis: Basic Documents* (Cambridge: Cambridge University Press, 1991), 55.

11 See: Nahla Yassine-Hamdan and Frederic Pearson, *Arab Approaches to Conflict Resolution: Mediation, Negotiation and Settlement of Political Disputes* (London: Routledge, 2014), 117–125.

12 David Finnie, *Shifting Lines in the Sand: Kuwait's Elusive Frontier with Iraq* (London: I.B. Tauris, 1993), 139.

13 Istvan Pogany, *The Arab League and Peacekeeping in the Lebanon* (Aldershot: Avebury, 1987), 159.

14 Pogany, *The Arab League and Peacekeeping in the Lebanon*, 161.

15 As Elmandjra points out, the League is not reticent in passing resolutions on a range of issues, including foreign issues outside of the immediate Arab orbit, passing 993 resolutions in its first ten years alone. Elmandjra, *The League of Arab States, 1945–1955*, PhD thesis (London School of Economics, 1957), 250, cited in Marco Pinfari, "Nothing but Failure? The Arab League and the Gulf Cooperation Council as Mediators in Middle Eastern Conflicts," *LSE Working Paper* No. 45, March 2009, 10, www.lse.ac.uk/internationalDevelopment/research/crisisStates/download/wp/wpSeries2/WP452.pdf. This tendency to pass resolutions but provide rather less implementation or even concrete proposals is often considered a symptom of the League's ineptitude but can also be seen as a sign of its utility as a forum for discussion, unity and rhetorical expression.

16 "Mauritania: Arab League Mission to Mediate with Junta," *ADN Kronos*, 8 August 2008, www1.adnkronos.com/AKI/English/Politics/?id=1.0.2402866201.

17 Hesham Youssef, "Mediation and Conflict Resolution in the Arab World: The Role of the Arab League," in *Yearbook on the Organization for Security*

and Co-operation in Europe (OSCE), ed. IFSH (London: Bloomsbury, 2013), 307.

18 See: Amor Boubakri, "The League of Arab States and the Electoral Gap," in *The Integrity of Elections: The Role of Regional Organizations*, International Institute for Democracy and Electoral Assistance (2012), 75–92.

19 "Document: Arab Peace Initiative," *Middle East Policy* 9, no. 2 (2002): 25–26.

20 For a detailed discussion on the language used in the declaration see: Ilai Alon, "A Linguistic Analysis of the 2002/2007 Arab Peace Initiative Documents," Institute of Israel Studies, University of Maryland, Position Paper 1 (2010), http://israelstudies.umd.edu/articles/linguistic-analysis-Alon.pdf.

21 See: Gawdat Bahgat, "The Arab Peace Initiative: An Assessment," *Middle East Policy* 16, no. 1 (2009): 33–39.

22 On the Saudi role in the peace process see: Joseph Kostiner, "Saudi Arabia and the Arab–Israeli Peace Process: The Fluctuation of Regional Coordination," *British Journal of Middle Eastern Studies* 36, no. 3 (2009): 417–429.

23 The League even tried to mediate between the various factions in the aftermath of the invasion of 2003, with a somewhat inevitable absence of success. See: Ibrahim Al-Marashi, "Regional Organizations as Conflict Mediators? The Arab League and Iraq," in *Beyond Regionalism?: Regional Cooperation, Regionalism and Regionalization in the Middle East*, ed. Cilja Harders and Matteo Legrenzi (Farnham: Ashgate, 2008), 139–155.

24 Hakim Almsmari, "Arab Peace and Security Council Reaches no Agreement over Fighting Piracy," *Yemen Post*, 10 November 2008, www.yemenpost.net/55/LocalNews/20081.htm.

25 See: Farah Dakhlallah, "The Arab League in Lebanon: 2005–2008," *Cambridge Review of International Affairs* 25, no. 1 (2012): 53–74.

26 Abbas Assi and James Worrall, "Stable Instability: The Syrian Conflict and the Postponement of the 2013 Lebanese Parliamentary Elections," *Third World Quarterly* 36, no. 10 (2015): 5 and 18.

27 Rodrigo Tavares, *Regional Security: The Capacity of International Organizations* (London: Routledge, 2010), 110.

28 Farah Dakhlallah, "The League of Arab States and Regional Security: Towards an Arab Security Community?" *British Journal of Middle Eastern Studies* 39, no. 3 (2012): 410.

29 "Who is Attending the Arab Summit?" *The New Arab*, 28 March 2015, www.alaraby.co.uk/english/news/2015/3/28/who-is-attending-the-arab-summit.

4   The Arab League
Economic, social, and cultural cooperation

- **Economic cooperation**
- **Socio-cultural cooperation: Human rights**
- **Technical cooperation: The specialized agencies**
- **Conclusion**

The League's efforts in promoting Arab unity were always likely to bear more fruit in the economic, social, and cultural spheres than in those of peace and security. Yet even here the League has faced considerable difficulties in some areas and progress, especially in the economic sphere, has clearly not been as extensive as it could have been, which is a cause of much frustration and has created a feeling that if progress is limited in these spheres then there is little hope for advancement elsewhere. In large part this lack of progress is a result of the distrust that is so often a key characteristic of regional relationships, thus making cooperation in areas that elsewhere would be relatively uncontroversial much harder; but also because, especially in the economic sphere, there has at times appeared to be relatively little to gain from greater economic cooperation or attempts at integration, thus creating a slightly paradoxical situation of nothing to gain and there being too much suspicion to risk cooperation. This chapter explores the League's activities in these three spheres, examining some of the structures, initiatives, and programs that the League has shaped in these areas in order to pursue its goals, while offering an analysis of the progress achieved. To this end it begins by exploring the cooperation in the field of economic integration and economic development before moving on to explore League initiatives in the sphere of human rights, as a key socio-cultural arena. It ends by examining the less political areas of cooperation in the form of the functionalist specialized agencies of the League, and the League's fostering of cooperation with other Arab bodies—namely the so-called Arab Unions. Often working well below the radar, the chapter assesses the contributions made by some of these specialized agencies to the cause of Arab unity, and to social, cultural, and economic development in the Arab world.

Economic cooperation

From the very earliest days economic cooperation and moves towards integration of the economies of the Arab States were high on the agenda of the League. There have been, therefore, a number of initiatives made in this direction. As discussed in Chapters 2 and 3, the 1950 Joint Defense and Economic Cooperation Treaty was designed to provide the impetus and architecture behind economic arrangements at League level, thus fulfilling aspirations outlined in the League's founding pact. The treaty established the Economic Council as a key body at the heart of the League itself. It first met in 1953 and has consistently tried to move forward in economic cooperation, mainly through the promotion of a range of other initiatives. The Economic Council was renamed in 1980, seemingly to match the usage prevalent elsewhere, namely the UN and EU, of having an Economic and Social Council (ESC). It plays a joint coordinating and supervisory role of a range of structures and initiatives in the economic sphere, two of which are discussed here.

The Council of Arab Economic Unity was established in 1957 by the Economic Council of the League, although it did not hold its first meeting until 1964. It emerged from the Economic Unity Agreement signed on 3 June 1957 with the aim of organizing and consolidating "economic relations among the States of the Arab League on bases that are consistent with the natural and historical links among them; and to provide the best conditions for flourishing their economies, developing their resources and ensuring the prosperity of their countries."[1] Reading this treaty it is very easy to get the impression that it is both comprehensive and extremely ambitious. Thus, article 1 discusses the establishment of complete economic unity with movement of people, capital, and goods (although no specific mention of services is made). Article 2 though immediately appears to row back from the ambitions outlined in article 1, focusing on a customs union and a harmonized tariff regime. The language speaks much of coordination and of the possibility of exceptions being made to some of the general principles. It states that the Council of Arab Economic Unity can only adopt measures by two-thirds majority, thereby setting the bar high. Additionally, there is no mention of any kind of arbitration or court and certainly nothing like the EU's qualified majority voting, all of which further hobbles progress towards the lofty goals outlined in article 1. Furthermore, the Economic Unity Agreement does not enjoy universal membership, thus geographically limiting what the body can achieve in terms of promoting Arab Economic Unity.

The Economic Unity Agreement appears to be essentially frozen at best, with little information about its activities available. Given this, it was perhaps unsurprising that alternative, less ambitious attempts at kick-starting intra-Arab trade as a precursor to deeper forms of integration had to be pursued.

In February 1978 the Agreement to Facilitate and Develop Trade Among Arab Countries was adopted by the ESC to act primarily as a customs facilitation tool. The agreement did this time explicitly include services. It also discussed both tariff and non-tariff barriers. The immediate tariff abolitions only concerned five limited classes of goods including agricultural products, raw materials, and goods produced by the Arab joint venture companies established by the League as it began to push alternative models of economic integration during the 1970s. This time the Agreement received widespread adherence but states were able to opt in and out of a whole raft of measures, making this a deeply piecemeal and limited effort, which could do little more than establish an absolute minimum level of economic cooperation. This more pragmatic approach did lay some groundwork for the more significant attempts made to move Arab Economic Unity forward during the 1990s. These efforts culminated in 1998 with the beginning of the Greater Arab Free Trade Area (GAFTA), which was supported by 14 of the 17 member states that agreed the proposals at the League's Cairo summit in 1996. Thus while not universal, the membership does mean that the vast majority of intra-Arab trade is conducted by states within the GAFTA framework. Despite this, according to the International Monetary Fund (IMF), intra-Arab trade represented just 8.2 percent of the value of all Arab exports in 1998,[2] this total had barely moved in 2007 when it stood at 8.5 percent of Arab exports,[3] which speaks volumes for the lack of momentum created by the new initiative. Meanwhile, while many reports highlight the potential that intra-Arab trade has for regional economic growth,[4] other modeling has suggested that growth in intra-Arab trade produces significantly less gross domestic product (GDP) growth per capita than extra-regional trade by almost 17 percent,[5] which might explain why business seeks extra-regional trade growth first and foremost. However, while the percentage figures on their own seem gloomy when compared to the EU figure for intra-regional exports of around a quarter of trade, when one examines the percentage value of the Arab region's exports to the EU in 2007, which took just 11.6 percent of the value of all Arab exports, the figures seem a little less gloomy.[6] It should also be borne in mind that GAFTA did not become fully operational until 2005, when agreed tariffs reached zero.[7]

GAFTA is interesting on two levels: first, because it indicates a strong residual will of Arab States to at least be seen to be making progress on Arab integration; and second, because the agreement deals with both tariff and non-tariff barriers to trade. The agreement does, however, contain measures that can be applied to prevent dumping and has other safeguards built in. However, it did lead to a 10 percent reduction in tariffs each year, has led to the creation of a system for the sharing of national standards, and moves have been made towards standardization in some areas, especially agricultural products. The agreement is overseen by the ESC through technical and executive committees and in 2004 members agreed to the establishment of a formalized dispute resolution structure, although it is unclear whether this has yet been created.[8] There seem to have been a number of initial problems with tariffs being replaced, in some instances, by other taxes that had a similar effect; many states made extensive use of exceptions granted to them, and non-tariff barriers have largely remained, although progress has been made in these areas since 2005. One of the bigger problems is that GAFTA has long been running on temporary Rules of Origin arrangements and significant progress is needed in this area.[9] It appears that the League itself has been working to try to make progress in a number of these areas. Thus, for example, according to Anja Zorob: "In 2003/2004 the A[rab] L[eague] General Secretariat sent delegations to GAFTA member countries to identify all non-tariff and para-tariff restrictions applied in each country based on the results of which it shall be decided on how to pursue its future elimination."[10] Institutionally, though, the structures underpinning GAFTA continue to lack key enforcement and monitoring tools on competition policy, rules on procurement by the states and on capital transfers. It also lacks the ability properly to monitor and oversee clashes between agreements outside the Arab region and GAFTA member states. This is important given the existence of other trade agreements and more comprehensive programs with the United States and the EU, and especially the burgeoning Euro-Med agreements, especially the Mediterranean Arab Free Trade Area (MAFTA).

Despite GAFTA's continuing issues, we should remember that a number of Arab States[11] have actively pursued bilateral trade agreements, even fairly comprehensive free trade agreements, with other Arab countries[12] and that 13 Arab States are now members of the

World Trade Organization (WTO), along with a further seven that have observer status, a requirement which obliges the opening of accession talks within five years.[13] Thus, even excluding sub-regional trade agreements through the GCC and AMU, there is a clear platform for trade between most Arab States already in existence, meaning that the League's existing efforts in this area now have to be more ambitious than the WTO's minimum requirements, setting the bar even higher than before for Arab League initiatives to promote greater intra-Arab trade and investment.

Given the inability of GAFTA to drive intra-Arab trade it is also important to recognize the very real constraints facing attempts to drive greater trade between Arab countries. These are often hurdles that require significant investment of both economic and political capital, and which cannot easily be overcome. George Abed attributes the region's weak intra-regional trade growth to five key structural factors: weak institutions, dominance of the public sector, underdeveloped financial markets, highly restrictive trade regimes, and problematic exchange rate regimes.[14] To this list can also be added high transaction costs from inadequate infrastructure and expensive transport costs, difficult bureaucracies, geographical distance, engrained import-substitution structures in most Arabs states outside the GCC, reliance on trade taxes rather than direct taxation, lack of complementarities, and product differentiation, as well as a general lack of focus on exports more generally within many Arab economies.[15] There is perhaps more promise in the potential liberalization of trade in services than goods given these barriers and common regional cultures and language, but progress in this area has been negligible in comparison to agreements on the trade in goods. An Arab Agreement for the Liberalization of Trade in Services was agreed in 2003 with 11 signatories but there is much work still to do in this area overall.[16]

As we know, improving intra-Arab trade is a challenging task and while many headline initiatives of the 1950s and 1960s fell far short of expectations, away from the limelight many other initiatives were pursued which have been more successful. Much of this work came in laying elements of the groundwork for better industrial integration and in the support mechanisms to underpin intra-Arab trade.

Two key elements here come in the form of the Arab Monetary Fund (AMF) and the Arab Trade Financing Program (ATFP). The former, founded in 1976, and with universal League membership, aims to assist states in managing their balance of payments accounts, helping states to remove restrictions on current payments, encouraging better communication and offering technical advice, developing Arab financial markets, and explicitly written into its objectives is the promotion of trade between member states.[17] It also has as an aim the facilitation of the development of a single Arab currency, which was clearly unlikely to occur. Essentially the AMF was founded to correct imbalances between those Arab States that were net oil importers and those that were net oil exporters after the quadrupling of the oil price in the early 1970s. It was therefore partly an intra-Arab solidarity mechanism and partly a body explicitly designed to facilitate regional trade. The organization, based in Abu Dhabi, is among the more active of the League's bodies and publishes a large number of studies.[18] Complementing the AMF, the ATFP, also based in Abu Dhabi, is also designed "to promote Arab trade and to increase the competitive capabilities of the Arab producers and exporters."[19] Established in 1989 with over US$1 billion in capital, the organization is designed to support GAFTA and the earlier Agreement for the Facilitation and the Development of Trade between Arab Countries. It offers regular forums for buyers and sellers to meet, offers lines of credit, risk-sharing facilities for national agencies and supports the Intra-Arab Trade Information Network (IATIN), which works with local Arab chambers of commerce and industry and a network of export promotion centers to collect and make available data that can facilitate trade. The IATIN is a joint venture with the UN Development Programme (UNDP) and the Geneva-based International Trade Centre, demonstrating the willingness of the ATFP to make real progress in this area. Clearly the AMF and the ATFP fall far from the political and even the academic limelight. There are no studies specifically on the ATFP and most work on the AMF dates from the 1980s and early 1990s, yet these organizations provide vital foundations for the encouragement of intra-Arab trade. They are evidence of the existence of a regional desire to continue to work at economic integration.

We can also examine the recent series of Arab Economic and Social Development Summits, which demonstrate a renewed interest in practical issues of economic integration and development in the Arab world. While there remains a continuing element of grandstanding, messaging, and the continuation of the Arab "talking-shop" in these initiatives, a series of summits focusing solely on these issues is an interesting development. Proposed in March 2007 by Egypt and Kuwait, a great deal of preparation went into the holding of the first summit in Kuwait in January 2009. The fact that it included private-sector organizations and a range of other regional organizations such as the Arab Banks Federation was encouraging, and a dedicated high-level and regular forum for the discussion of economic integration and development in the Arab world is clearly crucial for the exchange of ideas and the creation of momentum around these issues. Since the first meeting in 2009 there have been further summits in Cairo, Riyadh, and Tunis, creating at least the sensation of momentum in these areas with the usual flurry of announcements and rhetoric.

With the failure of the more grandiose schemes of the high years of Arab Nationalism came smaller steps towards economic integration through specialized agencies, smaller schemes, and programs of Arab industrial integration including frameworks for integration in specific industries.[20] Another attempt was made through the creation of joint venture companies under the auspices of the League. These were designed to create clear momentum around concrete projects that could be delivered and spur rapid benefits, the theory being that trust could be built between states with inevitable spillover effects into wider attempts at economic integration on a larger scale. To this end, over the course of the 1970s and 1980s a number of these Arab joint ventures were created, many of which continue to exist to this day.

Other similar firms have also been established outside the auspices of the League and have also included foreign partners. Those listed in Table 4.1 are expected to develop economies of scale, can issue shares, and are expected to be profitable.[21] There are also extensive legal frameworks in which they operate which provide considerable privileges.[22] During the 1970s OAPEC pushed particularly hard in this area but was not always successful, with the Arab Engineering Investments Company folding in 1989.[23] Others such as the Arab Investment Company seem to be working well with sizable capital resources available.[24] While the creation of these joint ventures was clearly designed to kick-start practical cooperation and integration, the extent of the spillover effects appears to be rather modest and the companies ended up in some cases being something of a passing phase, inevitably used more for political grandstanding than concrete action. This is evident in the legal immunities and concessions granted to them on many occasions, which were unwarranted. As Salem Ghumidh puts it, "privileges and immunities are not just benefits granted to the Joint Companies, but are efficient instruments to assure proper functioning of the companies and their independence vis-à-vis Member States. Therefore, it should not be more than they really deserve. And in general, partners should deal with Joint Companies as commercial and economical [sic] entities not as political organizations for mutual co-operations [sic]."[25]

As can be seen from the discussions above, the League's attempts at moving forward integration at the economic level has been a slow process, with many initiatives that appear to have had little impact on

Table 4.1 Arab joint companies

Company	Established
Arab Company for Drug Industries and Medical Appliances	1976
Arab Company for Electronic Commerce	2001
Arab Company for Industrial Investment	1974
Arab Company for Livestock Development	1974
Arab Mining Company	1974
Arab Shipbuilding and Repair Yard Company	1977
Arab Petroleum Services Company	1977
Arab Oil Tanker Company	1972
Arab Petroleum Investments Company	1974
Arab Engineering Investments Company	1981
Arab Petroleum Services Company	1975

improving the rate of intra-Arab trade. Indeed, a recent UN Economic and Social Commission for Western Asia report on Arab integration and unity issued a rather damning verdict on attempts at economic integration, which is worth quoting at length:

> The early commitments of Arab countries to regional integration fell well short of their ever-greater hopes and plans, a trend that has continued since. Regional integration plans have been partial, lacking an integrated strategic vision for human development and regional prosperity. A successful vision would take into account the political and security specificities of the Arab region. It would include the establishment of transnational institutions capable of strengthening and guiding Arab economic integration; implementing relevant decisions; and addressing shortcomings, notably by drawing upon the experiences of other regional groupings. Little of this has actually happened.[26]

This, perhaps rather harsh, verdict has largely become the consensus in the academic literature too and there is clearly plenty of evidence to support this belief. It is, however, a rather pessimistic view. Frequently the League has been overly ambitious in this field, its hand often forced by states that want to generate a greater feeling of momentum than is politically or economically possible in the short term. This naturally leads to disappointment and the creation of multiple initiatives. It also does not help when the (seemingly successful) model of the EU is right on the doorstep and is the natural yardstick by which success and failure are measured both within the Arab world and often by commentators from without. If we take a closer look at what has been achieved in the area of economic integration and cooperation by the League the picture looks a little more promising, especially in more recent decades—all the more so when the political, economic, structural, and geographical constraints facing intra-regional trade between the Arab nations are considered. It is clear that a lot of groundwork has been put in place to support intra-Arab trade both in terms of legal and political structures such as GAFTA, which has reduced tariffs dramatically, and in terms of the infrastructure to support trade, especially in terms of information and technical support from the AMF and ATFP. While there is much still to do to encourage greater Arab economic integration, progress has been made and there is still a willingness to continue to advance, however slowly and whatever a realistic end point may be.[27]

Socio-cultural cooperation: Human rights

All regional international organizations have some level of concern with issues of human rights from the Organization of American States (OAS) and AU, to the Association of Southeast Asian Nations (ASEAN), and the EU (which delegates many responsibilities in this area to the Council of Europe). The Arab League for many years had no remit in this area, and no mention of human rights is made in the League's founding pact. Most states in the region had little desire to talk about these issues and it was largely left to civil society groups to discuss the potential of various mechanisms for monitoring the protection of human rights in the Arab world. As human rights rose up the agenda internationally during the 1960s, discussion began at the League about the possibility of an Arab Charter of Human Rights. This appeared to come more from a desire to affirm difference between the UN human rights system, which has received less than universal Arab adherence, than as a means of strengthening the provisions in the UN human rights regime. The first formal move towards creating some kind of Arab human rights system came in 1968, and even then it was at the initial instigation of the UN, when the then secretary-general wrote to all organizations without a permanent commission on human rights issues in late 1967. The League's response was swift, with the decision to establish the Permanent Arab Commission for Human Rights being taken in Beirut in December 1968. The new body began with some initial vigor, having been approved by the League's Council and was projected to be made up of a single representative from each member state.[28] The Commission had the right to propose recommendations to the Council and by its second session in April 1969 had drawn up a plan of action, which was subsequently approved by the League's Council that September. It was proposed to set up a series of National Commissions which would report directly to the Permanent Commission in Cairo, and the Commission soon after began work drawing up a draft of a Charter of Arab Human Rights. This produced a version by 1971 that attracted no interest or support from the League's members, then nothing much happened for more than a decade. Further drafts were worked on until in 1983 a revised draft treaty was submitted to the League's Council.

Given the changes in the region in the intervening years and the rise of Islamic sentiment and the fact that the OIC, established in 1969, was working on its own human rights charter, the League's Council decided to await the outcome of these discussions before deciding on a separate Arab Charter. As Leila Zerrougui notes, various Arab non-governmental organizations (NGOs) stepped into this vacuum with draft declarations of their own and much invective was launched against the League for failing to make progress in this sphere.[29] The OIC arrived at an Islamic perspective on human rights in 1990, which was adopted as the Cairo Declaration on Human Rights in Islam.

Somewhat inevitably in the absence of the adoption of the proposed charter, and constrained by budgets, lack of independence and political difficulties, the Permanent Arab Commission for Human Rights focused extensively on Palestinian rights and the condemnation of Israel, and was blind to many other rights violations across the Arab world.[30] Until 2007 the Commission did not have its own statute and ran under the statute governing the League's specialized agencies.

Once the OIC had come to a decision the League began to consider again its own human rights charter and on 15 September 1994 the Arab Charter on Human Rights was actually approved by the League's Council. This, however, came with the objections of seven member states and was followed by a resounding lack of ratification from the League's member states.[31] It was also prefigured by a structural change in the League's secretariat when the secretary-general established a Department of Human Rights in April 1992, which coordinates with the Permanent Commission.

Despite these problems with a broad Arab Charter on Human Rights though, progress was made in other areas and human rights clearly began to become part of the work of other League bodies. The League also managed to agree on other instruments, including a Charter on the Rights of the Arab Child in 1983 and work in this area has proceeded with a number of high-level conferences under League auspices having taken place.[32] Although it could easily be argued that since every League member with the exception of Somalia has ratified the UN equivalent there appears little need to "create an Arab instrument parallel to every international instrument."[33]

Against the more active backdrop of the League, at the beginning of the new millennium, calls were made to push forward on the human rights front, and to this end on 24 March 2003 the Council called on the Permanent Commission to redraft and "modernize" the Arab Charter. Just over a year later this revised charter was adopted by the League's Council at the Tunis summit. While clearly an improvement on the 1994 version, the new charter attracted intense criticism from a range of Arab and non-Arab civil society groups for having deviated from international norms and human rights standards.[34] On the political front the new charter was ratified by seven states: Algeria, Bahrain, Jordan, Libya, Palestine, Syria, and the United Arab Emirates. This meant that 60 days later, on 15 March 2004, the charter entered into force, with Saudi Arabia, Yemen, Lebanon, Iraq, Kuwait, and Qatar also having ratified by the end of 2015.

The new charter does actually have a monitoring mechanism attached to it but does not allow for individual or group complaints to be brought and tellingly does not allow for states to raise concerns about human rights violations in other states. In other words the mechanism adheres strictly to the conditions of the League's pact and speaks to the paranoia of various regimes about human rights mechanisms, and as pertinently about the potential for neighbors to attempt to use human rights as a hostile foreign policy tool. The mechanism requires states-parties to submit tri-annual reports on their progress towards adherence to the charter, as well as a first report 12 months after ratification. There appears to be no mechanism for action if reports are not submitted.

The Permanent Arab Commission on Human Rights has also begun allowing NGOs to participate as observers but has placed a number of qualifying and participatory restraints upon them, meaning that fewer than 20 such organizations have this status. These NGOs can submit reports to be considered alongside the scheduled reports coming from the states. Thus the discourse of human rights, wider awareness and an increased mirroring of other regional and international systems for monitoring human rights has taken place in the Arab world, some of this led by the League, often pushed forward by concerted NGO action. The League's activities in the sphere of human rights have often drawn a lot of criticism as well as considerably more academic interest than any other area of activity outside peace and security. The Arab Charter of Human Rights and its weak monitoring structures, overseen as they are by the League's Council, have been further compromised by other decisions taken by the League. This is particularly the case when it comes to the Arab Convention on the Suppression of Terrorism,[35] adopted in 1998 and ratified by 16[36] of the League's 22 members.[37] With its extremely woolly definition of terrorism and in giving states opportunities to deviate from international standards in imposing their own special systems for dealing with terrorists, both of these are extremely problematic for human rights.[38]

Progress in the domain of human rights has been quite rapid since 2000 and there is now a functioning, if highly limited, system in place. This has rightly received both a tepid welcome and vitriolic denunciation from various quarters. There are clearly multiple problems with both the charter and the monitoring mechanisms from both a liberal perspective and when compared with most other regional human rights systems, but given that the League is mostly made up of autocracies and authoritarian regimes, getting human rights on the agenda at all, let alone a document that comes close to being acceptable to the wider world, and which is a significant improvement on the 1994 convention, marks significant progress. The way in which human rights discourses now influence not only the member states but also Arab societies and the work of the League means that in the longer term further progress may be possible. In many ways the case of the Arab Charter on Human Rights demonstrates both that the League is capable of evolution but that the core tenets underpinning its founding pact are unlikely to change in the near future, thus meaning that firm mechanisms in controversial areas will remain elusive. This does not mean that the League will not be able to use the new status that has been given to human rights within its technocratic functions, which connected as they are within systems of global governance are already subject to international normative discourses. These moves, and the very discourse and relevance now given to human rights, are likely to have some influence on the League in the future. Indeed as Chapter 11 explores, some impacts can already be discerned both during and as a result of the Arab Spring.

Technical cooperation: The specialized agencies

As part of its evolution over the past 70 years the League has created a number of specialized agencies to further its work in specific areas. Emerging from either Arab summits or Council decisions the agencies often, but not always, mirror those that have emerged from the UN and run the gamut of functional concern from culture to communications, and finance to health. These agencies, connected to the League but with their own staff and headquarters, have been the site of a good deal of cooperation and positive results in driving forward collaboration and a sense of Arab unity, as well as in producing positive outcomes within the Arab world. One of the most interesting factors at play with the creation of these agencies is that the pact allows those Arab States that do not wish to participate, to remain outside these structures. This creates a patchwork quilt of membership with only a few of these bodies having a universal League membership (see Table 4.2). This can be problematic at times, of course, and can lead to a proliferation of agencies that are begun as an eye-catching initiative but then receive little funding or support and are thus unable to function properly. Looked at another way though, the potential for opt-outs can reduce problems for agencies in having to deal with spoilers, and can mean that those states that are committed can move farther and faster. This means that any state that decides to join an agency at a later date is automatically expected to adhere to the rules of the body, which has evolved in ways it has been unable to influence. There have been some examples when domestic and international costs of remaining outside a specialized agency have been too high and states have been forced to join agencies that are more advanced in terms of levels of cooperation and bureaucratic structures than the new member state may have liked. For the League's members, then, specialized agencies provide opportunities for functional cooperation that attracts relatively little attention, and for the League they provide low-key spheres of cooperation in which tangible results and outcomes are realized, and the potential benefits of greater unity are advertised.

The scope and activities of the specialized agencies are a constant surprise. Some naturally are more active and organized than others, and while there is insufficient space to examine them all here, three of these agencies are briefly highlighted in order to offer further insights into the scope of activities that are engaged in: the Arab League Educational, Scientific and Cultural Organization (ALESCO), the Arab Bank for Economic Development in Africa (BADEA), and the Arab Administrative Development Organization (ARADO).

Established in 1964 when the League's Council ratified the organization's charter, and also agreed a Charter of Arab Cultural Unity,[39] ALESCO is a direct mirror of the UN's Educational, Scientific and Cultural Organization (UNESCO). The new body did not, however, hold its first conference and properly establish itself until July 1970,

Table 4.2 Arab League specialized agencies

Agency	Foundation	Headquarters	Membership
The Council of Arab Economic Unity	03.06.1957	Cairo	J, Su, S, So, I, P, E, M, Y
The Organization of Arab Petroleum Exporting Countries	19.01.1968	Kuwait	U, B, T, A, SA, S, I, Q, K, L, E
Arab Administrative Development Organization	01.04.1961	Cairo	All
The Arab States Broadcasting Union	15.10.1955	Tunis	All, ex. C
The Arab League Educational, Scientific and Cultural Organization	21.05.1964	Tunis	All
The Arab Center for the Study of Arid Zones and Dry Lands	03.09.1968	Damascus	J, T, A, SA, S, Su, So, I, P, Q, C, K, L, E, M, Ma, Y
Arab Academy for Science, Technology and Maritime Transport	26.04.1975	Alexandria	All
The Arab Labor Organization	12.01.1965	Cairo	All, ex. C
The Arab Organization for Agricultural Development	11.03.1970	Khartoum	All
The Arab Satellite Communication Organization	21.03.1976	Riyadh	All, ex. C
Secretariat General of Arab Interior Ministers Council	23.09.1982	Tunis	All
The Arab Atomic Energy Agency	26.03.1982	Tunis	J, B, T, SA, S, Su, I, P, K, L, Ly, E, M, Ma, Y
Arab Industrial Development and Mining Organization	06.07.1988	Rabat	All, ex. C
Civil Aviation Arab Commission	02.10.1993	Rabat	J, U, B, T, A, SA, Su, S, I, O, P, Q, L, Ly, E, M, Ma, Y

Agency	Foundation	Headquarters	Membership
The Arab Women Organization	12.09.2001	Cairo	J, U, B, T, A, Su, S, I, O, P, L, Ly, E, M, Ma, Y
Arab ICT Organization	10.09.2001	Tunis	J, T, A, D, Su, S, So, O, P, C, L, Ly, E, M, Ma, Y
The Arab Fund for Economic and Social Development	16.05.1968	Kuwait	All
The Arab Bank for Economic Development in Africa	05.12.1973	Khartoum	All, ex. So, C, Y, D
The Arab Investment and Export Credit Guarantee Corporation	16.12.1970	Kuwait	All, ex. C
The Arab Monetary Fund	08.12.1975	Abu Dhabi	All
The Arab Authority for Agricultural Investment and Development	1976	Khartoum	J, U, T, A, SA, Su, S, So, I, O, P, Q, C, K, L, E, M, Ma, Y

Key: A=Algeria, B=Bahrain, C=Comoros, D=Djibouti, E=Egypt, I=Iraq, J=Jordan, K=Kuwait, L=Lebanon, Ly=Libya, M=Morocco, Ma=Mauritania, O=Oman, P=Palestine, Q=Qatar, SA=Saudi Arabia, S=Syria, So=Somalia, Su=Sudan, T=Tunisia, U=United Arab Emirates, Y=Yemen.

when it first met and adopted its statute, elected its executive board and formalized its administrative and financial regulations. Its goals are partly intellectual, partly practical—in terms of promoting education, growth, and environmental protection—and partly about the wider promotion of Arab-Islamic culture globally.

Its institutional framework is tripartite in nature, revolving around a General Conference of Member States, an Executive Board, and a secretariat headed by a secretary-general. ALESCO maintains a series of specific programs, which have their offices around the Arab world; thus, for example, the Institute of Arab Manuscripts is based in Kuwait, the Program on the Environment of the Red Sea and the Gulf of Aden is based in Jeddah, and the Institute for the Arab Encyclopedia is based in Baghdad. In addition, each country has its own ALESCO national commission and the body also maintains a permanent delegation to UNESCO in Paris.[40] The agency has been very active in a number of spheres and has paid special attention to improving teaching standards, eradicating illiteracy, especially among women, and in translating technical documents and studies into Arabic. An Arab Strategy for the Development of Arab Culture has been adopted and a lot of work has been conducted to protect historic structures in cities such as Fez, Kaiouran, and Jerusalem, as well as promoting the study and protection of ancient manuscripts. On the scientific side ALESCO has sponsored research and the publication of a monograph series on marine conservation and protection, aquifers, and mineral extraction, and has focused much attention on the problem of desertification and the practical measures needed to combat its spread. The body also acts as an important information clearing house and has done much work on standardization of scientific language in Arabic, especially through its Documentation and Information Department. Its promotion of the development of libraries, the dissemination of books across borders and raising awareness through its own publication program, especially catalogues such as the *Bulletin of Arab Publications* have all been significant programs for ALESCO. This is all important and rather unsung work, which is foundational in encouraging cooperation, standardization, and increasing knowledge and awareness. In this sense ALESCO is very much at the coal face of promoting greater Arab unity and is often seen as one of the most successful of the League's specialized agencies.[41]

In one sense it should not be too surprising that the League has mirrored the UN, but it has also innovated and diverged from purely mimicking the structures and programs of other organizations. BADEA is symbolic of the need for the Arab States to maintain good relations with their African neighbors, and is a source of power and influence.[42] Established at the League's Algiers summit in November 1973, it began operating in March 1975 with the aims of financing development in Africa, providing technical assistance and encouraging Arab investments of all kinds in Africa.[43] While not having universal League membership, it still has an overwhelming majority participating. In part it functions to assist Arab exports to Africa but it also offers a range of low-interest loans for development projects, although the bank also has rules that restrict it from lending more than 60 percent of the total cost of a project, meaning that the Bank often works alongside other donors.[44] BADEA also has a role in research and the dissemination of a range of data, even sponsoring an annual prize for academic work relating to its areas of interest and operation. This specialized agency, although originating from the League, is essentially an independent entity demonstrating the flexibility of the League itself but also its wider importance as a forum for the promotion of initiatives which may go beyond the structures of the League itself. BADEA has lent more than $1.2 billion since its establishment, and while clearly a fairly small player in terms of development in Africa, has a role to play in encouraging Arab States to engage with Africa and to work more closely together in this regard.

The final specialized agency highlighted here, ARADO, is much more closely connected to the League and is something of a catch-all body which is unusual in its scope and remit. Established in 1961 it is one of the earliest specialized agencies of the League, and with universal League membership it has a long history of trying to fulfill its remit of assisting with administrative capacity building with the broader aim of improving wider development processes in the Arab States.[45] Interestingly, it works not only with governments and their bureaucratic machinery but also with publicly owned companies and a wide range of private-sector organizations, focusing on improving leadership. Its remit includes training, consultancy, information gathering and processing, dissemination of best practice, attempts at standardization and evaluation. Organized around the common tripartite structure, it comprises a General Assembly, an Executive Council, and a Directorate General (secretariat). The Executive Council, with just seven members elected for two-year terms, organizes the general direction and priorities of the agency. Given the broad remit, the range of issue areas touched by ARADO is significant, as are its relations with other aspects of the League's structures and those of a wide range of other international organizations. ARADO's role is essentially one of a house of expertise and the more its expertise is tapped, the more it can influence structures and working practices across a range of issue areas and across the Arab world. It is therefore very much at the heart of the ongoing standardization process, which is the critical foundation for any meaningful inter-Arab cooperation to occur. Its wide range of publications including a magazine, a bulletin, and an academic journal, alongside its conferences, workshops, and extensive range of training programs, both facilitate networks and dialogue but also spread common standards and practices across the region. ARADO has, for example, taken a lead in promoting e-government and developing standards in this regard for the Arab States. It is also worthwhile briefly listing some of the studies or programs the organization has undertaken in order to see how diverse ARADO's interests are. They have included studies on the management of hospital waste,[46] bureaucratic reform in Egypt,[47] the Arab Red Crescent and Red Cross Organization

Structure and Administrative and Financial Regulations Development Project, the development of performance framework and systems of the Ministry of Education, Bahrain, and even the reorganization of the Arab League secretariat in 2001.[48]

Arab Unions

Alongside the work of the specialized agencies, the League has also been active in other initiatives to promote greater cooperation between Arab bodies at the sub-state level. This is especially the case with the bodies that emerged largely during the height of the Arab Nationalist era from civil society efforts to accelerate ties between Arabs. These "Arab Unions" run the gamut of different foci and many are very active even today in their respective fields. A number of these were even established with assistance and encouragement of the League itself. The Union of Arab Banks founded in March 1974, for example, emerged out of a meeting held in Beirut under the auspices of ARADO. Despite remaining independent from the League it pursues many of the same objectives, including "[e]xerting all efforts towards the establishment of the Arab common market and the Arab economic integration and orchestrating the coordination and harmonization of legislation and regulations related to Arab banking and financial sectors."[49] The Union also has a Center for Arbitration and Conciliation, which has done good work in enabling inter-Arab banking trust and cooperation.

It is also worth highlighting the fact that these various Arab Unions not only work on issues of direct interest to the League but also work closely with the League's secretariat and its specialized agencies, often in highly functional fields. A good example of this is the Arab Iron and Steel Union (AISU) founded in 1971 whose members produce around 90 percent of iron and steel in the region. As the companies that make up its members (many of which are still state owned) diversified their activities, so this body has grown its interests. The role of such bodies, fostered, supported, and encouraged by the League, has important effects in the creation of forums, information sharing, and trust building. The AISU publishes its own magazine in both Arabic and English, holds regular meetings and specialized conferences, and has offices in Cairo, Damascus, and Riyadh.[50] It is easy to overlook these activities but they create the environment from which greater cooperation and trust can be built. Let us not forget that the roots of the EU lie within its forerunner, the European Coal and Steel Community (ECSC), and while this was a multilateral body rather than the NGO that is the AISU, important echoes remain.

These various unions in key industries (see Table 4.3), while representing the attempts of both private and public bodies to promote inter-Arab cooperation on matters of interest in the technical sphere where interests are shared, also represent the continuing appetite in the region for greater collaboration and solidarity between Arabs, and have laid a lot of important groundwork should there be political opportunities for greater intergovernmental cooperation at the level of the League in the future.

Table 4.3 Arab Unions

Union/federation	Established
Arab Cooperative Federation	1985
Arab Federation for Paper, Printing and Packaging Industries	1977
Arab Federation of Chemical Fertilizer Producers	1976
Arab Federation of Engineering Industries	1975
Arab Federation of Leather Industries	1978
Arab Federation of Travel Agents	1970
Arab Seaports Federation	1977
Arab Iron and Steel Union	1972
Arab Sugar Federation	1977
Arab Union for Cement and Building Materials	1977
Arab Union for Information Technology	1996
Arab Union of Electricity	1987
Arab Union of Fish Producers	1976
Arab Union of Food Industries	1976
Arab Union of Hotel and Tourism	1994
Arab Union of Land Transport	1978
Arab Union of the Manufacturers of Pharmaceuticals and Medical Appliances	1986
Arab Union of the Manufacturers of Tires and Rubber Products	1993
Arab Union of Railways	1979
General Arab Insurance Federation	1964
General Union of Arab Agricultural Workers and Cooperatives	1993
Union of Arab Contractors	1995
Union of Arab Investors	1995

Conclusion

Progress in the economic, social, and cultural domains should, on paper at least, be much easier for the Arab nations than the more sensitive issues of peace and security, but as this chapter has shown, cooperation in these spheres is clearly influenced by a continuing desire to preserve sovereignty, as well as the complex animosities that have divided the region in the post-war period, creating mistrust and competition that has shaped the League and its attempts in these domains. Despite these problems, however, the wider political recognition of the need for some cooperation and integration coupled with the popular desire for states to pursue these goals has led to a large number of initiatives in these areas. While this chapter has only been able to cover a fraction of these attempts at greater economic, social, and cultural cooperation, the diversity and persistence of moves on these issues demonstrates that the picture is not entirely gloomy as it initially appears. The depth of integration and cooperation may be decidedly patchy but a great deal of work has been done in these areas, and in the least contentious areas, often seemingly the most technical and uninspiring work, the achievements have often been the greatest. The League's specialized agencies, supported by the aligned Arab Unions, have laid much groundwork for concrete examples of cooperation, which has brought benefits to the Arab world. While major obstacles to cooperation remain, there does still seem to be enough willpower amongst governments and peoples for continuing moves to be made in all of the fields discussed in this chapter. That these gains may be piecemeal and incremental in nature should not lead us to despair. By focusing more on the incremental gains, rather than the failures of more grandiose designs and projects, we gain a more balanced picture of the League's activities and a more realistic idea of what level of Arab unity is possible in the future.

Notes

1 Prelude of the Economic Unity Agreement, http://caeuarab.org/docum ents/agreements/1-eng.pdf.
2 Hasan al-Atrash and Tarik Yousef, "Intra-Arab Trade: Is it Too Little?" *IMF Working Paper*, WP/00/10 (2000), www.imf.org/external/pubs/ft/wp/ 2000/wp0010.pdf, 4.
3 United Nations, COMTRADE database, Statistics Division, 2009.
4 See, for example, in agriculture: Assem Abu Hatab, "The Impact of Regional Integration on Intra-Arab Trade in Agrifood Commodities: A Panel Data Approach," *Egyptian Journal of Agricultural Economics* 25, no. 2 (2015): 21–36.

5 A study of 13 Arab countries between 1990 and 2007. Hossam Younes, "The Contribution of Trade to Growth of the Arab Countries" (2010), www.eiit.org/WorkingPapers/Papers/Other/FREIT097.pdf.

6 United Nations, COMTRADE database, Statistics Division, 2009.

7 Some exceptions to zero tariffs remain for poorer states such as Sudan, Yemen, and Palestine.

8 Nsour thinks not, see: Mohammad Nsour, *Rethinking the World Trade Order: Towards a Better Legal Understanding of the Role of Regionalism in the Multilateral Trade Regime* (Leiden, the Netherlands: Sidestone Press, 2010), 220.

9 For more information on this see: Bashar Malkawi, "Rules of Origin in the Greater Arab Free Trade Area" (2015), www.researchgate.net/publication/287318987_Rules_of_Origin_in_the_Greater_Arab_Free_Trade_Area.

10 Anja Zorob, "Intraregional Economic Integration: The Cases of GAFTA and MAFTA," in *Beyond Regionalism? Regional Cooperation, Regionalism and Regionalization in the Middle East*, ed. Cilija Harders and Matteo Legrenzi (Farnham: Ashgate, 2008), 176.

11 There is also the attempt at a sub-regional Free Trade Area, established in 2004 as a result of the "Agadir Declaration" between Morocco, Jordan, Tunisia, and Egypt in 2001, a copy of the agreement is available at: www.agadiragreement.org/CMS/UploadedFiles/10ac3206-5a49-4dd8-833e-0783d2ea4190.pdf. This in turn is linked to the EU seemingly rather more than to the League and the agreement is supported by an EU-funded Technical Unit.

12 This was actively called for in the GAFTA Agreement to speed up integration and lowering of barriers to trade. For details on these agreements see: Steffan Wippel, "The Agadir Agreement and Open Regionalism: The New Forum for Integration on the Southern Shore of the Mediterranean in the Context of Multiple Regional Orientations," EuroMeSCo Research Paper No. 45 (Lisbon: EuroMeSCo Secretariat, 2005), www.euromesco.net/euromesco/media/euromesco_paper_45.pdf.

13 The 13 are: Bahrain, Djibouti, Egypt, Jordan, Kuwait, Mauritania, Morocco, Oman, Qatar, Saudi Arabia, Tunisia, the United Arab Emirates, and Yemen. Observers are: Algeria, Comoros, Iraq, Lebanon, Libya, Sudan, and Syria.

14 George Abed and Hamid Davoodi, *Challenges of Growth and Globalization in the Middle East and North Africa*, IMF (2003), www.imf.org/external/pubs/ft/med/2003/eng/abed.htm.

15 For more discussion on this see: Anja Zorob, "Intraregional Economic Integration: the Cases of GAFTA and MAFTA," in *Beyond Regionalism? Regional Cooperation, Regionalism and Regionalization in the Middle East*, ed. Cilija Harders and Matteo Legrenzi (Aldershot: Ashgate, 2008), 173–174; and Nasser Saidi, "Arab Economic Integration: An Awakening to Remove Barriers to Prosperity," Economic Research Foundation Working Paper 0322 (Cairo: ERF, 2003).

16 UN Economic Commission for Western Asia, *Annual Review of Developments in Globalization and Regional Integration in the Countries of the ECSWA Region* (2003), 27–29.

17 Regional monetary funds are seen as important factors in regionalization: Raj Desai and James Vreeland, "Global Governance in a Multipolar

World: The Case for Regional Monetary Funds," *International Studies Review* 13, no. 1 (2011): 109–121.

18 See for example: Philippe Karam, *Exchange Rate Policies in Arab Countries: Assessment and Recommendations* (Abu Dhabi: Arab Monetary Fund, December 2001), www.mafhoum.com/press7/216E13.pdf.

19 See the ATFP website, available at: www.atfp.org.ae.

20 For deeper discussion of these projects see: Elias Ghantus, *Arab Industrial Integration: A Strategy for Development* (Beckenham: Croom Helm, 1982).

21 Samir Makdisi, "Arab Economic Co-operation," in *Arab Industrialisation and Economic Integration*, ed. Roberto Aliboni (London: Croom Helm, 1979), 128–129.

22 Salem Ghumidh, "Privileges and Immunities of Multilateral Arab Public Joint Investments,"*Journal of Law* 10, no. 1 (2012): 1–26.

23 Saadallah al-Fathi, "Arab Economies Pay Price of Slow Integration," *Gulf News*, 4 May 2014, http://gulfnews.com/business/analysis/arab-economies-pay-price-of-slow-integration-1.1327789.

24 See: www.taic.com/index.php?lang=en.

25 Salem Ghumidh, "Privileges and Immunities of Multilateral Arab Public Joint Investments,"*Journal of Law* 10, no. 1 (2012): 25.

26 UN-ESCWA, "Arab Integration: A 21st Century Development Imperative" (2014), 33. www.unescwa.org/sites/www.unescwa.org/files/publications/files/e_escwa_oes_13_3_e.pdf. See also for a critique: Adam Hanieh, "Development Through Unity. Assessing ESCWA's Arab Integration: A 21st Century Development Imperative," *Development and Change* 46, no. 4 (2015): 979–992.

27 For detailed (and realistic) economic discussion of the potential for the Arab States to emulate the EU see: Bernard Hoekman and Patrick Messerlin, "Initial Conditions and Incentives for Arab Economic Integration: Can the European Community's Success Be Emulated?" in *Arab Economic Integration: Between Hope and Reality*, ed. Ahmed Galal and Bernard Hoekman (Washington, DC: Brookings Institution Press, 2003), 102–147.

28 For more on the specifics see: Mohamed Amin al-Midani, "Human Rights Bodies in the League of Arab States," in *Regional Protection of Human Rights*, ed. Dinah Shelton, Paolo G. Carozza, Paolo Wright-Carozza, Volume 1, second edition (Oxford: Oxford University Press, 2013), 159–168.

29 Zerrougui served as chairperson of the Committee of Experts in charge of drafting the revised Arab Charter on Human Rights and has worked extensively in the UN Human Rights system. Leila Zerrougui, *The Arab Charter on Human Rights* Lecture given at the University of Essex, July 2008, http://projects.essex.ac.uk/ehrr/V7N2/Zerrougui.pdf, 2.

30 David P. Forsythe, *Human Rights in International Relations*, third edition (Cambridge: Cambridge University Press, 2012), 191. Forsythe states on the same page that "the League and its human rights agency ... does not merit analysis here."

31 The Open Society Foundations have recently published a useful guide to the human rights mechanisms of the League: Mervat Rishmawi, *The League of Arab States Human Rights Standards and Mechanisms, Towards Further Civil*

Society Engagement: A Manual for Practitioners (Cairo, 2015), www.openso cietyfoundations.org/sites/default/files/league-arab-states-manual-20151125.pdf.

32 For the text of the "Marrakesh Declaration" which emerged out of the Fourth High Level Meeting on The Rights of the Child, held 19–21 December 2010 see: http://srsg.violenceagainstchildren.org/sites/default/files/documents/ma rrakech_declaration_english.pdf.

33 Mervat Rishmawi, *The League of Arab States in the Wake of the "Arab Spring"* (Cairo: Cairo Institute for Human Rights Studies, September 2013), www.cihrs.org/wp-content/uploads/2013/09/Arab-Leage.pdf.

34 For a detailed examination of one key pan-Arab human rights group, see: Mohsen Awad, "Pan-Arab Civil Organizations: The Arab Organization for Human Rights," *Contemporary Arab Affairs* 1, no. 4 (2008): 621–630.

35 Available here: www.unodc.org/tldb/pdf/conv_arab_terrorism.en.pdf.

36 Algeria, Bahrain, Djibouti, Egypt, Jordan, Lebanon, Libya, Morocco, Oman, Palestine, Saudi Arabia, Sudan, Syria, Tunisia, United Arab Emi-rates, and Yemen. The Convention entered into force on 7 May 1999, with Qatar joining in 2004.

37 Lynn Welchman, "Rocks, Hard Places and Human Rights: Anti-Terrorism Law and Policy in Arab States," in *Global Anti-Terrorism Law and Policy*, ed. Victor V. Ramraj, Michael Hor, Kent Roach and George Williams (Cambridge: Cambridge University Press, 2012), 621–655.

38 See further discussion on these issues in Javaid Rehman, *Islamic State Practices, International Law and the Threat from Terrorism* (Oxford: Hart, 2005); and Amnesty International, *The Arab Convention for the Suppres-sion of Terrorism: A Serious Threat to Human Rights*, 31 January 2002, www.amnesty.org.uk/press-releases/arab-convention-suppression-terrorism-ser ious-threat-human-rights-0.

39 For the text of the charter see: J.D. Pearson, "D. Miscellany," *British Society for Middle Eastern Studies Bulletin* 3, no. 1 (1976): 63–64.

40 More information is available on ALESCO's structures, on its website: www.alecso.org/site/.

41 M.T. Khafagi, "ALECSO and its Activities in the Field of Information," *IFLA Journal* 15, no. 3 (1989): 246–250.

42 Peter Kragelund, "The Return of Non-DAC Donors to Africa: New Pro-spects for African Development?" *Development Policy Review* 26, no. 5 (2008): 555–584.

43 Eric Neumeyer, "Arab-related Bilateral and Multilateral Sources of Development Finance: Issues, Trends, and the Way Forward," *The World Economy* 27, no. 2 (2004): 281–300.

44 Arab Bank for Economic Development in Africa, www.badea.org/index.htm.

45 Arab Administrative Development Organization, www.arado.org/Default.aspx.

46 A.I. Altabet, "Medical and Chemical Waste in Dental Clinics," in *Pro-ceedings of the Third Arabic Conference of Environmental Administration: New Trends in Management of Environment Contamination Waste*, Arab Administrative Development Organization, 23–24 November 2004, Sharm el-Sheikh, Egypt.

47 Jamil E. Jreisat, "Faltering Bureaucratic Reforms: The Case of Egypt," *Journal of Developing Societies* 11, no. 2 (1995): 221–232.

48 For wider discussion of leadership development in the Arab world, see: May Al-Dabbagh and Christine Assaad, "Taking Stock and Looking

Forward: Leadership Development in the Arab World," NYU Abu Dhabi (2010),   http://wagner.nyu.edu/files/leadership/LeadershipDevelopmentPro gramsArabWorld.pdf.

49 For more on the Union of Arab Banks, see: www.uabonline.org/en/about.
50 For more on the AISU see: www.arabsteel.info/index.php?VAR=en_about_us.

5 The Arab League
Problems and prospects

- **The Arab League in the twenty-first century**
- **Obstacles and achievements**
- **Prospects?**

Having now seen the range of the Arab League's activities and explored its background, structures, and evolution, this chapter begins by bringing together the League's progress in the twenty-first century, in order to set the scene for further analysis. By drawing upon the tools contained in Chapter 1, we then proceed to explore the problems and opportunities that the Arab League has faced. In offering an assessment of the obstacles to progress experienced by the League, by examining both internal and external factors, the scene is set for a realistic assessment of the League's achievements. Using this analysis, the chapter then concludes with an examination of the outlook and prospects for the Arab League created by more recent events.

The Arab League in the twenty-first century

With the seeming final death of Arab Nationalism in the 1970s[1] and the final nail having been hammered home in the aftermath of the Iraqi invasion of Kuwait in 1990, pressure to engage in grandiose schemes of large-scale Arab cooperation lessened and the Arab League looked like it would decline in authority, function, and relevance. After all, the progress within the region at this time seemed to be made through the creation of the more dynamic sub-regional organizations. In just a decade after its creation the GCC appeared both more ambitious than the League's seemingly moribund dreams, and also more advanced, having already made concrete progress. In 1989 the western end of the region drew together through the AMU, against the odds and with a practically focused functionalist agenda. This happened almost simultaneously with the creation of the Arab Cooperation Council between North Yemen, Iraq, Jordan, and Egypt. As Charles Tripp puts it, "the founders of all three organizations laid great emphasis on the need for economic co-operation and suggested that it made sense for states situated geographically in close, or fairly close proximity to each other [to] group together into a single block."[2] It is therefore no real surprise that against these twin backdrops the League appeared to have run out of steam in the early 1990s with a series of failed initiatives such as those on human rights and a general lack of dynamism and focus. The League, though, still had its uses and from the late 1990s began to regain the initiative and become a focus for inter-Arab discussions and cooperation. The ACC was effectively stillborn, falling apart as it did with Saddam's invasion of Kuwait (an event that strengthened the GCC). It was already a slightly odd grouping, lacking geographical coherence, and with membership open to all Arab States it was difficult to see what it offered that the League did not already.[3] Although, in its first year it appeared to be very active indeed, perhaps wishing to show that progress was being made. Yet the odd combination of regime types always made the new body an unlikely vanguard for Arab cooperation; in many ways it seemingly amplified some of the League's existing issues in a new organization.[4]

Meanwhile, as explored in Chapter 10, the AMU quickly began to experience problems, which restricted its growth and potential, leaving the GCC as the only competition to the League. However, with its restricted membership, the financial clout of its member states, and their continuing desire for wider regional influence, it seemed that there was easily enough space for both bodies. From the late 1990s onwards the Arab League slowly began to make more headway. While Arab leaders had not given up their tendency towards the grandiose gesture, a new realism began to creep into activities conducted under the League's auspices with initiatives like GAFTA being more focused and achievable than previous attempts at cooperation. In the early 2000s there was a flurry of summits and initiatives, culminating perhaps in the Arab League's Tunis Declaration. This outlined an important agenda of modernization: the first key pledge is to "amend the Arab League charter and to modernize its work methods and its specialized institutions based on the various Arab initiatives and ideas included in the proposals put forward by the Secretary General as well as on a consensual and coherent vision and on a gradual and balanced approach."[5] The declaration also focused on issues of poverty, information technology, education, human rights, youth issues, and women's rights, and emphasized the need to work with civil society organizations.

While the Tunis Declaration may be "a timid reaction to the [sic] US democracy promotion,"[6] containing no real mechanisms to make it happen, it is remarkable that these regimes were able to agree even on this and that they were willing to promulgate it via the Arab League. This of course could be seen both ways—that the League is simply an instrument of the states, controllable and useful, but also that the League is the natural area in which progress, however limited, can be made around issues of common concern. These regimes were perhaps cognizant of the Arab Human Development Report, which was published by the UNDP from 2002 onwards. These reports painted a dire picture of the region's social and economic malaise. The subheadings of each year's report are certainly reflected in the priorities of the Tunis Declaration, thus 2002 was *Creating Opportunities for Future Generations*, 2003 was *Building a Knowledge Society*, 2004 was *Towards Freedom in the Arab World* and 2005 was *Towards the Rise of Women in the Arab World*. Recognition that these problems required at least some element of intra-Arab cooperation and that the League provided the best venue for this gave the body a new confidence, which lasted into the early years of the Arab Spring.

Obstacles and achievements

As we have seen, most of the academic literature on the League focuses on its failings and the obstacles posed by the regional environment to its success. These are important arguments that frame the ability of the League to make progress towards its goals.

Given this context and our awareness of the arguments put forward by realists and constructivists, and many area studies specialists, in terms of the structural and ideational barriers to the League's achievement of its objectives, it makes more sense here to concentrate on the achievements of the organization against these seemingly overwhelming odds. As we have seen in the foregoing chapters, these achievements have tended to be small, functionalist, and unobtrusive. Arab League peacekeeping has clearly been a welcome addition, and attempts at dispute resolution have sometimes borne fruit. In the economic sphere GAFTA has been a step in the right direction, reducing tariffs. Meanwhile in the social and cultural spheres the specialized agencies have done some excellent work on a range of issues, from education to industry, and especially in exchanging information and standardizing processes and training. These are not negligible achievements; indeed, they fit perfectly with the role of IOs as an arena, whereas in other areas the League clearly remains an instrument of the membership. In some areas this work has, especially when conducted in cooperation with the Arab Unions and other NGO actors, exhibited elements of greater autonomy and independence. The Arab League has shown an ability to evolve and does not fully fit Haas's model of "turbulent non-growth."

It is also clear that the League is now so well established institutionally and in the mind of the region that it does have the ability to structure discourse and thought by its very presence. The Arab League has, as Silvia Ferabolli rightly points out, "managed to project itself as the international representative of the Arab States and has acted as a unified group in several international forums, summits and conferences."[7] The League does operate bilaterally and is able to coordinate a range of activities including trade between the Arabs and other states. Indeed, it is clear that there is such a thing as Arab regionalism, which has shaped the "topographic and ideational boundaries of the Arab region," the League has been an important component and arena in this process, and membership and participation are therefore still important to Arab States.[8]

Thus, while it is all too easy and common to decry the "failures" of the League, most studies either label the organization a failure through unfair comparisons or expectations, or by examining the League through one theoretical prism, which inevitably paints a particular picture. Viewing the League as an arena and focusing on the nuts and bolts of cooperation, bureaucracy, and ideas creates a different picture—one which is less of a failure and more a work in progress, having laid foundations despite those overwhelming odds.

Prospects?

Around the turn of the millennium the Arab League seemed to have been given fresh purpose as a body that would begin to focus on more practical matters designed to improve Arab lives and connections. This tempered optimism continued right into the early years of the Arab Spring but has seemingly now come up hard against the regional environment once more. The League pessimists were never convinced, given the souring of the Arab Spring, heightened sectarian tensions and a return to authoritarianism which have encouraged a turn back to doom and gloom. In a recent report *The Economist* asked, what is the point of the Arab League? Its response was extremely negative, with the report stating that: "now something seems rotten not just in the institution but the ideology it represents. 'The league is obsolete'," says Khairallah Khairallah, a veteran Arab opinion-writer from Lebanon.

"It was built to respond to the 1940s and we're now in the 21st century. The idea of Arab Nationalism is dead."[9] Yet the article did not explore this point, instead focusing on the region's economic weaknesses, conflicts, and the presence of Western forces in the region.

Clearly the League cannot transcend these issues itself, many states seem perfectly content to host Western forces. Measuring the body against the supposed founding tropes of anti-Westernism, anti-Zionism, and Arab Nationalism is an outdated way of examining its purpose. If the original Arab Nationalist *project* is dead then it probably has been for quite some time. The basic ontological purpose of the League is essentially misunderstood in many quarters. Far from a being a vehicle of Arab Nationalism it was, as we have seen, created to control and shape it by providing some outlets for Arab cooperation—it was designed first and foremost to protect state sovereignty and satisfy some of the demands for Arab unity. These demands have changed. Now the wild dreams of Arab Nationalism are dead (having played an important role in shaping discourse and the League), more practical visions are possible and perhaps the League can, at last, escape from the shadow of Arab Nationalism.[10]

While Ahmed Aboul Gheit, the new League secretary-general, was elected unopposed on 11 March 2016 and indeed was the only candidate, there was for the first time real discussion among League members about the need for new blood rather than retired politicians treating the League as some kind of sinecure.[11] This discussion reflects an increased degree of awareness of the need to change but also an awareness in an era of great uncertainty and security concerns that change brings risks. At present, then, the League is somewhat trapped, as it always has been, by the regional environment but this does not mean that it cannot continue quietly to pursue functionalist ends wherever possible; it has shaped (and will continue to do so) the region in complex and often little-appreciated ways. The League defies easy categorization when viewed through multiple prisms. When the time comes the League is clearly best placed to act as a vital arena and tool of cooperation once circumstances allow. In the meantime, perhaps the Gulf Cooperation Council is best positioned to thrive in the post-Arab Spring era.

Notes

1 Fouad Ajami, "The End of Pan-Arabism?" *Foreign Affairs* 57, no. 2 (1978–79), www.foreignaffairs.com/articles/yemen/1978-12-01/end-pan-arabism.
2 Charles Tripp, "Regional Organizations in the Arab Middle East," in *Regionalism in World Politics: Regional Organization and International*

Order, ed. Louise Fawcett and Andrew Hurrell (Oxford: Oxford University Press, 1995), 282.

3 For the Agreement establishing the ACC see: https://treaties.un.org/doc/ Publication/UNTS/Volume%201530/volume-1530-I-26558-English.pdf.

4 There is virtually no literature on the ACC. One useful article examining Jordan's role is the only focused academic piece on the organization, see: Curtis Ryan, "Jordan and the Rise and Fall of the Arab Cooperation Council," *Middle East Journal* 52, no. 3 (1998): 386–401.

5 The Tunis Declaration of the 16th Arab Summit, 23 May 2004, Article 2.1, www2.ohchr.org/english/law/compilation_democracy/league.htm.

6 Larbi Sidiki, *Rethinking Arab Democratization: Elections Without Democracy* (Oxford: Oxford University Press, 2009), 281.

7 Silvia Ferabolli, *Arab Regionalism: A Post-Structural Perspective* (London: Routledge, 2015), 71.

8 Ferabolli, *Arab Regionalism*, 77.

9 "Snoozing While the Region Smoulders: What is the Point of the Arab League? The Sad Decline of a Once-Bold Organisation," *The Economist*, 29 April 2016, www.economist.com/news/middle-east-and-africa/21698047-sad-decline-once-bold-organisation-what-point-arab-league.

10 Dr Khalid Abdullah, Chief Representative of the Arab League to the United States outlined a range of practical steps and lessons learnt in a speech entitled: "The Challenges Facing the Arab Nation on the Threshold of the 21st Century," at the Los Angeles World Affairs Council on 27 October 1999, www.alhewar.com/KhalidAbdullaChallenges.htm.

11 "Arab League Elects Ahmed Aboul-Gheit as New Chief," *Al Jazeera*, 11 March 2016, www.aljazeera.com/news/2016/03/arab-league-elects-ahmed-aboul-gheit-chief-160311090316874.html.

6   The Gulf Cooperation Council
Structure and evolution

- **Founding the GCC**
- **Role and purpose**
- **Structures**
- **Conclusion**

The Gulf Cooperation Council (GCC), formally known as the Cooperation Council for the Arab States of the Gulf, is the second international organization of the Middle East. Formed on 25 May 1981, it is also the Middle East's first sub-regional IO, comprising the six monarchies with coastlines on the southern shore of the Persian/Arabian Gulf[1]—namely the Kingdom of Bahrain, the State of Kuwait, the Kingdom of Saudi Arabia, the Sultanate of Oman, the State of Qatar, and the United Arab Emirates. It is the region's most successful institution in terms of the progress achieved both in practical cooperation schemes and the beginnings of real integration. By the terms of its own charter, the GCC is keen to stress that its vision is greater unity, with its members having "the conviction that coordination, cooperation, and integration between them serve the sublime objectives of the Arab Nation." The charter also feels obliged to clarify that the founding of the GCC is in "conformity with the Charter of the League of Arab States which calls for the realization of closer relations and stronger bonds."[2] This chapter begins by briefly exploring the foundation of the organization, with special emphasis on the regional environment in the run-up to its formation in 1981. By drawing upon some of the key colonial, political, and intellectual contexts laid out in Chapter 1, while also exploring the specific dynamics of the Gulf region which drove its early years, the chapter provides important context to the ongoing challenges, opportunities, and constraints facing the GCC explored in the following chapters. The second part of the chapter then proceeds to outline the role, purpose, and scope of the GCC in terms of the ambitions contained in its charter but also the various communiqués that accompanied its foundation. This is then followed by an outline of the structures of the Council and how they have developed since the organization's foundation. Linking together the way in which the organization began with its structures and framework subsequently enables an examination of the evolution of the role of the GCC and the frameworks within which it operates in the chapter's conclusion.

Founding the GCC

Arab Nationalism spread to the Gulf quite early, its anti-colonial sentiments having particular resonance in a region so dominated by the *Pax Britannica*. The effect was amplified by the existence of large numbers of Arab migrant workers, particularly those working in education and in the oil industry. This was especially the case in Kuwait and Bahrain, which had developed their oil industries much sooner than those of the other Gulf States. This meant that despite the monarchical governance systems of the region there was considerable pressure to participate in pan-Arab causes. Kuwait, in particular, embraced and funded Arab Nationalist movements after its independence from Britain in 1961,[3] and Bahrain experienced serious unrest inspired by Arab Nationalism and socialist movements during the 1950s and 1960s with waves of strikes, protests, and agitation on a regular basis.[4] Quite how deeply Arab Nationalist sentiment went amongst the indigenous Gulf Arab population is harder to judge; certainly some parts of society were strongly influenced by these themes, even amongst elements of the merchant and ruling families. In Oman, however, awareness of Arab Nationalism remained very low, largely because of the country's isolation from the Arab world and its traditional preference for trade with India and East Africa. The ruling regimes of the region, alongside popular sentiment for Arab causes, also faced direct security threats sponsored by Arab Nationalist regimes elsewhere in the Middle East. Thus, for a time, Nasserist-inspired or -directed plots appeared to be everywhere, Iraq hosted training camps for Arab Nationalist guerrilla liberation movements, and the Yemeni civil war essentially became a proxy battleground between Egypt and Saudi Arabia. Meanwhile, as Britain withdrew from its Aden colony and South Arabian protectorates in November 1967 the internecine strife that broke out between Marxist and Nasserist insurgent groups upon Britain's departure left a Marxist regime in Aden, which had the avowed aim of toppling the Gulf monarchies, and immediately began supporting an existing irredentist rebellion in the southern Omani province of Dhofar, which dramatically increased the threat posed as it became Marxist and dramatically more effective.[5]

Against this backdrop of regional strife and direct threats to the Gulf monarchies during the period of the "Arab Cold War," the region's oil was fueling greater wealth and development. As the world became more and more dependent upon oil, this made the region much more important than ever before in terms of the West's economic and military power, while also making the Gulf a tempting prize for the Soviet Union. In short, the stakes were rising and the Gulf monarchies, facing a series of external threats and a rise in Arab Nationalist and socialist sentiment from those living within their borders knew that they had to satisfy some of the demands of the Arab Nationalists and be seen to be Arab players on the regional stage, while also taking measures to protect themselves from both external threats and internal discord. Adding to this combustible mix, in early 1968 Britain announced its intention to withdraw "East of Suez" by the end of 1971, thus dismantling its bases and ending its treaties of protection with Bahrain, Qatar, and the sheikhdoms of the Trucial Coast, and its ability to defend Kuwait (as it had in 1961).

With the febrile atmosphere in the region already, both Britain and the rulers sought to find ways of increasing the security of the Gulf States, and drawing the United States more deeply into the region. This latter fact, and the monarchies' continuing friendship and security relations with Britain, hardly played well with Arab Nationalist elements. Britain's plan before its withdrawal was to solve many of the complex land and sea border disputes between the Gulf States and (as it had with other colonies in the past) to attempt to cohere the lower nine sheikhdoms into a federation of some kind. This would be a more potent military force than the tiny armed units attached to each state at that time. It would also mean that the poorer sheikhdoms without hydrocarbon resources would benefit from direct fiscal support from the richer emirates such as Abu Dhabi. This attempt to create a single Arab State from the nine lower emirates of the Gulf inevitably proved complex and eventually both Qatar and Bahrain opted out of the structure before its formation in 1971. The creation of the United Arab Emirates, initially made up of six emirates, which were joined just over a year later by Ras al-Khaimah, was an important step towards cooperation in the Gulf and remains the only successful experiment in the cohering of Arab States into one country.

There is no doubt that Britain's military withdrawal from the Gulf was a significant catalyst in the long-term project of the creation of the GCC. As Britain left the Gulf in 1971 the region soon began the process of increasing cooperation between its states. While the death of Nasser, as we have seen, reduced the fervor of Arab Nationalism, the Gulf still faced multiple threats during the 1970s, which meant it was sensible for the Gulf's monarchies to work together in defending themselves. After a short period of inward focus on consolidating their new states, for Oman and the lower three Gulf States moves began to be taken towards cooperation.

Part of the problem the Gulf States faced as they began to come together, and a legacy which still has impacts upon the pace and extent of Gulf integration, is the history of Saudi expansionism in the region. Having itself formed so rapidly as a state, Saudi Arabia had made multiple claims on the territories of its neighboring Gulf States and had even been implicated in subversion against neighboring rulers in the 1950s. While Britain had been the protecting power of the Gulf States these claims had lain in abeyance but the other Gulf States remained fearful of the reactivation of these territorial disputes, some of which still exist to this day despite a long process of negotiation and settlement of some of the most contentious. This history, along with Saudi Arabia's overwhelming superiority in population size, military power, economic strength and size of territory, naturally makes its smaller neighbors wary of being subsumed. Given the wider regional environment, and a more cautious approach from Saudi Arabia, the more pressing security issues led to deep and complex discussions around security, often assisted and encouraged by Britain and the United States. This also spilled over into other areas of collaboration.

One of the earliest initiatives was the foundation of the Gulf Organization for Industrial Consulting (GOIC). Established in 1976 and still separate from the GCC itself, GOIC was aimed at encouraging industrial cooperation and coordination between the six nations of the Gulf (Yemen joined the organization in 2009). In order to facilitate collaboration it collects and disseminates information about industrial development projects and policies. It also encourages joint industrial projects, and acts as a research and technical consultancy on industrial issues.[6] The establishment of the GOIC was part of a range of functionalist attempts to encourage cooperation among the Gulf States in the late 1970s. The contacts that were generated, alongside the momentum in a number of issue areas during this period, were essential groundwork to the formation of the GCC itself in 1981. Often the literature focuses on the worsened security environment from 1979 onwards and while this clearly played a role, the increased trust and dynamism created through bilateral and multilateral Gulf initiatives in the years prior to 1979 are arguably more important—indeed, many of the structures created and the methods of policy agreement in the run-up to their creation are directly mirrored in the structures of the GCC itself. One can also argue that some of these experiments, which at the time sometimes included Iran and/or Iraq, also demonstrated to the Gulf rulers the wisdom of banding monarchies together.[7] Some, but not all, of these institutions were later absorbed into the GCC; others continue to operate separately. All constituted important steps, especially in the industrial, cultural, and educational fields towards the construction of the GCC.

These discussions led to attempts at wider processes, thus for example, in 1976 Sultan Qaboos of Oman organized a security conference for the region in Muscat, while the Kuwaitis began to propose an organization similar in scope to the GCC and to lobby actively for its creation, gradually building up enthusiasm for the project over the course of 1978. The Iranian Revolution of 1979, and the rise to power of Saddam Hussein in Ba'athist Iraq that same year, transformed the regional security environment, giving fresh impetus to the work that had already been done towards regional cooperation. With Iraq and Iran actively hostile to the Gulf monarchies, working together made even greater sense. The outbreak of the Iran–Iraq War in 1980 took regional tensions onto a different plane but also meant that there was no longer any need to make any pretense of including Iraq as a fellow Arab Gulf State. Given this combination of external circumstances, existing contacts, and previous groundwork, discussions were begun in Kuwait in February 1981 for the formation of a sub-regional organization for the six monarchies of the Gulf. These benefits still did not mean that the six states viewed the shape of the new organization through the same prisms, however, and each presented differing visions in terms of the scope and specific focus of the new body. Oman wanted this to lie on defense, the Saudis on cooperation over internal security, and the Kuwaitis wanted more overt focus on economic and cultural projects. A compromise (albeit slightly fractious) was reached surprisingly quickly, meaning that by 9 March the basic structure of the GCC had been approved: it was decided to focus on economic, cultural, and social aspects, leaving room for security and defense cooperation as the new organization grew.[8] Just a month and a half later the GCC held its first summit meeting and the body was formally established.

Role and purpose

These tensions over the exact purpose of the GCC have diminished over time, only to be replaced by tensions regarding the speed and depth of integrative projects in the region. It is often argued that the GCC is a club for autocrats; indeed, it is easy to argue that the GCC is indeed "an organization constituted chiefly to help sheikhly regimes maintain their grip on power through security and economic means."[9] The GCC Charter itself within article 4 defines the new organization's role and purpose widely. It specifies that the basic purpose is "to effect coordination, integration and inter-connection between member states in all fields in order to achieve unity between them." Clearly this rhetoric is driven by the wider linguistic norms of Arab Nationalism. It is debatable quite how far towards unity the states would actually be willing to go. This is effectively made clear in the rest of article 4, which states the formulation of "similar regulations" (i.e. there is still room for variation between states) in various fields, including the following: "Economic and financial affairs, Commerce, customs and communications, and Education and culture." The article concludes by also outlining the final purpose as being "to stimulate scientific and technological progress in the fields of industry, mining, agriculture, water and animal resources; to establish scientific research; to establish joint ventures and encourage cooperation by the private sector for the good of their peoples." Article 4 is the only one within the main text of the charter that specifies its purpose. Aside from the general vague ambitions and declarations in the preamble of "being fully aware of the ties of special relations, common characteristics and similar systems founded on the creed of Islam which bind them; and desiring to effect coordination, cooperation and integration between them in all fields; [in the] pursuit of the goal of strengthening cooperation and reinforcement of the links between them," what is conspicuously absent from the charter is any notion of security cooperation, although in theory this (and a wide manner of other subjects) is covered by the phrase "all fields." What we have, then, is an inherently flexible organization, which can expand or contract according to the desires of its members. As Abdul Khaleq Abdulla puts it, "the GCC is not an economic integration body, nor a military alliance, nor a full-fledged security community ... it has vacillated among various functions and expectations."[10]

Structures

Like the Arab League and the AMU, the GCC is structured to ensure that decision-making power remains with the states, and more specifically with the rulers themselves. The organization is made up of three central bodies, the Supreme Council, the Ministerial Council and the

Secretariat General, although the GCC Charter makes it clear that each of these central bodies has the right to establish such sub-agencies as they consider necessary.

The Supreme Council (SC)

As the name implies the SC is the most powerful and important body within the GCC. Comprising the heads of state of its six members, the body must meet at least once per annum with emergency sessions able to be called with the agreement of a minimum of two member states (see Table 6.1 for a list of regular summits). The presidency of the SC rotates through alphabetical order of the members and sessions can be held in any member state. This stipulation has led to the various rulers trying to outbid each other in terms of the extravagant venues and preparations made for Supreme Council meetings. According to article 7 of the charter an SC meeting is considered valid if attended by two-thirds of members. At its 1998 meeting in Abu Dhabi the SC decided to hold an interim consultative meeting each year around halfway between normal annual meetings. This was a useful innovation encouraging greater contact and ensuring that annual meetings were more productive. This is especially the case since article 9 of the charter specifies that voting in the SC requires unanimity for any substantive matter to pass, while procedural matters are settled by simple majority.

Article 8 lays out a number of the powers, functions, and objectives of the SC, which include appointing the secretary-general, amendments to the charter, approving the organization's budget, outlining the organization's policy directions and basic means of reaching objectives, reviewing and commissioning reports from the secretary-general, receiving and approving reports from the Council of Ministers, and agreeing to GCC relationships with other states and international organizations. In short, then, the rulers have contrived to keep all important decision-making powers under tight control and each retains a veto over integrative moves with which he is not comfortable.

The Ministerial Council (MC)

Composed initially of the foreign ministers of the member states, the MC has effectively expanded over time into a series of MCs based on subject area. Nowadays these specific MCs feed their findings direct to the SC more often than going through the MC of foreign ministers. Like the SC, the MC can call extraordinary meetings but it meets on a

Table 6.1 GCC regular summits

Place	Date(s)
Abu Dhabi	25–26 May 1981
Riyadh	10–11 November 1981
Manama	9–11 November 1982
Doha	7–9 November 1983
Muscat	3–5 November 1985
Abu Dhabi	2–4 November 1986
Riyadh	26–29 December 1987
Manama	19–21 December 1988
Muscat	18–20 December 1989
Doha	22–24 December 1990
Kuwait City	23–25 December 1991
Abu Dhabi	20–22 December 1992
Riyadh	20–22 December 1993
Manama	19–21 December 1994
Muscat	4–6 December 1995
Doha	7–9 December 1996
Kuwait City	20–22 December 1997
Abu Dhabi	7–9 December 1998
Riyadh	27–29 November 1999
Manama	30–31 December 2000
Muscat	30–31 December 2001
Doha	21–22 December 2002
Kuwait City	21–22 December 2003
Manama	20–21 December 2004
Abu Dhabi	18–19 December 2005
Riyadh	9–10 December 2006
Doha	3–4 December 2007
Muscat	29–30 December 2008
Kuwait City	14–15 December 2009
Abu Dhabi	6–7 December 2010
Riyadh	19–20 December 2011
Manama	24–25 December 2012
Kuwait City	10–11 December 2013
Doha	9 December 2014
Riyadh	9–10 December 2015
Manama	6–7 December 2016

more regular basis, every three months. It is chaired by the member state that presided over the last normal session of the SC. The MC has a vital role in preparing the detail of decisions to be agreed by the SC, ensuring that many decisions can be ratified with little further discussion by the rulers. It actually sets the agenda for the (now) twice-yearly meetings of the SC. Although it should of course be recognized that each minister holds his state's veto, so proposals tend to get vetoed at this level rather than at SC level, the rulers, already having such power in their own states, therefore effectively have a high degree of influence at this level of the organization as well.

In many senses the MC(s) have become the focal points of cooperation with the organization. This structure has also encouraged greater contact, consultation, and preparatory work further and further down the hierarchies within ministries, as ministers of state, secretaries-general and heads of department from within individual ministries in the member states now meet on a regular basis to exchange views, cooperate on technical matters and prepare more detailed ground for proposals. Clearly the spillover benefits of greater trust, frequency of meetings, and technical-functional requirements have led to much greater cooperation at all levels and thus made the organization's impact more far-reaching than the centralization of power in the SC would lead one to expect.

The MC has 11 key functions as outlined in article 12 of the charter, and can create technical or specialized committees to assist in its work. Its main role is in proposing policies, commissioning studies, and identifying projects. It also has a joint coordinating role between the six member states, develops action plans for executing decisions that have been approved, submits to the SC recommendations for charter changes, approves the secretary-general's choices for assistant secretaries-general, approves its own and the Secretariat General's rules of procedure, responds to specific requests from the SC, recommends the budget to the SC and approves internal reports. It also organizes and prepares the SC meetings and finally, and slightly surprisingly, it is charged with encouraging coordination between the countries' private sectors—largely through the chambers of commerce and industry, and encouraging the movement of workers within the GCC. This wide remit shows a mixture of desire of the member states to keep tight control at all levels over the organization that they have created, but also expresses the open-ended nature of the project. This is especially evident in the remit to attempt to coordinate the region's private sector.

The Secretariat General

Based in Riyadh, the Secretariat General largely functions to assist the MC, although it naturally does work for the SC as well. Its role is in the drafting of reports, planning and programming common action, preparing occasional reports that review the achievements and progress of the GCC, responding to requests from the SC or the MC, following up the implementation of GCC action plans and legislation with the member states, drafting administrative and financial regulations, preparing the organization's budget, and preparing meetings, agendas, and draft resolutions for the MC. It can also recommend the convening of extraordinary sessions of the MC. In theory the Secretariat's power to follow up on implementation is potentially significant and could become so in the future, but as Matteo Legrenzi points out, "the number of decisions taken at the Ministerial Councils that have not been implemented, particularly in the economic realm, is vast."[11] The absence of any real structure within the GCC to properly monitor implementation and to impose sanctions upon states that fail to comply, is clearly designed to allow maximum flexibility to the states.

The Secretariat itself is small, comprising staff in the low to mid-hundreds,[12] especially considering the scope of cooperation envisaged by the GCC and the wealth of its members. Article 18 provides that the organization's budget is funded equally by all six member states. There is no weighting of contribution for GDP size as in many other IOs. It can be speculated that this is a measure that ensures that Saudi Arabia with a significantly larger GDP cannot use its funding share as leverage. This control over the budget also serves to limit the size of the Secretariat and its potential for following up too closely on the states' implementation of decisions.

The secretary-general represents the organization overseas and is in charge of the functioning of the Secretariat General. He appoints, upon the approval of the MC, eight assistant secretaries-general. The secretary-general himself is appointed directly by the SC, supposedly on a three-year term, which is renewable. As the list of secretaries-general in Table 6.2 suggests, this theoretical six-year term is often exceeded. Assistant secretaries-general are appointed on the same terms and are in charge of specific areas of business. At present this is organized with two associate secretaries-general (a relatively new innovation) heading the Political Affairs and Economic Affairs Directorates. These are complemented by departments dealing with military, security, humanitarian, environmental, legal, media, culture, information, finance and administration, strategic dialogue and negotiations. These in turn are sub-divided and run by directors-general for specific

Table 6.2 List of GCC secretaries-general

Name	Nationality	Period of office
Abdullah Yaccoub Bishara	Kuwaiti	26 May 1981–1 April 1993
Fahim bin Sultan al-Qasimi	Emirati	1 April 1993–1 April 1996
Jamil Ibrahim Hejailan	Saudi	1 April 1996–1 April 2002
Abdul Rahman bin Hamad al-Attiyah	Qatari	1 April 2002–1 April 2011
Abdullatif bin Rashid al-Zayani	Bahraini	1 April 2011–

functional departments, including for example: intellectual property rights, the Office of the Technical Secretariat for Anti-dumping, the Technical Office of Communications, located in Bahrain, and the Office of the Consultative Commission, located in Oman. The GCC also maintains permanent diplomatic missions to the UN in New York and the EU in Brussels.

Additional bodies

Article 10 of the charter provides for the creation of a Commission for the Settlement of Disputes. This quasi-judicial body, which is attached to the Supreme Council, is designed to express an opinion or a set of recommendations to the SC. It is used solely on an ad hoc basis to offer assistance should there be a disagreement over the interpretation or implementation of the charter that has not been resolved at the MC or the SC. It remains, however, entirely up to the SC whether or not it accepts the commission's advice.[13]

In addition to these core bodies other key elements have been developed over time. The SC has created a further permanent body, which is designed to assist with its functions. The Consultative Commission of the Supreme Council, which was established in 1997, comprises five experts from each of the six member states serving for three-year terms to act as an advisory body to the SC. The commission appears to have been used less for detail than in terms of more blue-skies ideas and is perhaps best known for its work on two major studies on the collective processes of the GCC.[14]

The GCC has also established the GCC Standardization Organiza-tion (GSO), which interestingly also includes Yemen.[15] Headquartered in Riyadh with a further office in Jeddah, its role is to examine inter-national standards, recommend Gulf standards, and work to monitor and compare standards present in member states; it has no enforcement mechanism, however.[16] Founded in November 1982 as the Gulf Standards Organization, it is effectively the transformation of the Saudi standards body into a regional organization—hence the locations of its headquarters and branch office. It was re-founded under its current name in 2003. In 2009 the GSO agreed to the establishment of a Gulf Meteorology Organization,[17] which is designed to improve technical capabilities in the member states' meteorology departments and coordinate with other international bodies in the field.

The other two subordinate bodies that have been created by the GCC are the Patent Office of Cooperation of the Council for the Arab States of the Gulf and the GCC Commercial Arbitration Center (GCCCAC). The former, based in Riyadh within the GCC's headquarters, was approved at the Gulf summit in 1992 but did not begin receiving applications until October 1998. A patent granted by the body secures legal protection in all member states and the body is tasked with encouraging foreign direct investment (FDI) across the region and offering advice on wider patent application in other jurisdictions.[18] The GCCCAC, based in Manama, was approved at the 14th GCC summit in December 1993 and began its work in March 1995, offering a quick and transparent mechanism to resolve commercial disputes. Clearly this body is designed both to encourage FDI and to ensure that local companies feel comfortable in trading in other member states.[19]

Proposals for institutional evolution

The degree of flexibility inherent within the structures has led to the creation of both ad hoc and permanent committees to serve various purposes; the specific technical committees created at the first GCC summit have generally proven quite effective. The GCC, though, is unlike the Arab League or other general purpose regional or international organizations in that it has not spawned the kind of institutional structures seen elsewhere, thus there is nothing like an economic and social council and certainly no sign of a GCC parliament.[20] The core of the GCC's structures remains simple and tightly under the control of the member states.

In terms of potential expansion of the GCC, there has traditionally been great reluctance to include other states—Yemen in particular has been especially keen to join. In the midst of the Arab Spring in May 2011 Jordan's application to join the GCC, which had been submitted more than a decade earlier, was suddenly accepted and Morocco was invited to join the organization. Since then little progress has been made and some states that were already somewhat unimpressed with this Saudi initiative have lost interest.[21] Yemen is a slightly different matter. Clearly closely connected to the Gulf States, its level of development and different political system represents a real stumbling block to membership. While the GCC has made some efforts to include Yemen in some initiatives, it seems very unlikely that Yemen could ever become a member; indeed, if it did it would clearly put back attempts at regional integration.[22] In fact, membership for any of these countries would require the charter to be amended and the preamble itself speaks of the GCC as a grouping of "similar regimes," which is a definition that essentially automatically excludes Yemen.

Conclusion

From its foundation in 1981 the GCC has exhibited a degree of flexibility that has enabled it to develop organically. Clearly regional integration in the Gulf region has been strongly influenced by external regional factors but the desire of the citizens of the Gulf States for more integration and cooperation, initially driven by Arab Nationalist ideals, has also been a factor at times. In terms of its scope the GCC has been able to encompass a wide range of areas of cooperation and it is its institutional flexibility that has been especially useful in enabling initiatives to be brought under its banner as and when required. The GCC still suffers somewhat from a tendency of the member states towards grandiose gestures, which often simply remain on the drawing board; this is especially the case when dynamics within the organization mean that members wish to move ahead at different speeds. The veto held by each state at both Ministerial Council and Supreme Council levels enables the states to retain ultimate control of the project. The GCC's institutional simplicity can, when accord is present, lead to extremely swift decision making but at other times, if trust is weakened, the pace and scale of cooperation are damaged, which has led to bursts of enthusiasm followed by more fallow periods. Clearly, though, the GCC has clear advantages which have made its progress and its prospects brighter; the socio-political similarities of the states are a clear advantage for the construction of a sub-regional organization in the Arabian Gulf.

The following three chapters build on the structures, dynamics, and constraints explored in this chapter by exploring the specific structures, provisions, and evolution of the GCC's activities in terms of its cooperation on matters of diplomacy, peace and security, and with regard to its economic, social and cultural activities, thus beginning an assessment of the Council's achievements and difficulties in these various areas, before a final assessment of the problems and prospects facing the organization.

Notes

 1 There is extreme contention over the naming of this stretch of water. This chapter chooses "Arabian" simply because it is in most common usage in the literature on the GCC.
 2 Charter of the GCC, Preamble.
 3 See: Saad al-Shehabi, *The Role of Merchants in Kuwaiti Politics: Between Decline and Influence*, unpublished PhD thesis, King's College London, 2015.
 4 See: Bernard Burrows, *Footnotes in the Sand: The Gulf in Transition, 1953–1958* (Salisbury.: Michael Russell, 1980), 58–71.
 5 James Worrall, *Statebuilding and Counterinsurgency in Oman: Political, Diplomatic and Military Relations at the End of Empire* (London: I.B. Tauris, 2014).
 6 GOIC: www.goic.org.qa/GOICCMS/About_EN.html.
 7 Matteo Legrenzi, *The GCC and the International Relations of the Gulf: Diplomacy, Security and Economic Coordination in a Changing Middle East* (London: I.B. Tauris, 2011), 21.
 8 Legrenzi, *The GCC and the International Relations of the Gulf*, 32–33.
 9 Legrenzi, *The GCC and the International Relations of the Gulf*, 3.
10 Abdul Khaleq Abdulla, "The Gulf Cooperation Council: Nature, Origin, and Process," in *Middle East Dilemma: The Politics and Economics of Arab Integration*, ed. Michael Hudson (New York: Columbia University Press, 1999), 155.
11 Legrenzi, *The GCC and the International Relations of the Gulf*, 38.
12 Exact figures are hard to find. This is a composite of other accounts and my own research via LinkedIn, which suggests that Saudi nationals comprise more than 40% of the total, Omanis are very under-represented and that perhaps a dozen GCC employees are female.
13 There is some confusion in the literature over whether or not this body was ever activated. Laura Guazzone suggests that it was and played a role in settling some intra-GCC territorial and a GCC–Yemen border dispute but Richard Schofield stated that in 1995 it was suggested that the Commission be activated and based in Muscat to deal with territorial disputes (it seems it never was though). It seems that if the Commission has ever been activated, it has left little trace, being convened solely as needed and creating no legal precedents. See: Laura Guazzone, "Gulf Co-operation Council: The Security Policies," *Survival* 30, no. 2 (1988): 146; and Richard Schofield, "Boundaries, Territorial Disputes and the GCC States," in *Gulf Security in the Twenty-First Century*, ed. Christian Koch and David Long (London: I.B. Tauris, 1997), 149.
14 Bernard Savage, "Monitoring Regional Integration and Cooperation in the Gulf Region," in *Governing Regional Integration for Development:*

Monitoring Experiences, Methods and Prospects, ed. Antoni Estevadeordal *et al.* (Farnham: Ashgate, 2008), 167.

15 Gulf Standardization Organization (GSO), www.gso.org.sa/gso-website/?la ng=en.

16 Bernard Hoekman and Khalid Sekkat, "Arab Economic Integration: The Missing Links," Sciences Po Working Paper (April 2010), 5, http://gem.scien ces-po.fr/content/publications/pdf/Hoekman_Sekkat_Arab_RI042010.pdf.

17 Gulf Meteorology Organization (GMO), www.gulfmet.org/gulfmet/gulfm et/calibration.

18 GCC Patent Office (GPO), www.gccpo.org/AboutUsEn/AboutUs.aspx.

19 GCC Commercial Arbitration Centre (GCCCAC), www.gcccac.org/en/.

20 The closest to this are annual meetings for the Speakers of the various parliaments, consultative councils, and assemblies of the Gulf States. The wide differences between the Kuwaiti parliament and the Qatari consultative assembly, for example, make this kind of institutional innovation rather unlikely. See "GCC parliament speakers' meeting," *The Peninsula*, 1 December 2014, http://thepeninsulaqatar.com/news/qatar/309959/gcc-parliament-spea kers-meeting.

21 Curtis Ryan, "Jordanian Foreign Policy and the Arab Spring," *Middle East Policy* XXI, no. 1 (2014): 144–153.

22 Matteo Legrenzi, "Did the GCC Make a Difference? Institutional Realities and (Un)intended Consequences," in *Beyond Regionalism?: Regional Cooperation, Regionalism and Regionalization in the Middle East*, ed. Cilja Harders and Matteo Legrenzi (Aldershot: Ashgate, 2008), 121.

7 The Gulf Cooperation Council
Security, peace, and defense

- **GCC defense and security evolution**
- **Structural obstacles to cooperation**
- **Conclusion**

There is a certain paradox in examining the GCC's role in peace and security in that the organization's founding charter makes no mention of any role for the organization in this sphere and yet it is also clear that living in the classic "dangerous neighborhood" was an important spur to the creation of the organization. Indeed, the GCC is often seen as the classic case of "defensive integration," a group of states coming together as an initial symbolic gesture designed to create a structured and lasting sense of security for all members over the longer term.[1]

The GCC is unlike the Arab League in that it has no collective security mechanisms, no structured dispute resolution systems and seemingly aspired to play no role in issues of foreign policy by engaging with other states. Despite appearances, however, the GCC has gradually developed a role in defense and security issues, although that role is often hidden and pursued under the banner of the GCC but not necessarily through its institutional mechanisms. This chapter explores the evolution of the GCC's role in this important area of activity, offering an assessment of the extent and quality of cooperation in this issue area before examining the prospects for deeper cooperation in the areas of defense and internal security, as well as the development of a GCC foreign and diplomatic policy.

GCC defense and security evolution

As we have seen, the disagreements at the organization's founding between those members that wished to focus cooperation on defense and security and those that wished to focus on economic and cultural integration, were an early and important fault line. This was in part about the external messaging the states wished to send to neighbors and to the great powers given the Cold War context at the time. Given the GCC's institutional flexibility and opacity, though, there remained plenty of space for the new organization to be an important arena for the discussion of the various internal and external security threats facing the member states.[2] Perhaps this arena function of the GCC, alongside the corporate personality, which has at times given the organization a more significant level of international standing in the area of security than it perhaps deserved, have been the most significant contributions of the GCC to defense and security concerns.

The first Gulf security conference was held on 24 February 1982, less than a year after the GCC's foundation—perhaps not surprising given the ferocity of the Iran–Iraq War. The conference laid down the basic principles and objectives of GCC cooperation in the military sphere and expressed the aspiration of drawing up some form of comprehensive security agreement.[3] This was followed in November 1982 at the GCC summit with a declaration that the GCC states would be creating a combined military force of around 5,000 personnel, which would be designated the "Peninsula Shield" (PS).[4] The new force was constituted quite rapidly, beginning its first exercise in 1983. The mid-1980s saw some combined exercises that did not include Western forces as part of the new force's creation, which created some momentum behind greater military cooperation at all levels, but it remained limited despite the shifting of the Iran–Iraq War into the waters of the Gulf with Iraqi attacks on Iranian shipping in the so-called "Tanker War." The PS later acquired a permanent headquarters in the north of Saudi Arabia near Kuwait in 1986; around 3,000 of its troops took part in both Operations Desert Shield and Desert Storm to help liberate Kuwait from Iraqi occupation, although the force had clearly proven entirely ineffective in preventing the invasion, either as a symbolic structure or in terms of its combat preparedness.

After the shock of the Iraqi invasion of Kuwait, the mid-1990s saw moves in other areas of military cooperation. This largely focused on improving communications and information sharing. The establishment of a secure communications network among GCC armed forces was proposed in December 1995 and was launched in 2000; this included the creation of a coordination office, which was largely focused on the technical side of ensuring the system developed. The system was expanded to include a back-up satellite communications system in 2014. Alongside this, in 1997, the proposed creation of cooperation systems in air defense was announced, with the first phase of this so-called "Cooperation Belt" system coming into effect in 2001. However, it does little more than increase communications between existing air defense structures in the member states.[5]

With the fall of Saddam Hussein in 2003, though, there were even suggestions in 2005 that the PS unit should be disbanded, with each country's contribution returning to its home forces with the potential of a rapid reassembly of the unit if required. Just a year later, though, the Saudis proposed the expansion of the PS with the creation of a joint command and control system for the force. In 2008 the creation of a Rapid Intervention Force was proposed, which would see PS forces being reinforced with units that would be on standby within the member states, thus taking its theoretical strength to around 22,000.[6]

At present though, the PS force is still making steps towards a proper unified command structure, and proposals to move forward on a joint defense strategy at Gulf level remain very much on the drawing board. This is despite the GCC Joint Defense Agreement having been signed at the GCC's Manama SC meeting in 2000. This agreement, however, is rather vague, containing aspirations rather than a concrete roadmap; these aspirations include the idea of collective defense and the development of a common defense industry with private-sector involvement. In more recent years moves in the defense sphere have been more regular, thus in 2009 a GCC Defense Strategy was adopted, attempting to create a common perception of strategic risk and the beginnings of deeper coordination of defense issues. This agreement also accelerated moves to develop the PS force with naval and air units, and the creation of the Rapid Intervention Force.

The turmoil in Bahrain during the Arab Spring saw the activation of the PS force and its deployment to Bahrain, supposedly to deter any act of foreign aggression. This was clearly a symbolic move to show support for the embattled Bahraini royal family and it was interesting that Oman and Kuwait did not send troops; the force was essentially entirely United Arab Emirates (UAE) and Saudi troops. Since this successful deployment, moves on GCC defense have accelerated further in the face of a worsening regional situation, especially the growing tensions between Iran and Saudi Arabia. Thus in December 2013 the creation of a Unified Gulf Military Command[7] was announced and at the same conference some steps were taken to move forward with some of the plans made in 2000. These steps included the announcement of the creation of a GCC Unified Defense Command,[8] the GCC Academy for Strategic and Security Studies to be based in Abu Dhabi, and the GCC Joint Defense Council, which held its first meeting in May 2014.[9] There has also been recent discussion of the potential for a joint-GCC Missile Shield, which is likely to prove too costly and technically difficult in the short-to-medium term but has generated a lot of interest.[10]

This more rapid progress, at least in terms of announcements, has been followed up by some action. In addition, earlier more functionalist agreements in 1988 and 2012 in terms of military medical cooperation, and in 2010 to facilitate transfer of military personnel between forces and on human resources issues such as training, certification, and insurance systems are beginning to lay the foundations for more meaningful day-to-day interactions between the militaries of the GCC states.

There is a natural difficulty in studying the levels of cooperation between the Gulf States on matters of both internal and external security given the security situation in the region and the often secretive nature of the states involved. What we have seen quite consistently since shortly after the GCC's foundation has been talk of cooperation over defense. The actual results of these discussions have often been rather minimal. What tends to happen is that cooperation does happen but only really occurs when Britain and the United States are also involved and can drive cooperation forwards at a practical level. There remains a preference for working with external partners on defense matters. This is in part due to the greater abilities of foreign forces but also a lack of common threat perception amongst members, which has not diminished even given the current tense regional situation.

Internal security cooperation

The situation is slightly different when it comes to internal security concerns. Here there are regular bilateral meetings and information sharing between intelligence agencies and police. The GCC itself, though, plays little formal role in these processes and there has been no real institutional development in this sphere at the supra-national level. What coordination there is at GCC level amounts to an occasional liaison function for the head of the Security Department of the Political Affairs Section.[11] Multilateral as opposed to bilateral cooperation over internal security issues in the GCC states tends to focus on the internal dimension of external threats, or especially since 9/11 on the threat to the Gulf from Al Qaeda and more recently *Daesh*, the so-called Islamic State. That said, as Matteo Legrenzi outlines, in 1987 a multilateral agreement covering intelligence sharing, training, and extradition was approved at the 1987 SC meeting. Naturally enough, the agreement is eminently flexible, outside the structures of the GCC, and used infrequently in favor of less formalized coordination, especially at the bilateral level. At the 2014 GCC summit in Doha, alongside the proposal for the creation of a joint Gulf Naval Force, the announcement of the creation of a GCC Police Force, to be known as GCC-Pol, was made. This new force, as its name suggests, seems designed to be an Interpol-like joint coordinating body rather than a real shared police force.[12]

Structural obstacles to cooperation

There have been a number of stumbling blocks to the deepening of coordination efforts when it comes to defense and security, which range from the technical to the political. On the technical side the longstanding approach of hedging bets has meant that the Gulf States have procured weapons and training from a wide range of Western states, which has led to some issues with interoperability and differing training structures, not to mention the differing sizes, capabilities, and reputations of each nation's armed forces.

More importantly, however, on the political side, has been the lack of a common perception of who the shared enemy might be. While all Gulf States were nervous of Iran and Iraq, this was very much a matter of degree. The Gulf nations have formed a spectrum from the obsessed to the merely watchful when it comes to Iran in particular, with Oman and Kuwait striving for cordial relations with Iran at one end and Bahrain and Saudi Arabia exhibiting a degree of paranoia about Iranian subversion at the other. Qatar has moved increasingly towards the Omani position of constructive engagement while the UAE oscillates between a middle ground and supporting the Saudi viewpoint. This reflects an internal division between Dubai, which has strong trade links with Iran, and Abu Dhabi, which is more deeply skeptical of Iranian intentions. Furthermore, the deposition of Saddam Hussein has also removed a defensive unifying concern. It is difficult to see how a coherent unified position on defense can be agreed without a shared threat perception. There has been more agreement over security issues, especially terrorism and some evidence in more recent years that where this shades into regional security issues the GCC states have been more willing to take a common stand. Thus in March 2016 the GCC declared Hezbollah a terrorist group because of Iran's use of the movement in Syria and reportedly in Yemen. The GCC's secretary-general, Abdullatif al-Zayani, said the step was taken because "the [Hezbollah] militia recruited young people [from the Gulf] for terrorist acts."[13] This is perhaps a sign that Iran's growing interference across the Middle East is causing a more converged outlook from the Gulf

States. It remains to be seen quite how this affects defense cooperation in the GCC, however.

Internal GCC disputes

One of the recurring problems faced by the GCC in terms of cooperation in general, and defense and security in particular, has been continuing tension between member states and a tendency to interfere in each other's internal affairs. While this trend has been improving, the Arab Spring saw a return to some of these problems. A few examples will suffice to suggest the depth and complexity of these issues, although it should be noted that despite these issues there remains a will to try to surmount them. The classic example of these issues has been the tensions between Bahrain and Qatar, which led to a Qatari boycott of the 1995 closing meeting of the GCC summit in Muscat. This feud, which emerged in part because the ruler of Qatar had been deposed by his son, led to Bahrain offering the deposed emir a warm welcome.[14] In return Qatar allowed exiled Bahraini opposition leaders sanctuary. Tensions between the two nations originated in tribal politics of the past and ongoing territorial disputes over the status of the Hawar Islands. This dispute was finally settled by an International Court of Justice judgment in 2001.[15] Likewise, during the Arab Spring Qatar took a very different viewpoint on issues of which rebel groups to support, backing the Muslim Brotherhood in Egypt in the teeth of Saudi opposition.[16] This has led to a degree of Qatari isolation in recent years, although the situation improved over the course of 2015 with the arrival of a new emir.

The diplomatic front

Recent years especially have seen the GCC engage in direct negotiations with the EU[17] and establish diplomatic offices in Brussels and New York. It has also been a convenient umbrella for negotiations over Yemen in the wake of the Arab Spring (explored in more detail in Chapter 11). Indeed, this latter role has been used in the past to assist with brokering settlements over the border between Oman and Yemen in 1982, engagement with elements of the Arab–Israeli peace process, and assisting with internal GCC border disputes such as that between Qatar and Saudi Arabia, which was successfully resolved. The extent of GCC agency as an organization in this, as opposed to it being a forum or a symbol, is up for debate, however,[18] although it does seem that the various secretaries-general have attempted to make use of their good offices to encourage dialogue and resolution of disputes.[19] That said, there is clearly potential for the GCC to develop a wider role in jointly coordinating and representing unified GCC foreign policy positions on a range of issues, and to act as an umbrella for negotiations on regional disputes, even if it seems unlikely to be able to develop the institutional structures or agency to adjudicate on disputes between GCC member states.

Conclusion

Given the complexities and instability of the Gulf region's security and the pressures that most observers believe were the driving force in attempts at regional integration of the Gulf Arab monarchies, it appears to be deeply contradictory for the GCC still to have so little focus as an organization upon security matters. The lack of real depth of progress towards proper region-wide military interoperability and command and control functions, alongside the seemingly determined focus on keeping defense and security concerns outside the structures of the GCC is unusual given the perceived regional threat levels.

As we have seen, cooperation on matters of defense and security has been problematic despite seemingly being an area of natural shared interests in such a "dangerous neighborhood."[20] Cooperation in these fields is spurred by changes in the regional environment and comes in fits and starts, while the remaining internal tensions between member states and their differing strategic outlooks act as a brake on deeper cooperation.[21] This is likely to remain the case, especially since ultimately the GCC states themselves have continued to work hard to ensure the continuing validity of their insurance policies. Every state in the region has a bilateral defense arrangement with the United States, and in recent years both Britain and France have deepened and strengthened their military engagement in the Gulf with new military bases. Having these three states maintain a strong interest in the region remains the central defense strategy of the Gulf States, meaning that collaboration under the nominal umbrella of the GCC itself is of less concern. While matters of defense and internal security have been a spur to wider cooperation within the framework of the GCC, paradoxically that driving force has been felt much less on security matters, although it could be argued that the economic, social, and cultural integration efforts explored in the next chapter have gone a long way in creating the "corporate identity" of the GCC, which adds to a sense of defensive purpose.

Notes

1 Melani Cammett, "Defensive Integration and Late Developers: The Gulf Co-operation Council and the Arab Maghreb Union," *Global Governance* 5, no. 3 (1999): 379–402.

2 For a theoretical examination of the way in which regional threats played into the creation of the GCC see: David Priess, "Balance-of-Threat Theory and the Genesis of the Gulf Cooperation Council: An Interpretative Case Study," *Security Studies* 5, no. 4 (1996): 143–171.

3 Zafer Alajmi, "Gulf Military Cooperation: Tangible Gains or Limited Results?" Dossier, Al Jazeera Centre for Studies, 31 March 2015, http://stu dies.aljazeera.net/en/dossiers/2015/03/201533164429153675.html.

4 This was renamed in 2005 the Peninsula Shield Force.

5 Matteo Legrenzi, *The GCC and the International Relations of the Gulf: Diplomacy, Security and Economic Coordination in a Changing Middle East* (London: I.B. Tauris, 2011), 76.

6 Habib Toumi, "GCC leaders to meet on May 11 in Riyadh," *Gulf News*, 18 April 2010, http://gulfnews.com/news/gulf/saudi-arabia/gcc-leaders-to-m eet-on-may-11-in-riyadh-1.614003.

7 Brahim Saidy, "GCC's Defense Cooperation: Moving Towards Unity," *Foreign Policy Research Institute*, October 2014, www.fpri.org/article/2014/ 10/gccs-defense-cooperation-moving-towards-unity/.

8 "Gulf Nations Announce Joint Military Command," *Atlantic Council*, 13 December 2013, www.atlanticcouncil.org/blogs/natosource/gulf-nations-a nnounce-joint-military-command.

9 "GCC Joint Defense Council's Inaugural Meeting—Media," *Saudi-US Information Service*, 20 May 2014, http://susris.com/2014/05/20/gcc-joint-defense-councils-inaugural-meeting-media/.

10 Alajmi, "Gulf Military Cooperation."

11 Legrenzi, *The GCC and the International Relations of the Gulf*, 79.

12 Justin Vela, "GCC to set up regional police force based in Abu Dhabi," *The National*, 9 December 2014, www.thenational.ae/world/gcc/gcc-to-set-up -regional-police-force-based-in-abu-dhabi.

13 "GCC Declares Lebanon's Hezbollah a 'Terrorist' Group," *Al Jazeera*, 2 March 2016, www.aljazeera.com/news/2016/03/gcc-declares-lebanon-hezbolla h-terrorist-group-160302090712744.html.

14 Abdul Khaleq Abdulla, "The Gulf Cooperation Council: Nature, Origins and Process," in *The Middle East Dilemma*, ed. Michael Hudson (New York: Columbia University Press, 1999), 150–151.

15 Krista Wiegrad, "Bahrain, Qatar, and the Hawar Islands: Resolution of a Gulf Territorial Dispute," *The Middle East Journal* 66, no. 1 (2012): 79–96.

16 Kristian Coates Ulrichsen, *Qatar and the Arab Spring* (London: Hurst & Co., 2014).

17 These negotiations have not been especially successful in agreeing a Free Trade Agreement, however. See for example: Silvia Colombo (ed.), *Bridging the Gulf: EU-GCC Relations at a Crossroads* (Rome: Edizioni Nuova Cultura, 2014); and Gerd Nonneman, "EU-GCC Relations: Dynamics, Patterns and Perspectives," *The International Spectator: Italian Journal of International Affairs* 41, no. 3 (2006): 59–74.

18 Marco Pinfari, "Nothing but Failure? The Arab League and the Gulf Cooperation Council as Mediators in Middle Eastern Conflicts," LSE Working Paper No. 45, March 2009, 17–18, www.lse.ac.uk/internationa lDevelopment/research/crisisStates/download/wp/wpSeries2/WP452.pdf.
19 Frauke Heard-Bey, "Conflict Resolution and Regional Co-operation: The Role of the Gulf Co-operation Council, 1970–2002," *Middle Eastern Studies* 42, no. 2 (2006): 213.
20 Scott Cooper, "State-Centric Balance-of-Threat Theory: Explaining the Misunderstood Gulf Cooperation Council," *Security Studies* 13, no. 2 (2003): 306–349.
21 Kristian Koch, "The GCC as a Regional Security Organization," *KAS International Reports* no. 11 (2010), www.kas.de/wf/doc/kas_21076-544-2-30.pdf? 101110135754.

8   The Gulf Cooperation Council
Economic, social, and cultural cooperation

- **Economic cooperation and integration**
- **Socio-cultural cooperation**
- **Technical cooperation**
- **Conclusion**

Somewhat ironically given the defensive drivers of the organization, it is in the economic, social, and cultural arenas that the GCC has made the most progress. Indeed, in some areas this progress has been startling. In fact, when compared to the Arab League or the Arab Maghreb Union the GCC's achievements in these spheres is on an entirely different scale.

Given the scope and scale of the work that has been done in terms of the integration of the Gulf States' economies, and the increased coordination over key socio-cultural developments, it would be impossible to explore these achievements fully in just one chapter. Instead, here an approach is taken which is designed to demonstrate the broad development trends of the GCC in these areas over time, while also focusing on areas in which cooperation has proven especially fruitful or especially difficult. The chapter thus aims to provide the reader with an impression of the surprisingly rapid progress made in these areas in less than four decades, along with a sense of the scope of cooperation in these areas, and some of the difficulties that the GCC has faced in these fields.

The chapter therefore explores the GCC's activities in these three spheres thematically at the risk of losing some chronological coherence. By examining some of the structures, initiatives, and programs that the GCC has shaped in these areas it can then offer an analysis of the progress achieved. Given that the achievements in economic integration are the most considerable of the organization, the chapter begins by exploring the cooperation in the field of economic and industrial activities, focusing in particular on the creation of the Gulf market, and discussions over a common currency and joint companies. It then moves on to explore GCC initiatives in the spheres of migration, research, and culture as key socio-cultural arenas that have dovetailed and reinforced economic cooperation. The chapter ends by examining the often overlooked technical areas of cooperation in the form of the functionalist specialized bodies created by the GCC. Finally, the chapter offers an analysis of what GCC activities in these three areas tell us about the GCC and the cause of Gulf unity.

Economic cooperation and integration

It is interesting to open with a brief examination of what economic integration in the GCC currently looks like before outlining the developments that led to this situation and an examination of particular issue areas. The GCC today is without question the most integrated economy of the Middle East. Partly this is down to historical interconnections in the Gulf area,[1] but mostly it is the work of the GCC itself and a range of civil society networks and private-sector initiatives, which have paved the way for this situation. Indeed, according to Scott Cooper:

> Forming a regional trade arrangement is, by itself, no difficult accomplishment: dozens of regional agreements have been made in the Third World in the last forty years. Many, however, have never been implemented at all, and fewer still have been meaningful in practice. Forming a regional trade agreement that substantially lowers trade barriers is rare. There have arguably been only three such trade institutions formed in the Third World since the Second World War: the Central American Common Market in the 1960s, Mercosur in the 1990s, and the Gulf Cooperation Council in the 1980s.[2]

Today the Gulf not only has a free trade zone but has moved on to the creation of a customs union and the beginnings of a common market. Capital now flows with relative ease around the GCC states, as do its peoples who have the right to travel freely in the GCC, as well as to marry, own land, buy and sell shares, and have banking facilities in other Gulf States. These are very real achievements in terms of the free flow of goods, services, capital, and people around the region.

Despite this progress, though, we should acknowledge that in this issue area, as in others, the tendency to over-promise and under-deliver remains evident. Indeed, there are some important questions remaining about the quality of implementation in some areas and a number of loopholes, exceptions, and opt-outs still remain, which can make the assessment of the exact extent of harmonization and integration difficult to ascertain fully. We should also recognize that while the GCC has reduced or eliminated many barriers to intra-regional trade, the amount of exports that leaves member states bound for other Gulf monarchies remains only a small fraction of the volume and value of exports leaving the Gulf region bound for elsewhere in the world.

Clearly this level of integration has not come about overnight and has often come through a combination of large steps forward and periods of slower movement towards economic cooperation, alongside continual incremental gains in terms of the harmonization of detailed requirements to enable initiatives to move forward. None of this has been either politically or practically easy to accomplish, yet gains were made almost from the organization's foundation in 1981. Thus from March 1983 onwards visa requirements between GCC states were abolished and soon afterwards ownership rules for companies were changed to allow cross-border control of companies.

At the institutional level the first significant step was taken in the economic sphere just weeks after the inauguration of the GCC. In June 1981 the Unified Economic Agreement (UEA) was approved, designed in part to make sense of a series of previous agreements pre-dating the foundation of the GCC. The UEA forms the foundation upon which all subsequent economic cooperation has been built. The strength of the UEA is its clarity in terms of the objectives envisaged by the member states and its scope is considerable, covering as it does the core areas of trade, capital, and movement of people. It also focuses on technical cooperation, transport, and communication links; monetary issues and the coordination of development. Covering areas as diverse as the elimination of customs duties, joint oil and industrial policy, the building of a common economic infrastructure, unified investment strategies, and even talk of jointly coordinating financial policy. Inevitably progress in some of these areas has been more comprehensive than in others. The concrete proposals have ranged from a free trade area (formally established in 1983), a focus on attempting to coordinate production chains, common legal frameworks for trade and investment, and the idea of a GCC citizenship, which confers certain common rights across the member states.

When judging the success of economic integration in the Gulf it is important to remember the starting point and early stage of state building of the countries involved. Most of the states had embryonic civil services and were seriously lacking the trained personnel, procedures, and in many cases administrative structures (even buildings) necessary for their work. As Frauke Heard-Bey reminds us:

> The governmental institutions and the administrative apparatus in every one of these six countries were mostly still in the formative stages even in the mid-1980s. In particular the legal framework, which had to provide for the transition from protected communities to sovereign states was still being formulated. Because there was no time to train nationals for all the urgently required legal and administrative tasks, the governments had to seek the help and advice of foreign Arabs, other Muslims or western expatriates. These foreign employees introduced the routines to which they were accustomed in their home environment, into the administration of the host country. In consequence the newly institutionalized administrative systems in these six states were even less easily co-ordinated.[3]

Given this background, the sheer ambition and progress made in the economic sphere is all the more startling. Economic integration has been driven by two Joint Action Plans: the UEA of 1981, and the Economic Agreement of 2001. The latter was designed to shift from the economic cooperation and coordination envisaged under the UEA to a more integrative phase through the implementation of specific programs. Thus the Economic Agreement laid out specific processes for the completion of the earlier attempts at a formal customs union whose implementation had never been fully completed. It also aimed to complete the common market in terms of the idea of economic nationality, laid out plans for monetary and economic union, deeper development integration across a range of sectors, and a focus on infrastructure. In essence, the schemes described and analyzed below largely flow from the Economic Agreement of 2001.[4]

When analyzing the success of economic integration schemes in the region it is easy to overlook the progress made in the development of common regulatory regimes, which underpin key aspects of the idea of a Gulf common market—thus, for example, standards in banking inspection, veterinary inspections, and port handling. Likewise there has been considerable development of legal structures when it comes to trade, for example in the field of commercial distribution law.[5] These basic structures, while often still needing further work, form a critical foundation of cooperation in the region and are key to the work of the GCC in the longer term.[6]

Common market—economic nationality

The implementation of article 8 of chapter 2 of the UEA in respect of free movement of GCC citizens represents a good example of a practical achievement of the organization. Although given the degree of commonalities around the Gulf it is surprising that so few GCC citizens are to be found residing or working in other Gulf States.[7] Article 8 specifies that "Member States shall grant citizens of all Member States the same treatment as is granted to its own citizens without any discrimination or differentiation in the following fields: 1) Freedom of movement, work, and residence. 2) Right of ownership, inheritance, and bequest. 3) Freedom of exercising economic activity. 4) Free movement of capital."[8] The ultimate goal is the completion of a regional labor market. The Economic Agreement of 2001 goes further in outlining the rights of GCC citizens to work in the public as well as the private sector in member states, to access pension and social security benefits, and the opening up of the professions through recognition of qualifications and training.[9]

Constantly attempting to move forward with economic integration even when the previous stage has not been fully implemented is both a blessing and a curse for progress towards economic integration in the GCC. The usual steps of free trade area, customs union, common market, and economic union[10] become muddled, which can make analysis difficult and also lead to knock-on effects, which could create uneven integration. Yet at the same time the element of momentum created means that progress is made organically, driving forward in areas where it can make greater strides without becoming permanently stuck when it comes to contentious aspects of integration at earlier stages.[11] That said, sometimes the problem comes when states feel pressured into rushing forward with announcements and initiatives, not wishing to break the solidarity among the leaderships of the GCC states but having no real intention of progressing with the initiative. This means that some aspects of integration remain very much on the drawing board as states uncomfortable with the schemes find ways to block progress through technicalities. Perhaps the classic example of this when it comes to the GCC is the issue of a common currency.

Common currency

A common Gulf currency, to be named the *khaleeji* (Gulf), was always likely to be a particular challenge, yet it has been on the drawing board of the GCC since the beginning. It was not until the Economic

Agreement of 2001 that real steps were made towards this goal, however, with completion scheduled for 2010, a relatively similar schedule to the establishment of the euro in theory.[12] Despite this initial impetus and a challenging target, progress in the development of a common currency has been very slow indeed. On the economic front there is clearly more work to do in synchronizing the region's economies. Emilie Rutledge identifies a core group comprising Bahrain, Qatar, and Saudi Arabia, with Oman and the UAE in a separate category, observing that "while the GCC economies have travelled a considerable way towards meeting the criteria for an OCA [optimal currency area], they have not done so sufficiently so as to be considered an OCA."[13] While clearly there is work still to be done in terms of the full completion of the customs union, the creation of a proper statistics agency and in the fields of fiscal and monetary convergence, all of which will take time, in reality the problems with the formation of a common Gulf currency are political. The level of political capital required to be invested for a long period is rather problematic.[14] It has become even more difficult given the struggles of the euro since the global financial crash of 2008 to create the right momentum behind the project. Even before economic reality intruded, however, some states were already retreating from the project; thus as early as 2006 Oman formally withdrew from the common currency plan, followed in 2009 by the UAE.[15] On the surface these withdrawals were over disputes about whether to peg the new currency to the dollar or a basket of currencies, and the planned headquartering of the currency's bureaucracies and new Gulf Central Bank in Saudi Arabia. In reality it was fears of loss of control that are at the heart of the formal withdrawal of the two states from the currency union. This is an important step because it breaks Gulf solidarity, it is rare for a Gulf State to withdraw publicly rather than simply drag its feet, and it also illustrates clearly for the first time the potential limits of GCC integration.[16]

Joint industrial projects

Much of the groundwork for industrial cooperation in the Gulf takes place outside the formal structures of the GCC itself, although often the decisions regarding strategy are taken within the MC or the SC. Some of these initiatives pre-date the foundation of the GCC, although there has been a strong tendency to increase cooperation in these areas since the GCC's foundation. The principal way in which cooperation in these areas is taken forward is through the creation of joint companies and many of these are coordinated, or run, through the GOIC (described in Chapter 6). These various companies owned by the member states have been at the center of economic cooperation in the Gulf region for decades. By 2013 there were 232 of these companies, employing almost 60,000 workers—with a joint value of around US$23 billion, coordinated by the GOIC alone.[17] Other successes in industrial coordination have come, for example, in the form of the 15-year Gulf metal smelting strategy.[18]

As we saw in Chapter 6, the flexibility of the GCC structure and the lack of any enforcement mechanism for the Secretariat General, not to mention its small size, means that there are difficulties in ensuring that agreements reached in the SC are fully implemented within the member states. The only real power held by the Secretariat General in this regard is that of persuasion and cajoling through both informal mechanisms and the publication of progress reviews, although given the requirements of Gulf diplomacy these are tools that have to be wielded with great care and skill. This leaves elements of a puzzle: why has integration been relatively extensive despite the absence of the kinds of mechanisms of enforcement being present within the GCC which are seen elsewhere? Perhaps the problem is that many studies tend to explore trade integration, which has risen but is still relatively small, rather than other drivers of integration such as joint industrial companies.[19]

It is also important to examine briefly the wider environment of the Gulf region because non-GCC drivers towards greater economic cooperation have long been a factor in delivering greater interconnectivity across the Gulf. Indeed, we will recall that article 4 of the GCC Charter states that one goal of the GCC is to work to encourage these joint coordinative practices. Thus the cooperation between chambers of commerce[20] has been important in a process of pre-harmonization creating expectations, norms, and standards across the Gulf, which at times have outpaced the formal mechanisms emanating from the GCC itself.[21] The drawing together of companies, sectors, and civil society groupings across the Gulf States precedes the development of the GCC and has been an important complement to it during its life.[22] Matteo Legrenzi highlights the example of the "Development Forum,"[23] which brings together people in business, academia, and the public sector in workshops and conferences to discuss a range of economic and social issues. In a sense it is almost a proto-think tank on these issues.[24] The diversity of the cross-GCC organizations is actually quite startling[25] as has been their impact on creating bonds and dynamics that have impacted on the GCC itself.[26] Although the GCC has been surprisingly successful in terms of economic integration, there is much work still to do.

At the GCC's 2016 consultative summit held in Riyadh in May 2016, the formation of an Economic and Development Affairs Commission was announced, designed to "boost coherence, integration and coordination between member states in all economic and development sectors" with a specific initial focus on completing the customs union and common market.[27] This came alongside announcements of a plan to simplify customs procedures with the aim of removing them completely in the coming years. The GCC states themselves clearly recognize the obstacles remaining but still seem determined (at least in public) to continue to make clear steps towards economic integration.

Socio-cultural cooperation

While economic integration has tended to capture both media and academic attention, the GCC has also encouraged cooperation in a range of socio-cultural areas. This section briefly explores five of these issue areas—namely, the environment, social protection, immigration, research and higher education, and sport—in order to assess the level and quality of cooperation in areas both connected to, and separate from, the drive for economic integration.

The environment

On the environment there have been a number of recent initiatives. One would have thought that this would be a relatively new area of cooperation for the GCC, having risen up the region's agenda alongside the increased global attention on climate change. Yet while the issue does receive more attention in the Gulf nowadays, GCC environmental cooperation actually dates from the early years of the organization's history. The SC adopted a document entitled, "The Policies and General Principles of Environment Protection at the GCC States" at its 1985 Muscat summit. Beginning by mandating the creation of common definitions and concepts of the environment, it also promoted the idea of a GCC environmental protection law. This document even went so far as stating that there should be a system developed to monitor the environmental impact of projects funded by the foreign aid given by the GCC states to other countries. This initiative was followed up through a series of action plans, which have led to a range of legislation being passed. This includes, for example, the Convention on the Conservation of Wildlife and Habitat in the Countries of the GCC, signed in 2001.[28]

The GCC has also produced a range of television programs focused on environmental issues, in conjunction with the Joint Program

Production Corporation of the GCC states, and even awards a series of environment prizes for work done in this area by GCC citizens. Connected to this environmental work the GCC has established a GCC Disaster Control Center in Kuwait, which is designed to help states coordinate policy and responses to both natural and man-made disasters.[29] It is natural that the GCC states should cooperate on research into desertification and measures of mitigation. There have also been a range of initiatives that do not fall under the auspices of the GCC itself but do use its name. One recent Saudi initiative, running since 2010, has been the creation of the GCC Environment Forum.[30] GCC work in this area is surprisingly advanced but there are some issues with the depth of commitment to some of these issues, with some member states being much more advanced on these issues than others, which can make cooperation more difficult.[31] One area where policy coordination is especially slow is in terms of energy policy where it merges into issues of climate change, with states such as the UAE being more (on the surface at least) committed to this agenda than others.[32]

Social protection

Connected to the environment and risk, but also a key part of moves towards a common market among the Gulf States, is the issue of social and consumer protection. Work has been ongoing in this sphere for many years but has received new impetus since the Arab Spring as consumer protection laws have been tightened across the Gulf States. One key area here is the control of food quality. A 2009 study found that the countries had made good progress on implementing international standards for national food control systems, and that despite differing approaches across the states real moves were being made. As the study stated, "cooperation is leading to increased harmonization of legislation and food control practices" across the GCC.[33] This is evidence of a growing momentum in a range of fields, which partly by design, partly by natural processes, and partly by luck the GCC states are cooperating and integrating in a range of fields. This has recently become evident also in the beginnings of harmonization of mobile phone roaming rates within the GCC.[34]

Immigration

With significant proportions of the population, and more so the workforce, of the Gulf States being expatriate workers, a key lever of control for the regimes has been in the strict regulation of migration and issuing of visas and work permits.[35] This has traditionally been an important tool for managing employment for locals, defending national identity, and also demonstrating the power and authority of the state. Needless to say with an issue that is perceived to go to the heart of state sovereignty in the region, cooperation on migration has been seen as a very difficult area for the GCC to work in. Clearly though, cooperation in this area would make sense given the region's reliance on migrant labor but also a need to create more jobs for GCC citizens, especially in the context of harmonization process and goals for common industrial policies and the already existing free movement of Gulf nationals. Migration governance though is too sensitive and is likely to be an issue area that receives little or no attention from the GCC until it becomes more obviously necessary as other initiatives advance.[36]

Research and higher education

The GCC began work in these fields in 1986 with a separate MC for Higher Education being established in 1996 once all member states had created Ministries of Higher Education. Since 2008 there has been an acceleration in cooperation in this field with a special committee of the heads of all universities in the Gulf States created, an information portal called "*jesr*" established, and work on exchange structures, common bylaws and working towards the formation of a federation of Gulf universities.[37]

Cooperation in this field has also extended to the establishment of the Arabian Gulf University in Bahrain. In fact, this organization pre-dates the foundation of the GCC by two years, being initially proposed in 1979 by the General Convention of Arab Education for the Gulf,[38] and established in 1980. Entry to the university is restricted to GCC and Yemeni nationals. While not directly connected to the GCC itself, it further demonstrates the web of connections that support, both directly and indirectly, the work and goals of the GCC.

Sport

The role of sport in creating connections should not be underestimated and this has been on the GCC's agenda since 1983. The primary focus was to develop a joint strategy for the promotion of sport, with a focus not just on participation, research, and regulation but also on the organization of competitions among the Gulf States. This has been institutionalized through the slightly unusual formation of a committee of all the heads of Olympic Committees of the Gulf States, supported by the Executive Office of the Council of Chairpersons of the Olympic Committees, which in turn oversees 24 separate committees focused on different sports. These bodies then act to coordinate, spread best practice and arbitrate in disputes.[39] In terms of concrete measures beyond this infrastructure, these are harder to see. Perhaps the biggest achievement is the organization of sporting contests in parallel to the Gulf Cup of Nations. This, Gulf States (plus Yemen), football championship takes place every three or four years depending on other major tournaments, and has been running since 1970, thus pre-dating the GCC, but its impact has been considerable in generating an awareness of Gulf identity. Parallel championships in other sports have been running since 2004, with the next Gulf Cup being held in Qatar in 2017.

Technical cooperation

In addition to the institutions discussed in Chapter 6 that come under the direct control of the GCC Secretariat in some sense, such as the Gulf Patents Office, the GCC Standardization Organization and the GCCCAC, in more recent years a number of bodies for technical coordination have been created, mostly in the sphere of infrastructure.

Perhaps the most significant of these is the Gulf Cooperation Council Interconnectivity Authority (GCCIA), which has been created in the form of a joint stock company by all six member states. Approved in 2001 and now operational, its website states that it is, "inspired by the principles and goals of the GCC and having the desire to realize more cooperation and fostering the links between them in the areas of trade and services in power."[40] Its focus is upon the gradual creation of an interconnected power grid and market for the Gulf, reducing costs and enabling emergency planning and greater efficiency. The new body was actually conceived as far back as 1986 with feasibility studies taking many years; since its formal establishment in 2002, however, it has awarded more than a dozen contracts worth more than $1 billion with many of the first phase contracts completed by 2009.

The Economic Agreement of 2001 also envisaged the creation of the Technical Office for Telecommunications,[41] the GCC ATM Network,[42] and the Office of the Technical Secretariat for Anti-Dumping. The latter is a body that has been established within the structures of the GCC Secretariat General. The former bodies are arm's-length organizations but with connections to the GCC itself; all are functioning and there have, for example, been clear results in a transition to a GCC payments system for banking, although much remains to be done.[43]

In addition, there have long been discussions around joint transport infrastructure projects,[44] with a particular focus since 2000 on the idea of a GCC rail network. To this end a Gulf Railway Authority was mandated at the 2009 GCC summit.[45] The construction of an inter-connected Gulf Rail Network was originally scheduled for completion in 2018, but this has since been pushed back to 2022.[46] Indeed, at present it seems that the project has rather fragmented, with each state pushing ahead with its own projects as the establishment of the Rail Authority only began in 2015.[47] The fact that construction is already underway or in some cases almost complete within some member states even in the absence of the Rail Authority perhaps demonstrates that existing cooperation through Ministries of Transport is already advanced enough given the pre-existing plans not to need additional coordination in the construction phase.

Pre-dating these technical initiatives is the Gulf Investment Corporation (GIC), which was established in 1983 with initial capital of $420 million and focused on encouraging the development of joint development projects, especially in the fields of power and industrial cooperation. It has had an important role in developing cooperation in the region and delivering elements of the GCC strategy to prevent duplication and encourage efficiency in industrial development in the region. It has made billions of dollars of loans and is an important symbol of cooperation among the GCC's member states, even though the GIC is run outside the immediate umbrella of the GCC.[48]

Conclusion

The GCC is often a puzzling organization, ambitious yet with little force to monitor compliance, the most advanced IO of the region and at times not even appearing like other international organizations at all. It is in fact a patchwork quilt of areas of considerable progress, part-completed plans, thriving cooperation and at times distrust, prone to the announcement of grandiose schemes, which take decades to establish properly, if they are not simply left on the shelf. A complex mix of the political and the practical drives the organization forward, with many aspects of cooperation announced at its meetings and yet run entirely separately from the organization. It is at times easy to be cynical about the GCC and it achievements, being as it is difficult to disentangle the rhetoric from the reality, yet the organization has made concrete steps towards integration, and cooperation in economic matters is increasingly the default position across the Gulf States.

Notes

1 See for example: Richard Sindelar and J.E. Peterson (eds), *Crosscurrents in the Gulf* (London: Routledge, 1988).

2 Scott Cooper, "State-Centric Balance-of-Threat Theory: Explaining the Misunderstood Gulf Cooperation Council," *Security Studies* 13, no. 2 (2003): 307.

3 Frauke Heard-Bey, "Conflict Resolution and Regional Co-operation: The Role of the Gulf Cooperation Council, 1970–2002," *Middle Eastern Studies* 42, no. 2 (2006): 217.

4 For more detail on these agreements see: Robert Looney, "The Gulf Cooperation Council's Cautious Approach to Economic Integration," *Journal of Economic Cooperation* 24, no. 2 (2003): 137–160.

5 Dahmane Ben Abderrahmane, "Commercial Distribution Law in the Countries of the Arab Gulf Cooperation Council," *Arab Law Quarterly* 8, no. 4 (1993): 303–314.

6 Maher Dabbah, *Competition Law and Policy in the Middle East* (Cambridge: Cambridge University Press, 2007), 193–236.

7 Numbers are commonly thought to be in the low tens of thousands.

8 Badr El Din A. Ibrahim, *Economic Co-operation in the Gulf: Issues in the Economies of the Arab Gulf* (London: Routledge, 2007), 33–58.

9 Zahra Babar, "Free Mobility within the Gulf Cooperation Council," Center for International and Regional Studies, Georgetown University School of Foreign Service in Qatar, Occasional Paper No. 8 (2011).

10 Matteo Legrenzi, *The GCC and the International Relations of the Gulf: Diplomacy, Security and Economic Coordination in a Changing Middle East* (London: I.B. Tauris, 2011), 60–61.

11 It should be noted that the GCC seems to see the process slightly differently, listing the goals as: 1 customs union, 2 economic citizenship, 3 banking co-operation, 4 convergence of financial and economic policy, 5 integration of financial markets. See: www.gcc-sg.org/en-us/Cooperatio nAndAchievements/Achievements/EconomicCooperation/FinancialandEco nomicCooperation/pages/Home.aspx.

12 Esteban Jadresic, "On a Common Currency for the Gulf Countries," *IMF Policy Discussion Paper*, PDP/02/12 (2002), www.imf.org/external/pubs/ft/p dp/2002/pdp12.pdf.

13 Emilie Rutledge, *Monetary Union in the Gulf: Prospects for a Single Currency in the Arabian Peninsula* (London: Routledge, 2009), 58.

14 Courtney Trenwith, "GCC Single Currency Comes Down to Politics, Says ex-IMF Boss," *Arabian Business*, 25 November 2014, www.arabianbusiness. com/gcc-single-currency-comes-down-politics-says-ex-imf-boss-572960.html #.V1L2M6T2amw.

15 Robin Wigglesworth, "UAE Quits Gulf Monetary Union," *Financial Times*, 20 May 2009, www.ft.com/cms/s/0/822cab2e-4534-11de-b6c8-00144 feabdc0.html.

16 There has been some talk of the other four states still continuing with the currency, although few signs of it progressing. There have also been symbolic attempts to re-engage the UAE and Oman in the project. See: Ghazanfar Ali Khan, "GCC Tries to Persuade UAE, Oman to Join Currency Talks," *Arab News*, 29 June 2014, www.arabnews.com/news/593931.

17 "GOIC: Cumulated Investments Worth 23 Billion USD in Joint Gulf Ventures," 20 April 2015, www.goic.org.qa/GOICCMS/WebsiteNews_175_EN. html.

18 Nancy Troxler, "The Gulf Co-operation Council: The Emergence of an Institution," *Millennium—Journal of International Studies* 16, no. 1 (1987): 17.

19 Humayon Dar and John Presley, "The Gulf Co-operation Council: A Slow Path to Integration?" *The World Economy* 24, no. 9 (2001): 1161–1178.

20 Steffen Hertog, *Benchmarking SME Policies in the GCC: A Survey of Challenges and Opportunities* (Brussels: Eurochambres, 2010).

21 The Federation of Gulf Chambers of Commerce and Industry, http://fgccc. org/en/.

22 This may be, as Hertog suggests, because the private sector remains relatively subordinate to the governments of the region. If this is the case then this might create a further puzzle if so much drive has come from these companies and less from the bureaucracies in terms of integration. See: Steffen Hertog, *The Private Sector and Reform in the Gulf Cooperation Council*, Kuwait Programme on Development, Governance and Globalisation in the Gulf States No. 30 (2013), http://eprints.lse.ac.uk/54398/1/ Hertog_2013.pdf.

23 Legrenzi, *The GCC and International Relations*, 59–60.

24 The story of the GDF is told in more detail in this article: Mohammed Al Rumaihi, "The Story of Gulf Development Forum," *The Peninsula*, 24 February 2016, www.thepeninsulaqatar.com/views/political-views/371741/ the-story-of-gulf-development-forum.

25 Abdulnabi Al Alekri, Abdullah Janahi and Mahmoud Hafith, *Civil Society in the Gulf Cooperation Council (GCC) Region: A Literature Review*, http:// foundationforfuture.org/en/Portals/0/Conferences/Research/Research%20pape rs/Civil_Society_in_Gulf_English.pdf.

26 Nir Kshetri and Riad Ajami, "Institutional Reforms in the Gulf Cooperation Council Economies: A Conceptual Framework," *Journal of International Management* 14, no. 3 (2008): 300–318.

27 "New Gulf Body to Tighten Economic Bond," *Arab News*, 1 June 2016, www.arabnews.com/node/932971/saudi-arabia.

28 Convention on the Conservation of Wildlife and Habitat in the countries of the GCC, www.sites.gcc-sg.org/DLibrary/download.php?B=335.

29 Berta Acero, "Gulf Cooperation Council Takes First Steps to Develop Risk Reduction Road Map," *UN Office for Disaster Risk Reduction*, 18 January 2013, www.unisdr.org/archive/30600.

30 GCC Environment Forum, www.gccenvironmentforum.com.

31 A. Kannan, *Global Environmental Governance and Desertification: A Study of Gulf Cooperation Council Countries* (New Delhi: Concept Publishing, 2012).

32 Danyel Reiche, "Energy Policies of Gulf Cooperation Council (GCC) Countries—Possibilities and Limitations of Ecological Modernization in Rentier States," *Energy Policy* 38, no. 5 (2010): 2395–2403.

33 D. Al-Kandari and D.J. Jukes, "A Situation Analysis of the Food Control Systems in Arab Gulf Cooperation Council (GCC) Countries," *Food Control* 20, no. 12 (2009): 1112–1118, at 1114.

34 Ewan Sutherland, "A Review of International Mobile Roaming to December 2011," *SSRN*, January 2012, http://papers.ssrn.com/sol3/papers. cfm?abstract_id=1894604.

35 Onn Winckler, "The Immigration Policy of the Gulf Cooperation Council (GCC) States," *Middle Eastern Studies* 33, no. 3 (1997): 480–493.
36 Mohammed Ebrahim Dito, "GCC Labour Migration Governance," United Nations Expert Group Meeting on International Migration and Development in Asia and the Pacific, United Nations Economic and Social Commission for Asia and the Pacific, Population Division, Department of Economic and Social Affairs, Bangkok, Thailand, September 2008.
37 David McGlennon, *Building Research Capacity in the Gulf Cooperation Council Countries: Strategy, Funding and Engagement*, http://citeseerx.ist. psu.edu/viewdoc/download?doi=10.1.1.485.2284&rep=rep1&type=pdf.
38 Arab Bureau for Education for the Gulf States, www.abegs.org/eportal/generalconference/index.
39 Gulf Joint Sport Action, www.gcc-sg.org/en-us/CooperationAndAchievem ents/Achievements/CooperationinthefieldofHumanandEnvironmentAffairs/ Pages/JointSportAction.aspx.
40 Gulf Cooperation Council Interconnectivity Authority (GCCIA), www. gccia.com.sa/P/company_profile/11.
41 GCC Telecom Bureau, www.gcctelecom.org.
42 GCC ATM Network, www.gcc-net.net/gcc-net/(S(ifwqqknqnthxo045eifljxbv))/ Default.aspx.
43 "UAE ATM Switch Connects to Other GCC Switches," www.atmmarketp lace.com/news/uae-atm-switch-connects-to-other-gcc-switches/.
44 In 2015 studies were commenced for a potential single GCC skies project, see: "Helios Begins Work on GCC 'Seamless' Airspace Study," *Helios*, 5 October 2015, www.canso.org/helios-begins-work-gcc-seamless-airspace-study.
45 John Lowe and Ibrahim Saud Altrairi, "The Gulf Cooperation Council Railway," www.arcom.ac.uk/-docs/proceedings/ar2013-1147-1157_Lowe_ Altrairi.pdf.
46 Ghazanfar Ali Khan, "New Timeline for 2,177-km GCC Rail Project," *Arab News*, 28 February 2016, www.arabnews.com/featured/news/887551.
47 Alicia Buller, "GCC Rail: A Train to Connect the Gulf," *Edgar Daily*, 4 August 2015, http://edgardaily.com/en/life/2015/gcc-rail-a-train-to-connect-t he-gulf-8079.
48 Gulf Investment Corporation (GIC), www.gic.com.kw/en/about-us/history/.

9 The Gulf Cooperation Council
Problems and prospects

- **Pinning down the GCC**
- **Obstacles and achievements**
- **Prospects?**

In less than 40 years cooperation in the Gulf region has expanded dramatically in both scale and scope. Having explored the structures and processes of the GCC and explored some of its work in the fields of defense, security, economy, and socio-cultural cooperation, this chapter begins by briefly attempting to capture the elusive nature of the GCC itself while also reflecting upon the wider environment in which Gulf cooperation takes place. Using tools from the framework outlined in Chapter 1, the chapter then proceeds to offer an assessment of the obstacles to progress experienced by the GCC through an examination of both internal and external factors. This then forms the backdrop to a realistic assessment of the GCC's achievements. Using this analysis, the chapter then concludes with an examination of the outlook and prospects for the GCC created by recent changes in the regional and domestic environments caused by the Arab Spring.

Pinning down the GCC

The GCC is often dismissed as a club for oil-rich monarchs in which they can air their differences, offer each other solidarity and make grandiose plans that rarely leave the drawing board. Without doubt security concerns have often been at the forefront of business in the GCC. The Arabian Gulf has long been subject to the impacts of global and Middle Eastern geopolitics which, combined with the withdrawal of British protection in 1971, left the Gulf experiencing an important period of political growth and transition. The creation of the GCC out of the environment of the late 1970s, influenced by Arab Nationalist rhetoric and the practical need for small states to cooperate was in turn spurred on by the rise to power of Saddam Hussein in Iraq and the creation of the Islamic Republic in Iran. This security narrative has often been deployed to explain the rise and the nature of the GCC as an organization.

A closer look at the structures, aims, and evolution of the GCC itself as an international organization leaves the impression of a body that in terms of its physical footprint is barely present. In its institutionalized form the GCC is a remarkably simple organization consisting of just three core elements on paper, and in reality is effectively simply a Supreme Council with a supporting apparatus. Yet this simplicity belies the complexity of both the organization itself and the wider structures, which make Gulf cooperation possible. As Chapter 8 demonstrated, the range of joint ventures, civil society groupings, international organizations that pre-dated the formation of the GCC, alongside more recent structures that have emerged from the GCC but which remain at arm's length to it, creates a series of interlocking and mutually reinforcing cooperative dynamics, which drive and are driven by the GCC itself.

In effect, the GCC is more than simply a sub-regional organization; it is in reality both a brand and a franchise. What we have seen since the foundation of the GCC in 1981 is the acceleration of a trend towards a growing identity among the citizens of the Gulf States. For while their national identities generally remain strong, with the waning of wider Arab Nationalist rhetoric and projects, what has grown is an awareness of a separate Gulf or *khaleeji* identity.[1] This has only been reinforced by the GCC and it initiatives.[2] Thus, for example, a very visible effect of the GCC's "common market," otherwise known as economic citizenship, has been the creation at passport controls of specific queues for "GCC Citizens" in the same way that there are specific queues for "EU Citizens" at airports across Europe. In turn, this increased sense of sub-regional identity has reinforced cooperation in a whole range of spheres both formal and informal across the GCC,[3] leading to a sense of dynamism in the region's cooperation and integration processes even when political issues create difficulties between the GCC states themselves.

The GCC's brand, with its moves towards greater cooperation, is now mixed up in the creation of this new sense of being Arab but being different—being a Gulf Arab. So successful has this brand become that even outside the region there is a marked tendency to refer to "the GCC states." This has made researching the GCC as an organization even more difficult than before, as academics across a range of disciplines use the GCC brand to refer to the group of states rather than the organization itself. As political and economic momentum has built across the region so too has the desire to be associated with the brand, thus there has been an explosion of companies, organizations, and NGOs using the terminology of Gulf cooperation in everyday speech, in their own branding activities, and as political and social tools when interacting with their own states.

These ideational realities perhaps represent the GCC's greatest success. There is undoubtedly now a clear identification with the GCC at all levels, and a momentum behind it, which is increasingly outside the control of the states themselves. While there may be limits to the extent of cooperation in some areas, in others the march of integration will be difficult to halt, clearly partly due to the visibility of some of the outputs of the GCC, its concrete achievements, which have contributed enormously to these dynamics.

Obstacles and achievements

The GCC is clearly an inherently flexible organization. While it may take inspiration at times from other regionalist experiments and particularly the EU, it works in an entirely different manner making comparisons extremely difficult. Some authors have said that the GCC's biggest achievement is simply its survival in the face of the pressures of the 1980s, facing such clear external security challenges and internal pressures with the collapse in oil prices. As Abdul Khaleq Abdulla puts it, "at the end of a turbulent decade, GCC states found themselves surprisingly unscathed. This was an undeniable success, and a great deal of the credit for it deservedly goes to the GCC."[4]

Clearly, though, the GCC had, even then, made great strides towards achieving its economic, social, and cultural goals, even though its progress in the defense and security realms was less impressive. Among the earliest achievements of the GCC was the creation of the free trade area, and it is in the economic sphere where the organization's progress has been most marked. As Scott Cooper puts it, the GCC's:

> most notable achievement is the complete elimination of intra-regional customs duties—an accomplishment with few parallels in the history of Third World regionalism. Nearly as important was the move to harmonize external tariff schedules by setting a common minimum tariff level of 4 percent and a maximum of 20 percent. This tariff band falls somewhat short of a common external tariff, but it has dramatically reduced variation in tariff rates.

Much of the remaining variation involves luxury goods. As a result of this market integration, intra-GCC trade increased from 3 percent of total trade in 1980 to 8 percent in 1990.[5]

Matteo Legrenzi is much more skeptical, pointing to what he terms the "saga" of the creation of the customs union and the difficulties in creating a coordinated oil policy among the GCC states. He explains the slow progress in the economic sphere through reference to the lack of dynamism in the periods when oil prices are high, and lack of political capital during periods of "slow motion crisis" in the economies of the region.[6] Fred Lawson, meanwhile, attempts to move away from the structuralist and historical institutionalist accounts of the foundation of the GCC drawn from Western experiences of regionalism and instead attempts to account for the up and down, or discontinuous, processes experienced by the GCC. He does this through the creation of a two-level game dynamic at play in the region at both the domestic and international levels.[7] He comes to the conclusion that "only in the face of extraordinary internal and external challenges have the six regimes created institutional arrangements designed to bind their respective states together" and it is this dynamic that has created the uneven progress in all of the spheres of the GCC's activity.[8]

The GCC has clearly faced some significant obstacles to progress, as well as having some inherent advantages. The regional environment can be both a blessing and a curse when it comes to cooperation through the GCC. Tensions between the Gulf States over both internal issues and the external politics of the Gulf region, or the wider Middle East, can have a big impact upon the organization at times, which often accounts for the somewhat stop-start nature of integration over time. On the other hand the continuing security threat posed by Iran, the rise of radical Islam, and the chaos in neighboring states ensures that cooperation remains essential. It is increasingly obvious that there are limits to integration among the GCC states—sovereignty remains a critical institution in the region, and this will ensure that in some areas integration is extremely limited or nonexistent.

Given all of this, it is clear that the GCC remains primarily an instrument of the member states, yet at the same time it has also become an important arena for cooperation. It may not have the bureaucratic structures to create the kinds of dynamics seen in other organizations but at times agency has been exercised and the GCC has had results through careful cajoling, coordination, and by setting expectations. The problem is that there are no studies of the GCC Secretariat due to access issues and secrecy so it is unlikely that we will see exactly how these dynamics work, or quite what influence the secretary-general has in pushing forward integration and cooperation.

Considering the multiple obstacles facing cooperation on all fronts in the region the depth and quality of interactions through the GCC are, when compared to the Arab League and AMU or even other Third World regionalist projects, of a surprising level. The GCC confounds expectations. Realists expect to see the GCC as an alliance and yet are confronted with an organization focused on economic, social, and cultural cooperation.[9] At the same time neoliberal institutionalism struggles to account for the depth of economic cooperation between non-democracies with low trade engagement and a similar economic focus on primary commodity production. Clearly an understanding of identity, internal security dynamics, and constructivist processes is also critical in understanding not only the formation but also the progress made by the GCC.[10] In many ways, then, the GCC has been remarkably successful, and yet it remains something of an enigma.

Prospects?

Having often been underestimated, the prospects for the GCC are actually quite bright. Clearly the organization is never going to be allowed to morph into something that resembles the EU. The rulers will remain in control but that does not mean that there will not be progress even if it might feel at times like one step back, two steps forward.[11] The GCC's founding goals were always likely to be unachievable and yet despite this, significant progress has been made in many fields. It is the flexibility and rapidity of decision making—which are both strengths and weaknesses of the organization at times—that will enable it to continue to make incremental progress in the coming decades. This, along with the wider environment and expectation of cooperation, which has become a broad form of norm in the Gulf region, will ensure that existing cooperation is maintained and developed in those areas that do not adversely affect the sovereignty of the nations involved. The elasticity of the GCC's goals mean that it can bridge high-flying rhetoric as well as the detail of day-to-day cooperation and functionalist interaction. As Abdullah puts it, "the fundamental operative logic of the GCC has been simple: if total political unity—theoretically at least the ultimate goal—is not immediately attainable, then co-operation is the second best goal."[12]

In the post-Arab Spring era drives towards greater unity have once again been made with the proposal of the formation of a "Gulf Union."[13] This has recently even morphed into proposals for a Middle

East Union.[14] Clearly neither of these things is likely—indeed, Oman has "bluntly" rejected the idea of a Gulf Union[15]—yet this rhetoric is a useful tool for the Gulf monarchies at times and even though it will seemingly inevitably not happen, these pronouncements do not seem fundamentally to harm the idea of greater Gulf cooperation and may even maintain the smaller, less visible forms of integration, which have been occurring in the Gulf since the 1970s.[16]

Notes

1 Neil Patrick, "Nationalism in the Gulf States," in *The Transformation of the Gulf: Politics, Economics and the Global Order*, ed. David Held and Kristian Ulrichsen (London: Routledge, 2012), 60–61.

2 Some have spoken of a *khaleej* capitalist class having been formed, see: Adam Hanieh, "*Khaleeji*-Capital: Class-Formation and Regional Integration in the Middle-East Gulf," *Historical Materialism* 18, no. 2 (2010): 35–76.

3 It has also reinforced historical connections in the region which were important already in making the right environment for the GCC to be formed, see for example: Madawi Al-Rasheed (ed.), *Transnational Connections and the Arab Gulf* (London: Routledge, 2005).

4 Abdul Khaleq Abdulla, "The Gulf Cooperation Council: Nature, Origin and Process," in *Middle East Dilemma: The Politics and Economics of Arab Integration*, ed. Michael Hudson (New York: Columbia University Press, 1999), 164.

5 Scott Cooper, "State-Centric Balance-of-Threat Theory: Explaining the Misunderstood Gulf Cooperation Council," *Security Studies* 13, no. 2 (2003): 316.

6 Matteo Legrenzi, *The GCC and International Relations: Diplomacy, Security and Economic Coordination in a Changing Middle East* (London: I.B. Tauris, 2011), 38.

7 Fred Lawson, "Theories of Integration in a New Context: The Gulf Cooperation Council," in *Racing to Regionalize: Democracy, Capitalism and Regional Political Economy*, ed. Kenneth Thomas and Mary Ann Tétreault (Boulder, Col.: Lynne Rienner, 1999), 7–31.

8 Lawson, "Theories of Integration in a New Context," 30–31.

9 David Priess, "Balance-of-Threat Theory and the Genesis of the Gulf Cooperation Council: An Interpretative Case Study," *Security Studies* 5, no. 4 (1996): 143–171.

10 For a deeper discussion of the different theories as applied to the GCC see: Matteo Legrenzi, "The Gulf Cooperation Council in Light of International Relations Theory," *International Area Studies Review* 5, no. 2 (2002): 21–37.

11 See: Fred Lawson, "Comparing Regionalist Projects in the Middle East and Elsewhere: One Step Back, Two Steps Forward," in *Beyond Regionalism?: Regional Cooperation, Regionalism and Regionalization in the Middle East*, ed. Matteo Legrenzi and Cilja Harders (Farnham: Ashgate, 2008), 13–32.

12 Abdul Khaleq Abdullah, "The Gulf Cooperation Council: Nature, Origin and Process," in *Middle East Dilemma: The Politics and Economics of Arab*

Integration, ed. Michael Hudson (New York: Columbia University Press, 1999), 152.

13 Middle East Policy Council, "GCC Debates Gulf Union," *Middle East in Focus*, 22 May 2012, www.mepc.org/articles-commentary/commentary/gcc-debates-gulf-union.

14 Sounak Mukhopadhyay, "Gulf Arab Leaders Push for EU-Style 'Middle East Union' at GCC Summit," *International Business Times*, 12 November 2015, www.ibtimes.com/gulf-arab-leaders-push-eu-style-middle-east-union-gcc-summit-2221397.

15 Paul Crompton, "Why is Oman Against a Gulf Union?" *Al Arabiya*, 10 December 2013, http://english.alarabiya.net/en/perspective/analysis/2013/12/10/Why-did-Oman-refuse-a-Gulf-union-.html; and "Oman Goes Blunt 'Against' a Gulf Union," *Al Arabiya*, 7 December 2013, http://english.alarabiya.net/en/News/middle-east/2013/12/07/Oman-says-it-opposes-union-of-Gulf-States.html.

16 Mustafa Al Zarooni, "GCC Chases 'Gulf Union' Dream at Riyadh Summit," *Khaleej Times*, 11 December 2015, www.khaleejtimes.com/region/gcc-chases-union-dream-at-riyadh-summit.

10 The Arab Maghreb Union

- Structures and evolution
- Economic, social, and cultural cooperation
- Problems and prospects
- Conclusion

This chapter forms a stand-alone examination of the *Union du Maghreb Arabe*, or Arab Maghreb Union (AMU) in English, a sub-regional organization founded in 1989 and comprising all of the Arab League's member states in the west of North Africa—namely, Algeria, Libya, Mauritania, Morocco, and Tunisia.[1] Often perceived as an essentially moribund body, this chapter explores some of the reasons for its difficulties while also examining the ambitious nature of the project and offering an assessment of its achievements and prospects.

The chapter is organized in a similar manner to our examinations of the Arab League and the GCC. We begin with an exploration of the founding of the AMU before moving on to examine its structures and evolution. Since the organization has been inactive in terms of peace and security this is not examined separately, although peace and security issues have clearly affected the AMU's development and are discussed where relevant. We then move on to explore the AMU's work in economic, social, and cultural cooperation before examining the organization's major problems and its prospects for the future.

Structures and evolution

Founding

The formation of the AMU on 17 February 1989 did not come completely out of the blue but given the politics of the sub-region and the scope of its ambition, the fact of its rapid creation certainly drew some attention. The region undoubtedly makes coherent geographical and cultural sense. Indeed, as Belaid and Zartman put it, the Maghreb "constitutes a region, an island of similar and self-identifying people, mutually interacting and interdependent."[2] Despite this, however, the region, which had essentially been under French control since the middle of the nineteenth century, had been since independence—in 1956 for Tunisia and Morocco, 1960 for Mauritania, and 1962 for Algeria; Libya had been released from Anglo-French supervision in 1951—a fractious mass of tensions, territorial disputes, and border wars. In the struggle for the independence of Algeria there had been many gestures of solidarity but the 1960s saw disputes over borders between Algeria and Tunisia, and Algeria and Morocco, followed by attempts at greater cooperation through the Maghrebi Permanent Consultative Committee and its attached body the Committee for Industrial Cooperation, which were both founded in 1964 and were seemingly initially very active. This was followed by an Arab Nationalist-inspired plan to form a union, the "Arab Islamic Republic," between Libya and Tunisia which, rather predictably, failed to make it off the drawing board having also tried to include Morocco and Algeria.[3] The fact that the constitutions of Tunisia, Morocco, and Algeria at this time had the ideal of Maghrebi unity built into them certainly shows the roots of the project, and it is perhaps only once these Arab Nationalist-inspired dreams[4] abated that the formation of the AMU could really become a practical reality. The 1970s were a difficult decade for the region. Ghadaffi's rise to power in Libya in 1969 certainly caused some disruption,[5] but in the early part of the decade Algeria and Morocco finally agreed on a border in the Sahara[6] and Morocco had belatedly recognized Mauritania in 1969; clearly these were "important preconditions to any construction of closer unity."[7]

The Spanish withdrawal from its territories of *Rio d'Oro y Saguia el-Hamra* (now known together as Western Sahara) and their subsequent Moroccan occupation in 1975/76, in spite of an International Court of Justice verdict that the native people had a right to independence, led to an ongoing conflict between Morocco and the native Saharawis' representative body the Polisario Front, with the latter backed by the Algerians (and a little later by the Libyans). The continuing implications of this conflict are explored in more detail in the third section of this chapter. The result at the time was to place Maghrebi cooperation, let alone unity, into the deep-freeze. The 1980s saw some attempts to revive cooperation: in 1983,[8] for instance, Morocco, Tunisia, and Algeria came together to celebrate the 25th anniversary of their agreement to work together to liberate Algeria and declared "the attachment of the three peoples to the unity of the Grand Maghreb."[9]

In reality, though, realist security concerns predominated and cooperation was seen as both a security threat and selectively as a potential security assurance. The polarization of the region between its two "great powers," Morocco and Algeria, which were evenly matched in terms of population and military strength meant that when Algeria attempted to draw itself, Tunisia and Mauritania closer,[10] Morocco responded by signing agreements with Libya. Neither of these experiments lasted very long. As Zartman puts it, "the dominant motor in cycles of relations has been the search for security within a structural dynamic, in which cooperation is as threatening as conflict, and unity as divisive as dispute."[11]

Despite this deeply inauspicious regional environment, some of the bilateral agreements, rather than the attempts at unions between two or three states, laid the groundwork for the founding of the AMU. These agreements included, for example, Algerian-Tunisian accords on the establishment of the "*Banque de cooperation du Maghreb arabe* (B.C. M.A.), the coordination of import-export policies towards the E.C. [European Community], and the establishment of common scientific institutions."[12] Tunisia also worked with Morocco to establish a series of joint companies across a range of sectors. There was a flurry of activity, which gradually laid the groundwork for deeper and more lasting ties, which were supported by more practical initiatives rather than over-ambitious rhetorically and diplomatically driven schemes.

In 1986 the three core states met again in Algiers, with momentum having been encouraged by a range of NGOs and civil society organizations. Eventually, in 1988 with relations having slowly warmed between Algeria and Morocco, full diplomatic ties were restored, and in early 1989 Algerian President Chadli Benjedid visited Rabat, signing various bilateral cooperation agreements along the lines of those that had already been proliferating between other Maghrebi states.

Momentum had therefore been clearly building in terms of cooperation, and with the warming of relations between Algeria and Morocco, Tunisia and Libya, Libya and Algeria, and Libya and Morocco during the 1980s, key impediments to more than just bilateral cooperation were slowly receding. This, combined with an effective stalemate in the war in Western Sahara, which caused Morocco to begin to look to the UN for a solution, meant a window of opportunity was opening. Thus in May 1988, in the aftermath of an Arab League summit on Palestine held in Algiers, the leaders of the five states held a summit to discuss Maghreb unity. The outcome was the establishment of "an Inter-Maghreb Commission (I.M.C.) to make proposals for, and to identify means of achieving, unity. Five subcommissions were created, each chaired and located in a different member-state, and their draft proposals were examined by the I.M.C. in Rabat in October 1988."[13] Progress thereafter was extraordinarily rapid, with a meeting in January 1989 approving all of the proposals and a treaty drafted and agreed at a summit in Marrakech, 15–17 February 1989, which came into force on 1 July the same year.

Role and purpose

The purpose of the AMU is, on paper, extremely wide ranging; indeed, in some senses it really feels more like attempts at Arab unity such as the UAR than an international organization like the League. Having said that, though, this is naturally mostly rhetoric with more than enough safeguards to sovereignty still being present. In terms of the issue areas the body covers, these are quite comprehensive in scope. Like the EU, the treaty planned for the gradual establishment of the free movement of goods, services, capital, and people; thus, for example, it would have a unified tariff by the end of 1991 and a full customs union by 1995,[14] followed by a common market by 2000.[15] It also envisaged the formulation of common policies in virtually all areas, including agriculture, diplomacy, culture, and even defense, although article 3 does specify that defense cooperation is designed to "safeguard the independence of each member country." What is especially interesting is that at the Marrakesh summit, alongside establishing the formal structures and roles of the AMU, a program of action was adopted, which attempted to map out the development of the new organization. This included the establishment of common research facilities, common universities, and joint venture companies.

The AMU is often seen as having been created in response to the expansion and consolidation of the European Economic Community (EEC) during the 1980s, which absorbed Spain and Portugal in 1986. As the region's largest trading partner the EEC/EC offered both a successful model for imitation and inspiration but also a potential economic threat that could harm the region's trade with higher tariff walls. Thus the AMU has been seen by people such as Melani Cammett as a form of defensive integration.[16] Offering more power and leverage in negotiations with the EU and other bodies[17] was seemingly an important goal of the new body, according to Abdulaziz Testas, providing a framework to coordinate policies regarding access to European markets, with the approach of the completion of the European Single Market in 1992 as a real spur to action.[18]

A slightly alternative viewpoint is put forward by William Zartman, who suggests that "Maghribi states draw together in an exercise of diplomatic integration when they need to emerge from a conflict which threatens the integrity of the region."[19] Both of these arguments have real merit in explaining the ups and downs of regional integration efforts. Yet at the same time, perhaps there were also some other genuine potentially positive impacts to derive from greater cooperation. Examining the AMU Constitutive Act and the Action Plans that went with it, we can see not only an ambitious agenda, especially in the economic sphere, but also real potential to encourage specialization rather than duplication of industries and exports. Rather than just leverage in negotiations with the EU or a stabilizing mechanism to reduce regional tensions, it is clear that cooperation also offered more positive reasons to come together over the longer term.

Structures

The institutional structures of the AMU are quite simple.[20] The executive body is the Presidential Council. This is modeled very much on the Arab League so it should be no surprise that under article 6 of the AMU's Constitutive Act decisions require unanimity and all of the AMU's other organs require some level of input from the Presidential Council. Indeed, article 6 states: "the Presidential Council is the sole body empowered to make decisions." This body meets biannually with the presidency rotating at the same interval. It is supported at the executive level by the Council of Foreign Ministers, which acts as a preparatory body for the Presidential Council, reviewing ideas for cooperation and action generated either by specialized ministerial groupings or other subordinate committees. In addition, under article 7 of the constitutive act, while not having a clear forum or specific place in the structure, the prime ministers are to meet "whenever so required." So far, the Presidential Council has only held six meetings (see Table 10.1). This lack of meetings since the first flush of the organization's youth is the reason most often cited for its failure.

This first, and clearly most important layer of the structure of the AMU is complemented by a *Comité de Suivi*, or Follow-Up Committee, whose job it is to submit studies to the Council of Foreign Ministers and implement resolutions adopted by the Presidential Council. There is also a Consultative Assembly, based in Algiers, comprising ten members from each state and meeting at least annually, which can make proposals to the executive organs and delivers opinions on draft resolutions of the Presidential Council.

Interestingly, there is also provision for a judicial organ, which is designed to act as a dispute settlement body in terms of the provisions

Table 10.1 AMU Presidential Council meetings

Location	Date
Tunis, Tunisia	21–23 January 1990
Algiers, Algeria	21–23 July 1990
Ras Lanouf, Libya	10–11 March 1991
Casablanca, Morocco	15–16 September 1991
Nouakchott, Mauritania	10–11 November 1992
Tunis, Tunisia	2–3 April 1994

and applications of the treaty, and for future agreements made by the AMU's member states. Surprisingly, article 13, which deals with this body, states that "its decisions will be executory and final." The judicial organ also acts as an advisory body on legal issues to the Presidential Council. Comprising two judges per state serving terms of six years and based in the Mauritanian capital Nouakchott, the court can hear cases brought by any member state or by the Presidential Council. On paper it represents an interesting experiment in mixed law, which given the right political environment could be a driving force in integration.[21]

The AMU's secretariat was originally supposed to move every six months to wherever the Presidential Council was meeting, but this was clearly impractical and it is now permanently headquartered in Rabat.[22] The secretariat is a less important body than those in many other international organizations because it interacts only with the Follow-Up Committee and the Special Ministerial Commissions. Its secretary-general was the Tunisian diplomat Habib Ben Yahia, who was replaced by the former Tunisian Foreign Minister Taieb Baccouche on 5 May 2016.[23] The secretariat is organized into five thematic sections: food safety; infrastructure; human resources; administrative and financial business; and information, political affairs and cabinet. These are largely to directly support the work of the Special Ministerial Commissions.

The Special Ministerial Commissions are designed to bring together groups of ministers to work on individual projects concerning largely functional cooperation. Thus, for example, there are committees for the governors of the central banks, and ministers of health. Away from the ministerial level and falling within the food security pillar there are a range of specialist councils working on cereals and vegetables, a permanent veterinary commission, and one on sustainable development and desertification.

In addition, the AMU also has the Maghreb University, the Maghreb Academy of Sciences (both based in Tripoli), and the Maghreb Bank for Trade and Investment (based in Tunis). These report directly to the Presidential Council and seemingly have no interaction with the secretariat.

From this brief overview we can see that the structure of the AMU has the ultimate safeguards present in the Arab League but at the same time differs in having a machinery that appears designed to continue to push for greater cooperation. At the fifth summit in Nouakchott, the Presidential Council decided to agree measures by a simple majority, except in the case of hostilities; however, given the absence of Presidential Council meetings since 1994, this has had little impact.

Economic, social, and cultural cooperation

Given the absence of Presidential Council meetings it is clearly sensible to lower our expectations of what the AMU can achieve. Having said this, however, in its first five years of life a great many schemes were passed, some of which are still functioning. So, for example, the AMU has established specialist energy committees to examine electricity cooperation and the development of renewable energy. The AMU also works with the separate framework of the *Comité Maghrébin de l'Electricité* (COMELEC), which works to strengthen the integrated electricity network of Maghreb countries.[24] In addition, there is now also AMU–Egypt cooperation on climate change and air pollution. This falls under the auspices of the Maghreb Environmental Charter, which was signed in Nouakchott in 1992.[25]

There have also been a range of practical initiatives, so for example, in January 2011 the Maghreb Virtual Science Library was launched in Algiers. The virtual library initiative is part of an AMU "effort to support development in science and technology by increasing the access to digitised scientific data and research, and encouraging partnership and networking."[26] In 2009 the AMU states along with France, Italy, Malta, Portugal, and Spain signed a digital education plan agreement.[27] The AMU has also worked on a comparative study of labor legislation within the union. Recently there have been concrete moves involving real investment, so in January 2013 the AMU launched a new investment bank focused on infrastructure with an initial US$100 million of capitalization and with advice from the IMF.[28]

Even in the absence of Presidential Council meetings the work of the Council of Foreign Ministers, the Special Ministerial Committees and the Follow-Up Committee have actually continued, albeit at times in fits and starts at the higher levels. Thus, for example, interior ministers have met regularly, especially since the Arab Spring.[29]

In addition, the AMU itself has taken the initiative and has signed agreements with other international bodies in order to fulfill its functions. For example, in 2011 it signed a cooperation agreement with the World Organization for Animal Health.[30] It regularly attends meetings in Brussels[31] and has been a useful joint coordinating body on issues of regional counter-terrorism while also working within wider international frameworks on security in the Sahel region, especially Mali, since 2011.[32]

Problems and prospects

Essentially, the AMU has been in the deep-freeze since 1995. Clearly there remain major obstacles to the proper functioning let alone to the concrete development of the AMU. The Western Sahara dispute, which goes through quiet spells, always has the potential to derail cooperation.[33] In recent years Morocco has attempted to end the dispute by offering the territory extensive autonomy in return for dropping claims to independence. This has not been accepted. The tensions between Algeria and Morocco remain at the heart of the obstacles to the AMU's progress, although both sides have made some efforts to make progress and Morocco backed away from an attempt to destroy the AMU in 1995.[34] This at least means that the organization has been able to continue elements of its work and has received funding.

Cooperation over trade in the region is clearly not the basis for successful regional integration. This is because there are insufficient incentives in this area and serious structural problems.

First, one must take into account the lack of consistency in the region's economies, the traditional focus on socialism in Algeria compared to freer forms of trade and the market economies of Tunisia and Morocco. Libya's bizarre political and economic systems under Ghadaffi would always have the potential to act as obstacles to cooperation[35] and the civil conflict across the country in the wake of the Arab Spring makes deep reform difficult. Likewise, Mauritania's weak economy and differences in GDP, and GDP per capita, make it difficult both to absorb and for it to implement many of the AMU's initiatives.[36] Things are further complicated by Mauritania and Libya's involvement in other African integration projects, which could cause legal, technical, and political difficulties for the AMU.

Second, there simply is not the volume of intra-regional trade for there to be enough of an economic push factor in deepening regional economic cooperation. Intra-regional trade represents only around 3 percent of the region's exports.[37] While there are many reports which suggest that intra-regional trade potential is lucrative enough for it to warrant attention, it is likely that a combination of political impediments, existing path dependencies and mindsets towards trade with Europe, along with competition (especially between Morocco and Tunisia) for FDI, all act as powerful counterbalances to the deeper investment of political capital in concrete moves towards economic integration. Likewise it seems the states have also been distracted by a range of other economic opportunities such as GAFTA with the Arab League, Morocco's free trade agreement with the United States, and the Agadir Agreement between Morocco, Tunisia, Egypt, Jordan, and the EU, in the absence of progress with the AMU.

This is clearly a shame as there is real potential in the AMU, especially between the economies of Morocco, Tunisia, and Algeria, which "share a robust and meaningful relation binding together their macro economies, their financial markets, and their monetary policies." Indeed it seems that the AMU has made some difference in terms of trade and economics with evidence suggesting that it "has apparently strengthened economic and financial ties among countries in the region."[38]

It is obvious that the AMU has largely been a disappointment, which has essentially been caused by it remaining an instrument of the states of the region. Its prospects for further development are thus entirely dependent upon regional relations improving dramatically.[39] Having said that, it is clear that "the Arab Maghreb Union ... has done a great deal to bring Maghreb countries closer to one another by establishing mechanisms for exchanges and common policies."[40] There have been increased attempts at reviving moves towards the free trade zone within the AMU from around 2005 onwards[41] and there is no shortage of reports on how the AMU can be revived.[42] The Arab Spring certainly seems to offer more hope (in both the short and longer term) in this regard than has been present for quite some time, with a dramatically increased number of meetings at a much higher profile than in many years.[43] Indeed in the longer term, as Yahia Zoubir suggests, current economic, social, security, and financial concerns may translate into both short- and long-term incentives for more meaningful cooperation.[44]

Finally it should also be noted that the new secretary-general, Taieb Baccouche, while a former Tunisian foreign minister, held that post for only one year—2015. Before that he made a career as a political activist, trade unionist, and academic; he was prominent in the revolution, helping found the political party *Nida Tounes*, which won almost 38 percent of the vote in the 2014 Tunisian parliamentary elections. In short, his background and drive could be a useful spark for the AMU in the coming years.

Conclusion

The AMU represents a rather depressing chapter in the story of the IOs of the Middle East. What began with such promise largely fizzled out in just five years. While the organization still survives, it has found it impossible to overcome the regional environment, which remains hostile to meaningful cooperation. Since 1995 the AMU has tried hard to continue cooperation as best it can, and while its institutional structures make it difficult for real progress to be made in the absence of Presidential Council decisions (impossible if there are no meetings), other elements of the organization have continued. Thus the various Special Ministerial Commissions have continued to meet, the AMU secretariat has continued to function in a range of useful ways, and some of the initiatives that got underway in those earlier, more hopeful years have proceeded and evolved. Having survived its years in the wilderness, the sheer tenacity of this small body can only be admired. It is difficult to see quite how it could now be uninvented, as it has set a benchmark for the sub-regional cooperation that is still desired by many in the Maghreb. Perhaps, with the Arab Spring having removed Ghadaffi from Libya, brought democracy to Tunisia and greater representation to Moroccan politics, as the region evolves, along with these changes will come new opportunities for trust and greater cooperation.

Notes

1 Article 17 of the Constitutive Act of the AMU allows membership for "other states of the Arab Nation, or the African Community." In November 1994 Egypt applied to join the AMU but has not yet been accepted.

2 Cited in: William Zartman, "The Ups and Downs of Maghrib Unity," in *The Arab Dilemma: The Politics and Economics of Arab Integration*, ed. Michael Hudson (New York: Columbia University Press, 1999), 171.

3 Ahmed Aghrout and Keith Sutton, "Regional Economic Union in the Maghreb," *The Journal of Modern African Studies* 28, no. 1 (1990): 115–139.

4 I say inspired here, of course, because while unions that merged states were supported as essential stepping stones towards a unified Arab State by many Arab Nationalists, there was some hostility towards this form of integration but even more so to projects that might Balkanize Arabs into sub-regional groupings.

5 Ghadaffi's meddling in the internal affairs of neighbors is of course legendary. His implication in a 1971 coup attempt in Morocco was especially damaging to trust and cooperation in the Maghreb.

6 For an in-depth examination of Moroccan-Algerian tensions see: Yahia H. Zoubir, "Algerian-Moroccan Relations and their Impact on Maghribi Integration," *The Journal of North African Studies* 5, no. 3 (2000): 43–74.

7 Zartman, "The Ups and Downs of Maghrib Unity," 176.

8 Also in 1983 Algeria, Tunisia and Mauritania came together, this time signing a treaty. See: Habib Meliani, "Le traité de fraternité et de concorde de 1983, ou un nouveau droit de la coopération maghrébine," *Annuaire de l'Afrique du Nord* XXIV (1985): 89–99.

9 Aghrout and Sutton, "Regional Economic Union in the Maghreb," 115.

10 Algeria settled a number of border disputes with Tunisia during the 1980s, for example.

11 Zartman, "The Ups and Downs of Maghrib Unity," 177.

12 Aghrout and Sutton, "Regional Economic Union in the Maghreb," 119.

13 Aghrout and Sutton, "Regional Economic Union in the Maghreb," 132–133.

14 Melani Cammett, "Defensive Integration and Late Developers: The Gulf Co-operation Council and the Arab Maghreb Union," *Global Governance* 5, no. 3 (1999): 391.

15 Claire Brunel, "Maghreb Regional Integration," in *Maghreb Regional and Global Integration: A Dream to Be Fulfilled*, ed. Gary Hufbauer and Claire Brunel (Petersen Institute for Global Economics, Policy Analyses in International Economics No. 86, 2008), 7.

16 Cammett, "Defensive Integration and Late Developers," 379–402.

17 The preamble states: "Aware of the fact that by virtue of this integration UMA will have a significance which will allow it to play an active role in the world balance of power through the consolidation of peaceful relations at the heart of the world community and through the strengthening of world security and stability."

18 Abdulaziz Testas, "The Production Impact of Economic Integration: A Comparison Between the EU and the AMU," *Development Policy Review* 16, no. 1 (1998): 61–72; and Abdulaziz Testas, *Problems and Prospects for Economic Integration in the Maghreb (North Africa)*, unpublished PhD thesis (University of Leeds, 1996).

19 Zartman, "The Ups and Downs of Maghrib Unity," 177.

20 The text of the AMU Treaty is available [in French] at: www.uneca.org/sites/default/files/uploaded-documents/ORIA/treaty_establishing_the_arab_maghreb_union_2.pdf.

21 Lazhar Bouony, "La Cour Maghrébine de Justice," *Revue Belge de Droit International* (1992/3): 351–373.

22 The secretariat remains very modest having begun with only 16 staff. Its offices being located in just a few small buildings near the center of Rabat.

23 Kamailoudini Tagba, "Maghreb: Taieb Bacchouche, New Chairman of Arab Maghreb Union," *The North Africa Post*, 6 May 2016, http://northafricapost.com/12050-maghreb-taieb-bacchouche-new-chairman-arab-maghreb-union.html.

24 Hussein Razavi, Emanuele Nzabanita and Emanuele Santi, "The Energy Sector," in *Unlocking North Africa's Potential through Regional Integration: Challenges and Opportunities*, ed. Emanuele Santi, Saoussen Ben Romdhane and William Shaw (Abidjan and Tunis: The African Development Bank, 2012), 43, www.afdb.org/fileadmin/uploads/afdb/Documents/

Project-and-Operations/Unlocking%20North%20Africa%20RI%20ENG%20FINAL.pdf.

25 "Regional Co-operation on Air Pollution and Climate Change in the Arab Maghreb Union and Egypt," *Atmospheric Pollution Forum*, www.unep.org/transport/pcfv/PDF/Tunis-Concept-Note_En.pdf.

26 Joao Duarte Cunha and Anja Linder, "Human Development," in *Unlocking North Africa's Potential through Regional Integration: Challenges and Opportunities*, ed. Emanuele Santi, Saoussen Ben Romdhane and William Shaw (Abidjan and Tunis: The African Development Bank, 2012), 149, www.afdb.org/fileadmin/uploads/afdb/Documents/Project-and-Operations/Unlocking%20North%20Africa%20RI%20ENG%20FINAL.pdf.

27 Wagdy Sawahel, "North Africa: Digital Education Plan Approved," *University World News*, no. 39, 18 October 2009, www.universityworldnews.com/article.php?story=20091015174431205.

28 "Arab Maghreb Union Launches Investment Bank," *Al Jazeera*, 10 January 2013, www.aljazeera.com/news/middleeast/2013/01/2013110101120697531.html.

29 "Terrorism Dominates Arab Maghreb Union Meeting," 26 April 2016, www.middleeastmonitor.com/20160426-terrorism-dominates-arab-maghreb-union-meeting/.

30 Available at: www.oie.int/fileadmin/Home/eng/About_us/docs/pdf/accords/UMA_ENG.pdf.

31 See for example: "European Parliament Resolution on Relations Between the European Union and the Arab Maghreb Union: A Privileged Partnership," (2001/2027(INI)), www.europarl.europa.eu/RegData/seance_pleniere/textes_adoptes/definitif/2002/06-11/0296/P5_TA(2002)0296_EN.pdf.

32 Interview, the head of the UK's Sahel Task Force, London, 19 June 2013.

33 Stephen Zunes, "Algeria, the Maghreb Union, and the Western Sahara Stalemate," *Arab Studies Quarterly* 17, no. 3 (1995).

34 For more detail on these efforts at reconciliation see: Robert Mortimer, "The Arab Maghreb Union: Myth and Reality," in *North Africa in Transition: State, Society and Economic Transformation in the 1990s*, ed. Yahia Zoubir (Gainesville, FL: University Press of Florida, 1999), 183–189.

35 Thus, for example, the AMU's consultative act contains only two footnotes, one of those is purely to explain the difference in the Libyan calendar under Ghadaffi which began on the date of the death of the Prophet Muhammed and named its months not by either the Western or the Muslim names but by ones of Ghadaffi's own devising, thus for example, February was *Annanouar* or "Flowers."

36 Kalid Sekkat, "Regional Integration Among the Maghreb Countries and Free Trade with the European Union," Working Paper 9504 (Cairo, Economic Research Forum, November 1994), 13.

37 Luis Martinez, "Algeria, the Arab Maghreb Union and Regional Integration," *Euromesco Papers*, no. 59 (October 2006): 6, www.euromesco.net/euromesco/images/59_eng.pdf.

38 Ali Darrat and Anita Pennathur, "Are the Arab Maghreb Countries Really Integratable? Some Evidence from the Theory of Cointegrated Systems," *Review of Financial Economics* 11, no. 2 (2002): 79–90, at 79.

39 Daniel Labaronne, "Les difficultés de l'intégration économique régionale des pays maghrébins," *Mondes en développement* 163, no. 3 (2013): 99–113.

40 Ali Yahyaoui and Mustapha Mezghani, "Information and Communication Technologies," in *Unlocking North Africa's Potential through Regional Integration: Challenges and Opportunities*, ed. Emanuele Santi, Saoussen Ben Romdhane and William Shaw (Abidjan and Tunis: The African Development Bank, 2012), 173, www.afdb.org/fileadmin/uploads/afdb/Documents/Project-and-Operations/Unlocking%20North%20Africa%20RI%20ENG%20FINAL.pdf.

41 Soumia Yousfi, "Maghreb Union Takes First Step Toward Creating Free-Trade Zone," *Al Monitor*, 20 September 2012, www.al-monitor.com/pulse/politics/2012/09/maghreb-union-moves-toward-greater-economic-cooperation.html#.

42 See for example: Wafa Ben Hassine, "Arab Maghreb Union: Overcoming Competition in Favor of Cooperation (Part II)," *Jadaliyya*, 17 September 2015, www.arabic.jadaliyya.com/pages/index/22675/arab-maghreb-union_overcoming-competition-in-favor (this article has attracted more than 850 comments in less than 12 months).

43 See for example: Lahcen Achy, "The Arab Spring Revives Maghreb Integration," *Carnegie Middle East Center*, 6 March 2012, http://carnegie-mec.org/2012/03/06/arab-spring-revives-maghreb-integration; and Younes Hassar, "Reviving the Maghreb Union," *Al Shawq al-Awsat*, 7 June 2013, http://english.aawsat.com/2013/06/article55304821/reviving-the-maghreb-union. *Al Jazeera* also conducted a conference on this theme, the proceedings of which are available here: http://studies.aljazeera.net/en/events/2013/04/201342104624548637.html.

44 Yahia Zoubir, "Tipping the Balance Towards Intra-Maghreb Unity in Light of the Arab Spring," *The International Spectator: Italian Journal of International Affairs* 47, no. 3 (2012): 83–99.

11 The Arab League, Gulf Cooperation Council, and the Arab Spring

The surprising rebirth of the Arab League as a security forum and the emergence of both the League and the GCC onto the international stage promoting varied types of humanitarian intervention in both Libya and Syria, as well as more covert efforts to promote dialogue and transition elsewhere in the region was perhaps one of the most interesting aspects of the Arab Spring. Given the importance of the uprisings in changing perceptions of the importance of the region, and the surprising role of the Arab League in sanctioning various interventions in Libya and Syria, as well as the key role taken by the GCC in Yemen and elsewhere, it is essential to examine the drivers behind the interventionist rhetoric coming from the staid and conservative IOs of the Middle East. The chapter begins by exploring the dynamics behind the new approaches to regional security governance displayed in 2011 and 2012, examining the impact and importance of these two regional international organizations, and discussing the reasons why these organizations were used as important arenas in the first part of the Arab Spring. The second half of the chapter explores why this interventionism proved to be short lived and briefly explores the longer-term impact of the Arab uprisings on the prospects for cooperation in both the League and the GCC.

The events

The outbreak of the Arab Spring in early 2011 posed a number of problems for both the Arab League and the Gulf Cooperation Council.

Having essentially remained what some observers described as "auto-crats clubs,"[1] suddenly being forced to deal with the rapid spread of revolutions throughout the region, especially as they became increas-ingly violent and threatened the rule of regimes that had in many cases been entrenched for decades, was to offer a whole range of dilemmas. That these organizations eventually took an activist stance in some cases was a surprise to a number of observers. The activism displayed by the Arab League and the GCC, especially in the cases of Syria and Libya had important consequences for the region and for international relations as a whole. There is a widely held contention that it was pure self-interest on the part of a number of the members of these organi-zations which drove this change. By examining how these decisions were affected by the wider geopolitical situation in the Middle East and then examining the important role played by considerations of internal security on the part of many states, we can build up a picture of how the League and GCC were essential tools for regimes con-cerned about their own survival to appear in control, to shape the agenda, and to secure their foreign policy interests. The chapter then juxtaposes this realist and regime survivalist viewpoint by examining the extent to which the activism of these two regional international organizations was driven by a sense of duty and humanitarianism, but also by continuing pan-Arabist sentiments.

The Arab League and GCC face the Arab Spring

The outbreak of protests in Tunisia in December 2010 did not appear to be anything too extraordinary but the speed at which events spiraled out of control left everyone rather breathless. By 14 January 2011 Tunisian President Zine el-Abidine ben Ali had fled to Saudi Arabia. At this early stage there appeared to be little need for either the Arab League or the GCC to do anything; indeed, there was little time for such ponderous organizations to react to such unexpected and unpre-cedented events. By giving ben Ali asylum, Saudi Arabia, a key player in both organizations, had in a sense facilitated a relatively bloodless transition in Tunisia. The first official reaction from the League to the events in Tunisia came during the Arab economic summit in Sharm el-Sheikh, which by coincidence was taking place from 16–19 January 2011. The host of the summit, Egyptian President Hosni Mubarak, made no explicit reference to the situation in Tunisia in his opening address, choosing to talk instead about threats to Arab national security because of lack of development in what appeared to be a coded recognition of the economic demands of the protestors, rather than any engagement with their political demands for freedom and justice. The then secretary-general of the League, Amr Moussa, was rather more blunt, stating his belief that "[t]he revolution that happened in Tunisia is not far from the subject of this summit. The Arab soul is broken by poverty, unemployment and general recession ... The political problems, the majority of which have not been fixed ... have driven the Arab citizen to a state of unprecedented anger and frustration."[2] He warned that "the Tunisian revolution is not far from us."[3]

In response to the emerging crisis, which was by now beginning to spark protests in Egypt, Jordan, Oman, Yemen, and Libya, the Arab League reached for the same old set of tools and promised the creation of a US$2 billion fund to boost economies and create jobs. This was, in fact, the re-announcement of an initiative that had already been proposed at a 2009 summit in Kuwait and had still not materialized. This time, though, promises of finance were made with alacrity, since governments wished to be seen to be doing something and because giving money was a much easier option than talking about the complex causes of the revolution in Tunisia and the protests that were emerging elsewhere. Both Saudi Arabia and Kuwait immediately pledged $500 million each for the fund. As ever with these kinds of Arab League initiatives there was no concrete form to how the idea might be implemented and the money disbursed in a way which might actually have some impact on the ground.

The outcome of the summit was viewed with the usual disdain by the Arabs in the streets, who had heard these kinds of promises before. The revolutions and protests were never likely to be halted because of a vague promise of jobs and development. The protests were becoming increasingly caught up in notions of freedom rather than demands for development; the narrative was changing and it would take some time for Arab leaders to understand quite how far-reaching the changes were going to be. The outcome of the Arab League summit was little more than the usual rhetoric and platitudes. In the final summit communiqué there was merely a call "for all political forces, representatives of Tunisian society and officials to stand together and unite to maintain the achievements of the Tunisian people and realize national peace."[4] This bland statement indicates the fear and paralysis among Arab League states; they simply did not have the tools to make a difference and their well-worn rhetoric failed to have any effect on the streets. The League's member states had lost control of the agenda and simply did not know how to engage with the discourses of freedom and justice, which were now driving the protests.

The GCC's reaction to events in Tunisia was essentially non-existent, it was left to individual states to issue statements, which were all remarkably similar to the sentiments expressed by the Arab League. Secretary-General Amr Moussa, on the other hand, was again more clear-sighted, stating in a press conference that "Tunisia's events are serious events and a development that has historical dimensions, and shapes the beginning of one era and the end of another."[5]

It is clear that there is something of a divergence between the League as an international organization with its own ethos and values, and the states that make up the League. This is, of course, in common with many international organizations, but in the case of the Arab League it is especially marked. It is difficult at times to divine the processes of the League itself as opposed to those of the member states, as the member states appear to maintain a much tighter rein over the secretariat of the League than is the case in other international organizations with more diverse funding streams, greater cultures of openness, and which are exposed to more opportunities for public scrutiny. At the time, though, it felt like the League itself had a much greater awareness of the gravity of the situation than the autocratic leaders who made up much of its membership.

In the aftermath of the Arab League economic and development summit, events in Egypt began to gather pace, and by 25 January 2011 mass protests had broken out in Tahrir Square. Just 17 days later, on 11 February, Hosni Mubarak stepped down as Egypt's president and retreated to one of his houses near Sharm el-Sheikh. The collapse of the Egyptian regime further emboldened protesters elsewhere in the region and led to larger and larger protests. The new focus for protests in the region, though, was Bahrain, somewhere far too close to home for the GCC states. Protests were also escalating rapidly in Yemen and looked likely to take hold in Morocco and Algeria as well.

Reaction to the fall of Mubarak was muted; it seemed as if the League and the GCC were paralyzed by the turn of events. Where in the past one might have expected there to be a desire to take some steps to prevent one of their own being overthrown, other Arab States did very little to support Mubarak beyond rhetoric. The Arab League itself did not even have an "emergency meeting" until 14 February, after Mubarak had resigned.

Amr Moussa, on the other hand, given the wider inaction, and with the certain freedom that his term in office would come to an end anyway in June 2011, seized the opportunity to express his views on the Egyptian revolution, in an interview with the website Democracy Now. In striking rhetoric he stated:

The young people, or the under people, of Egypt have expressed themselves differently. They talked about freedom. They talked about the future. They talked about the role of Egypt. This is very important. And this is the message. This is the message that now people can change. When they want to change, they are determined to change, they succeed in changing. This message is going around all over the world, and in particular in this region.[6]

At this point it is important to note that Moussa was much touted as a potential new Egyptian president and hinted strongly that he was likely to run.[7] Being seen to be on the side of the revolution, therefore, was essential to this process. The effect of the views of the secretary-general of the Arab League on the reactions of the League itself is difficult to quantify but it clearly helped to shape the wider discourse, and with the inertia inside the organization, undoubtedly aided others who were beginning to see the opportunities, as well as the threats, that the Arab Spring brought with it.

The fall of ben Ali, and more significantly Mubarak, meant that there was a certain vacuum created in the Arab League. The decapitation of two longstanding leadership figures in the League left it briefly paralyzed before others saw an opportunity to direct the League. With protests erupting in most member states, many leaders were focused on what was happening at home, so for those states that had escaped the contagion there was the perfect opportunity to take the lead. Thus far, events in the Arab Spring had been largely peaceful. It was in Libya that a new dimension to the evolving situation was to emerge—one which further enhanced the opportunity for determined actors to shape the discussion.

Events in Libya: The realist interpretation

The fall of the Tunisian regime was met with a fiery denunciation by Colonel Ghadaffi on 14 January 2011, who said in a television broadcast, "you have suffered a great loss ... there is none better than Zine to govern Tunisia." In a clear message to his own people he went on to say: "Tunisia, a developed country that is a tourist destination, is becoming prey to hooded gangs, to thefts and fire."

Soon what Ghadaffi described as "chaos with no end in sight" was to reach Libya.[8] The Arab Spring in Libya did not begin to take full flight until almost a month after Ghadaffi's broadcast on 16 February when major protests erupted in Libya's second city, Benghazi, after the arrest of a human rights activist. Over the following days the government initiated a widespread crackdown on protests and dissent, with dozens killed and injured. Protests soon spread from the east to Zintan, near the capital. The escalation of the protests and the violence of the repression from the regime was the worst yet seen in the Arab Spring. As protests began to build even in Tripoli, on 20 February, Ghadaffi's son Saif al-Islam made an incendiary speech on state television stating: "We will fight until the last man, the last woman, the last bullet."[9]

The scene was thus set not for exile or resignation, as in Tunisia and Egypt, but brutality and civil war. This impression was confirmed in a rambling and vitriolic address by Ghadaffi to the nation on 22 February, as the rebels managed to secure control of Benghazi and protests shaded into armed rebellion. In the now famous and widely parodied[10] address, Ghadaffi stated: "I will die as a martyr at the end ... I shall remain, defiant. Muammar is leader of the revolution until the end of time."[11] He continued: "we will hunt down these greasy rats inch by inch, house by house, home by home, alleyway by alleyway."[12] The revolution in Libya meanwhile was making increasing gains, shutting off oil exports on 24 February and occupying large parts of the east of the country. It had also gained traction in Tripoli with large demonstrations in the center of the city. At the same time alarming tales were emerging of acts of brutality and massacres, perpetrated by Ghadaffi's forces and mercenaries. By 27 February rebels had gained control of the city of Zawiyeh just 30 miles from Tripoli, startling progress since the start of the uprising just two weeks earlier, and also declared the formation of the National Transitional Council, an interim government for Libya.

The situation began to turn against the rebels soon after Ghadaffi's speech, however, as government forces began the fight back. Zawiyeh was one of the first targets in their sights and was surrounded and bombarded on 5 March. By 10 March rebel forces had been defeated in Zawiyeh and had retreated from the strategic oil town of Ras Lanuf. On 12 March government forces had defeated the rebels in Brega and the road was now open for an assault on Benghazi, the capital of the revolution. As the tide turned it looked increasingly likely that Ghadaffi would get the opportunity to carry out his threats against the rebels.

It is at this juncture of the campaign that the Arab League and the GCC came into play. Ironically, Libya was the chair of the Arab League at the time of the unrest and postponed indefinitely the summit that had been due to take place.[13] Ordinarily this might have given the League the perfect excuse not to have to take a position on the events in Libya, but on this occasion something quite different happened. On 22 February the League voted to suspend Libya. Amr Moussa condemned "crimes against the current peaceful popular protests and demonstrations in several Libyan cities" and expressed concern over the "grave breach of human rights" in the country.[14] Just four days later, on 26 February, the UN Security Council unanimously passed a resolution condemning Ghadaffi's violence against protestors, imposed sanctions, and referred the dictator to the International Criminal Court.

Momentum against the Ghadaffi regime was building rapidly at this point. On 6 March a GCC foreign ministers meeting issued a statement, which said: "The Gulf Cooperation Council demands that the UN Security Council take all necessary measures to protect civilians, including enforcing a no-fly zone over Libya."[15] The foreign ministers also urged Arab League foreign ministers "to shoulder their responsibilities in taking necessary measures to stop the bloodshed."[16] At its extraordinary meeting on 12 March the Arab League duly passed a resolution calling on the UN to pass a resolution imposing a no-fly zone.[17] Amidst inevitable attempts to pretend that this did not include the use of foreign forces, it was a remarkable step for an organization like the League to essentially authorize the Western powers at the very least to impose a no-fly zone, and in all probability to bomb the forces of a fellow Arab ruler.

On 17 March 2011, UN Security Council resolution 1973 was adopted imposing a no-fly zone over Libya and authorizing "all necessary measures" to protect civilians. It is highly unlikely that Russia and China would have abstained from this vote meaning that the resolution passed, had it not been for the direct support of the GCC and the Arab League. What followed, after commencement of the aerial campaign two days later, was the inevitable mission creep beyond what had so clearly been intended by the vast majority of Arab States that supported the no-fly zone. Ghadaffi's forces were driven back from the outskirts of Benghazi, initially chased by the rebels until a stalemate took hold mid-way between Libya's two main cities.

On 20 March Secretary-General Amr Moussa attempted to backtrack on the League's support for intervention in Libya, saying: "what is happening in Libya differs from the aim of imposing a no-fly zone, and what we want is the protection of civilians and not the bombardment of more civilians."[18] His protest and subsequent emergency meeting of the League[19] produced no unified Arab position against the airstrikes but remained in favor of the no-fly zone, however. This was especially the case since it was not just political support for UN resolution 1973 provided by both the League and the GCC; countries from both organizations, the UAE, and Qatar,[20] not only participated in both the implementation of the no-fly zone and airstrikes against

Ghadaffi's forces but also committed special forces to ground operations, and provided weapons and training to the rebel groups. The collapse of the Ghadaffi regime did not come until many months later, when the stalemate was broken over the course of August and the rebels were able to take the capital with extensive support from allied airpower. The National Transitional Council was recognized by the UN on 16 September and Ghadaffi himself was captured and executed on 20 October.

There is no doubt, then, that the GCC declaration supporting a no-fly zone created real momentum against Ghadaffi, and that this, alongside the Arab League's resolution on 12 March, provided the political legitimacy that enabled the Security Council to press ahead. In effect, the GCC and Arab League appeared to have become gate-keepers for external interventions in the Middle East, thereby being catapulted into global political relevance. Unpacking these diplomatic interventions shows that the Arab League and GCC were important instruments used by key Middle Eastern states to provide political cover, which ensured that the vital UN resolution was passed. It put these states on the right side of history both rhetorically and, in some cases, directly. By opposing Ghadaffi's brutal and discredited dictatorship both the states and the organizations could begin to get hold of the agenda in the Arab Spring, enhance their legitimacy, and demonstrate that the narrative was not as simple as people vs. regimes. It also greatly helped that Ghadaffi had long been a pariah and had essentially abandoned Arab causes for African concerns in recent years. In addition, it is clear that the Gulf States, and in particular Qatar, Saudi Arabia, and the UAE, saw the Arab Spring not only as a security problem but also as a clear opportunity for them to increase their influence on the region and promote their own security interests. As Mehran Kamvara sees it, "the Arab Spring has provided an opening for the Gulf Cooperation Council as a group and for Saudi Arabia as a long-time aspiring leader of the Arab world to try to expand their regional influence and global profile."[21]

Events in Syria: The realist interpretation

Syria during the initial stages of the Arab Spring is a much less clear-cut case for the Arab League, in terms of its use in a realist sense by certain states, than is Libya. We must remember that Syria is considered to be a state that is core to the region and one which has long been a supporter of Arab Nationalism. Unlike Ghadaffi, Bashar al-Asad was not absolutely despised by his neighbors. In addition, difficult as it may be to remember now, the civil war in Syria did not begin in earnest during 2011. Asad's forces had of course used extreme brutality but there remained a chance for dialogue and to avert the sectarian strife, degradation, displacement, and slaughter that later came to characterize the Syrian conflict.

Accordingly from early on, the League was very much involved in attempting to broker a peace deal. One of the first acts of the Arab League Secretary-General Nabil al-Arabi, upon taking up his new post in July 2011, was to go to Damascus for talks with Asad. Indeed, Arab League representatives "pushed for a peace plan involving the withdrawal of troops from urban areas, the release of prisoners, and a pardon for opposition leaders. The Syrian government formally accepted this plan but then refused to implement it."[22] It was only after this that the League began to take measures against the Asad regime. As Mark Heller puts it, this stance by the Asad regime "was inevitably seen as intransigence, and almost a year into the Arab spring, Arab governments [were] perforce more attentive to public sentiments about how governments should or should not behave."[23] Heller, though, is also quick to point out the sectarian tensions between Iran and Saudi Arabia and the realist goals of many Arab States in condemning Asad in the aftermath of his refusal to cooperate. The geopolitical observations of most analysts driving subsequent League actions to sanction and isolate the Asad regime seem to have more resonance than revulsion at the human rights abuses perpetrated by Asad's forces.[24] As Bruce Maddy-Weitzman puts it, "the league's actions have been not so much a result of the 'Tahrir spirit' as of the hardheaded, geopolitical calculations by the bloc of mostly monarchical Sunni Arab States headed by Saudi Arabia and Qatar."[25] Accordingly it was the Gulf States that began to ramp up the pressure on the Asad regime from late summer onwards. This pressure and Asad's failings to engage with the League led to a vote to suspend Syria from the League on 12 November 2011.[26] Lebanon and Yemen opposed the motion while Iraq abstained. This important move was followed on 27 November by League sanctions—travel bans, banking transactions being halted, and asset freezes on individuals and companies. Despite this, the League still managed to create an Arab monitoring mission, which was deployed to Syria but later fell apart in the face of multiple provocations by the regime and interference in its work.[27] These clear and decisive steps, later symbolically added to in 2013 by allowing the Syrian opposition to take up the regime's seat at the League, demonstrate the League's symbolic and real power in sanctioning an important member.[28]

Syria and Libya: Norm diffusion, adaptation, and co-optation?

In any examination of the discourses surrounding GCC and Arab League support for action in both the Libyan and Syrian cases it is clear that the language used, the approaches called for, and the results of decisions taken by both bodies had real impacts on the ground. One is thus left with the question of how far global norms and discourses on humanitarian intervention and the responsibility to protect have diffused into the region on a number of levels (elite conceptions within states, within international organizations, and of course with the wider Arab public), and how this has affected these two regional organizations. Can it really be that the realist interpretations offered above for the League's and GCC's role in Syria and Libya are the only explanation? Even if the diffusion of international norms of humanitarian intervention themselves have had little impact, what about residual Arab Nationalist sentiments and Islamic notions of solidarity with the *umma*, which might help to shape attitudes at both elite and street levels. One need only look at the surprisingly generous reception of millions of Lebanese refugees in Jordan and Lebanon to see that a realist account cannot fully capture the dynamics driving policy in the region. Indeed, the very use of these frames of reference, while a powerful cloaking tool for other realities, does help to shape discourse and expectation within, and outside, the region, creating certain obligations which must be fulfilled. Having used the GCC and the League as their instruments, certain precedents have now been set.[29]

The discourses suggest a high degree of overlap with global norms and it would seem that there is a series of logical explanations for this. Indeed, as Martin Beck points out:

> The Arab League's recent policies of membership suspension toward Libya—and then Syria—are not the least remarkable because they are inextricably linked with a substantial alteration of the organization's declaratory policy, which could be an indicator of a shift in identity. As any deviation from the principle of non-interference must be legitimized by norms beyond the mere *raison d'être* of a state, the Arab League referred to values such as the obligation of a government to refrain from using disproportionate violence toward its own constituency.[30]

In addition to these potentially important shifts, the increased standing of the League has led to a reinvigoration of some of its historic attempts at mediation. The fact that the UN and the League have worked so closely together in the diplomatic efforts to attempt (despite meager results) to broker a peace agreement between the Asad regime and the various rebel groupings demonstrates the League's perceived importance and potential utility in bringing a solution for Syria.[31]

The GCC in Bahrain and Yemen

While the GCC and the League have taken an interventionist stance on Libya and Syria, it is noticeable that the League has refrained from involvement in Bahrain and has largely ceded responsibility for Yemen to the GCC. The solidarity displayed towards the Bahraini government in the face of its uprising, which was one of the earliest in the Arab Spring,[32] is quite startling when compared to the rhetoric around human rights abuses and the promotion of international norms when it came to Syria and Libya. Indeed, Manama saw no comment from its Gulf neighbors and active support from Saudi Arabia and the UAE in the deployment of the GCC's Peninsula Shield Force to assist its own armed forces with quelling the protests, and sending a strong message of support to the wider region in the light of Saudi–Iranian tensions, with the possible use of Bahrain's Shi'a citizens as a fifth column, potentially destabilizing Saudi Arabia as well as Bahrain.[33]

As Silvia Colombo argues, this obvious double standard represents in reality two sides of the same coin. By supporting fellow monarchical regimes, whether inside the GCC, or outside in terms of Jordan and Morocco, with substantial financial donations, alongside support for friendly regimes in Egypt and elsewhere, whilst at the same time seeking to expand the influence and brand of the GCC is in itself an additional form of security. In this sense being actively involved in seeking a smooth transition in its backyard in Yemen is crucial for security and perceptions of prestige, which add to the GCC's insulation.[34] Concerned that the protests in Yemen in early 2011 would spiral out of control and turn into a civil war, the GCC states began to attempt to broker a diplomatic solution to the standoff between President Ali Abdullah Saleh and the protestors as the country's tribes increasingly began to choose sides.[35] In November 2011 a Saudi-led deal was agreed, which would see Saleh go into exile in early 2012 and be replaced by his deputy, with a presidential election with just one candidate on the ballot. Given this, the GCC states' aim was to "hasten Saleh's departure from power, while trying to carve out a role for themselves that would enable them to influence Yemen's future trajectory."[36] This deal, seemingly a real success for the GCC at the time, has proven illusory in the longer term[37] as the country fractured anyway and is currently in the midst of a complex civil war, increasing the operative space for terrorist groups such as Al Qaeda in the Arabian Peninsula, which explicitly targets the Gulf States. In 2015 this situation led to direct intervention by a coalition of the GCC states (excluding Oman), which has seen extensive aerial bombardment, ground intervention with armored units and special forces, and a naval blockade, not to mention the more than 8,000 civilian casualties[38] and more than half of Yemen's civilian population, around 14 million people, suffering malnutrition and deep food insecurity.[39] All of this deployment of military might is primarily aimed at a coalition between the Al Houthi Shi'a and former President Saleh and his tribal and military followers. The essential failure of the GCC intervention in Yemen over the medium term is clearly a cautionary tale about the ability of the organization and its member states really to deploy collective diplomatic power.

After the Spring: Problems and prospects for the Arab League and GCC

The League and GCC "moment" in the limelight was relatively short-lived. As Ghadaffi was toppled and Syria degenerated into deeper violence, the wave of euphoria of 2011 and 2012 rapidly ebbed. In pushing for greater intervention in Syria against the Asad regime the Arab League lacked the ability to generate momentum given Iraq's Shiite government's support for the Asad regime and Lebanon's desire not to be dragged into matters that could cause internal tensions. Even within the GCC tensions emerged on the way forward, with Saudi Arabia and Qatar pushing for more involvement, actively funding and arming rebel groups, while the Kuwaitis and Omanis took a more cautious approach. In addition to these internal tensions between member states making a unified approach less likely, the marked decline in the West over commitment to any deep intervention in Syria was more than matched by a new Russian determination to support a client regime and a desire shared by China to prevent the kind of "abuse" of the no-fly zone in Libya to bring about regime change, clearly a norm that they do not want to encourage. This block on intervention at the UN level essentially removed the brief window that had been created by the need to have local legitimacy derived from the League and GCC before intervention became politically possible.

While this level of legitimacy and freedom of movement created in the early days of the Arab Spring was short-lived, it does not mean that both organizations have not continued to play a role in attempting to manage in some way the multiple security crises that face the region.

Thus, for example, the Arab League has provided important cover again in the fight against *Daesh*, the so-called "Islamic State," which emerged out of the chaos of the Syrian civil war and the Iraqi government's disastrous mishandling of its own Arab Spring-style protests from its Sunni community. The League's firm resolutions against the group have been helpful in legitimizing the coalition of Arab and Western states that has been attempting to degrade the group's capabilities since September 2014.[40] This cover has not always evolved into real military action, however, although there have been some successes in dealing with factors such as funding. In 2015, with the rise of *Daesh* in Libya in the security vacuum there, the Arab League responded to a call for assistance from the Libyan government which were requesting Arab airstrikes by making a collective call for Arab nations to confront *Daesh* in Libya militarily. Almost a year later the League has not managed to develop a strategy to tackle *Daesh* in Libya and there have been no coordinated Arab airstrikes.[41] Thus in some ways it seems that little has changed. There is still a lot of talk but little action from the League, yet the increased standing and role in creating legitimacy for Western intervention, even though it is more muted than in 2011, is still an important boost for the League and the GCC on a number of levels.

At a wider level, some have seen the Arab Spring as a potential opportunity for the League. With the emergence of more stable forms of sovereignty in much of the region and the decline of Arab Nationalism, strangely it may be that the regional order is more stable than in the past, despite the current turmoil, which may potentially enable the construction of a security framework for the region in which the League plays a significant role.[42]

Conclusion

Since the heady flush of the early period of the Arab Spring, when it seemed that the GCC and Arab League had never been more relevant on the regional and international stages, both organizations' ability to shape and influence events in the region have been sharply curtailed by regional rivalries, inherent caution, and wider international geopolitical realities. It now seems obvious given what we know of the limitations of both organizations that this level of influence and coherence could not be sustained. This does not mean that the Arab League and the GCC have not continued to play an important role in the post-Arab Spring era, indeed they have become more important forums when it comes to regional politics and security than they have been in decades.[43]

Notes

1 Bill Law, "How the Arab League Embraced Revolution," *BBC News*, 2 December 2011, www.bbc.co.uk/news/world-middle-east-15948031.

2 Salma El-Awardany, "Arab Economic Summit: What they Said in Sharm El-Sheikh," *Al Ahram Online*, 19 January 2011, http://english.ahram.org. eg/NewsContent/3/0/4362/Business/Arab-economic-summit-What-they-said -in-Sharm-ElShe.aspx.

3 "Arab Leaders Warned of 'Revolution'," *Al Jazeera*, 19 January 2011, www.aljazeera.com/news/middleeast/2011/01/2011119165427303423.html.

4 "In Quotes: Reaction to Tunisian Crisis," *BBC News*, 15 January 2011, www.bbc.co.uk/news/world-africa-12197681.

5 "Arab League Calls for Unity Among Tunisians," *Arab News*, 15 January 2011, www.arabnews.com/node/365509.

6 "Arab League Secretary General Amr Moussa on Egypt's Revolution, his Potential Presidential Candidacy and Popular Uprisings Across the Middle East," *Democracy Now*, 24 February 2011, www.democracynow.org/blog/ 2011/2/24/arab_league_secretary_general_amr_moussa_on_egypts_revolution_ his_potential_presidential_candidacy_and_popular_uprisings_across_the_midd le_east.

7 "Egypt Protests—Tuesday 1 February," *The Guardian*, 1 February 2011, www.guardian.co.uk/news/blog/2011/feb/01/egypt-protests-live-updates.

8 Richard Spencer, "Gaddafi: Bring Back Ben Ali, There's None Better," *The Daily Telegraph*, 16 January 2011, www.telegraph.co.uk/news/worldnews/a fricaandindianocean/tunisia/8262859/Gaddafi-bring-back-Ben-Ali-theres-none-better.html.

9 Ian Black, "Libya on Brink as Protests Hit Tripoli," *The Guardian*, 21 February 2011, www.guardian.co.uk/world/2011/feb/20/libya-defiant-protes ters-feared-dead.

10 See the techno remix at: www.youtube.com/watch?v=PaFtpagQWu0.

11 Ian Black, "Muammar Ghadaffi Urges Violent Showdown," *The Guardian*, 22 February 2011, www.guardian.co.uk/world/2011/feb/22/muammar-ga ddafi-urges-violent-showdown.

12 Isabel Kershner, "Qadaffi YouTube Spoof By Israeli Gets Arab Fans," *The New York Times*, 27 February 2011, www.nytimes.com/2011/02/28/world/m iddleeast/28youtube.html?_r=0.

13 "Libya Puts Off Arab League Summit Indefinitely Amid Unrest," *International Business Times*, 18 February 2011, www.ibtimes.com/libya-puts-ara b-league-summit-indefinitely-amid-unrest-268449.

14 Ola Galal, "Arab League Bars Libya from Meetings, Citing Forces, 'Crimes'," *Bloomburg*, 22 February 2011, www.bloomberg.com/news/arti cles/2011-02-22/arab-league-bars-libya-from-meetings-citing-forces-crimes-.

15 "Statement by the GCC Concerning Libya," *AFP*, 7 March 2011, www.lcil. cam.ac.uk/sites/default/files/LCIL/documents/arabspring/libya/Libya_13_AFP_ Report.pdf.

16 "GCC: Libya Regime Lost Legitimacy," *Al Jazeera*, 11 March 2011, www. aljazeera.com/news/middleeast/2011/03/2011310211730606181.html.

17 "The outcome of the Council of the League of Arab States meeting at the Ministerial level in its extraordinary session on the implications of the current events in Libya and the Arab position," 12 March 2011, http://resp

onsibilitytoprotect.org/Arab%20League%20Ministerial%20level%20statem
ent%2012%20march%202011%20-%20english(1).pdf.

18 "Arab League Head Says Wanted No-Fly Zone Not Bombs," *Jerusalem Post*, 20 March 2011, www.jpost.com/Breaking-News/Arab-League-hea d-says-wanted-no-fly-zone-not-bombs.

19 Moussa backtracked on his statement just two days later. See: Martin Chulov, "Arab League to Reiterate Backing for Libya No-fly Zone," *The Guardian*, 22 March 2011, www.theguardian.com/world/2011/mar/22/ara b-league-libya-no-fly.

20 Jordan also provided warplanes but these appeared to be symbolic and were excluded from combat operations, Kuwait provided logistical support and Sudan allowed over-flight rights.

21 Mehran Kamvara, "The Arab Spring and the Saudi-Led Counter-revolution," *Orbis* 56, no. 1 (2012): 96–104.

22 Mark Heller, "Syria and the Arab League: Moral Censure and Identity Politics," *INSS Insight* no. 294 (16 November 2011): 1, www.inss.org.il/up loadimages/Import/(FILE)1321474887.pdf.

23 Heller, "Syria and the Arab League," 1.

24 See for example: "The New Politics of Intervention of Gulf Arab States," *LSE Middle East Centre Collected Papers* 1 (2015), http://eprints.lse.ac.uk/ 61772/1/The%20new%20politics%20of%20intervention%20of%20Gulf%20Ara b%20states.pdf.

25 Bruce Maddy-Weitzman, "The Arab League Comes Alive," *Middle East Quarterly* (Summer 2012): 71–78, at 71.

26 Bill Law, "How the Arab League Embraced Revolution," *BBC News*, 2 December 2011, www.bbc.co.uk/news/world-middle-east-15948031.

27 Maddy-Weitzman, "The Arab League Comes Alive," 71–78.

28 Ian Black, "Syrian Opposition Takes Arab League Seat," *The Guardian*, 26 March 2013, www.theguardian.com/world/2013/mar/26/syrian-oppositio n-appeals-nato-support.

29 El Hassan bin Talal and Rolf Schwarz, "The Responsibility to Protect and the Arab World: An Emerging International Norm?" *Contemporary Security Policy* 34, no. 1 (2013): 1–15.

30 Martin Beck, "The End of Regional Middle Eastern Exceptionalism? The Arab League and the Gulf Cooperation Council after the Arab Uprisings," *Democracy and Security* 11, no. 2 (2015): 197.

31 For an in-depth examination of the role and potential of the League in the Syrian Crisis, see: Matthias Vanhullebusch, "The Arab League and Military Operations: Prospects and Challenges in Syria," *International Peacekeeping* 22, no. 2 (2015): 151–168.

32 On 17 February GCC ministers of foreign affairs gathered in Manama to express their solidarity with the regime openly. See: Toby Matthieson, *Sectarian Gulf: Bahrain, Saudi Arabia, and the Arab Spring that Wasn't* (Stanford, Calif.: Stanford University Press, 2013), 34.

33 Simon Mabon, "The Battle for Bahrain: Iranian-Saudi Rivalry," *Middle East Policy* 19, no. 2 (2012): 84–97.

34 Silvia Colombo, "The GCC and the Arab Spring: A Tale of Double Standards," *The International Spectator: Italian Journal of International Affairs* 47, no. 4 (2012): 110–126.

35 Clive Jones, "The Tribes that Bind: Yemen and the Paradox of Political Violence," *Studies in Conflict & Terrorism* 34, no. 12 (2011): 902–916.

36 Colombo, "The GCC and the Arab Spring," 120.

37 Tobias Thiel, "After the Arab Spring: Power Shift in the Middle East?: Yemen's Arab Spring: From Youth Revolution to Fragile Political Transition," *IDEAS Reports* SR011, LSE IDEAS (London School of Economics and Political Science, 2012), http://eprints.lse.ac.uk/43465/1/After%20the%20Arab% 20Spring_Yemen%E2%80%99s%20Arab%20Spring%28lsero%29.pdf.

38 "Yemen: Civilian Casualties Top 8,100 as Airstrikes and Shelling Continue, UN Reports," *UN News Centre*, 5 January 2016, www.un.org/apps/news/ story.asp?NewsID=52938#.V1RpG6T2amw.

39 Megan O'Toole and Ali Aboluhom, "Starvation in Yemen: 'We are hoping just to survive'," *Al Jazeera*, 29 November 2015, www.aljazeera.com/news/ 2015/11/starvation-yemen-hoping-survive-151129070729907.html.

40 "Arab League Issues Proclamation on ISIS," *CBS News*, 8 September 2014, www.cbsnews.com/news/arab-league-agrees-to-take-urgent-measures-to-combat -isis/.

41 Guy Taylor, "Arab League Agrees to Use Military Force Against ISIS in Libya, Unsure on Airstrikes," 18 August 2015, www.washingtontimes.com/ news/2015/aug/18/arab-league-agrees-use-military-force-against-isis/.

42 See: Farah Dakhlallah, "The League of Arab States and Regional Security: Towards an Arab Security Community?" *British Journal of Middle Eastern Studies* 39, no. 3 (2012): 393–412.

43 For some examination of the AMU in the context of the Arab Spring but more on the Mediterranean and EU response see: Peter Seeberg, "Old Dogs, New Tricks? The Role of Regional Organizations in the Mediterranean after the Arab Revolts," *Democracy and Security* 11, no. 2 (2015): 208–226.

Conclusion

- **The five questions**
- **The framework**
- **The future?**

If the Arab Spring reminded the world of the existence of the region's international organizations, this book has been an attempt to go beyond the often shallow appreciations of these bodies to explore their histories, contextual environment, and structure, while also examining their functions, achievements, and limitations. It is hoped that the volume raises awareness about the complexities of the bodies and stimulates further study of organizations that have been too readily dismissed in the past as "failures." As Silvia Ferabolli rightly observes, "it is remarkable how every piece of work produced on Arab regional dynamics adds another element to the doomed Arab region narrative; it is even more remarkable how the imposed silences towards the successes of Arab regionalism serve as further evidence of the Arab region making *failure*."[1] Viewing the region's IOs through the prisms of realism and neoliberal institutionalism alone clearly creates path dependencies, which then fail to capture the range of dynamics on display.

This conclusion begins by revisiting the five questions developed in Chapter 1, examining these individually and attempting to engage with their complexity through the use of the analysis developed within the chapters of this volume. The conclusion then reflects on the framework that has been loosely applied throughout this volume, and what the book's detail tells us about the utility of the different approaches that have been taken in the IR and Middle Eastern Studies literature. Finally, the book then concludes with some thoughts on the utility, and prospects for the Middle East's international organizations.

The five questions

1 To what extent are Arab IOs connected to, and independent from, the regional environment?

The region's international organizations are clearly deeply connected to the region's environment but have also been inspired by other attempts at regionalism, and in the case of the Arab League by the discussions and drafts that led to the formal creation of the UN just a few months after the League's foundation in 1945. Regional politics also strongly influences the programs, agendas, and direction of all three of the organizations. The GCC and AMU in particular seem to be directly driven in many ways by regional interactions, animosities, fears, and dreams. Yet what we have also seen is the way in which all three of these organizations have also been able to exhibit some measure of independence and autonomy from the vagaries of Middle Eastern politics, which have affected high-level decision making. Even the AMU has been able to continue to pursue some initiatives despite the break-down of trust between its member states. In another sense, the regional environment itself, in terms of the legacies of Arab Nationalism and pan-Arabism, has continued to play a profound role, manifesting itself in continued public sentiment for Arab cooperation (at the very least), and some form of integration even if this no longer really means the kinds of experiments at Arab unity made in the 1950s and 1960s. This legacy also strongly influences those who work directly for all three organizations, in my conversations with their employees over the years I have been continually struck by their determination to make Arab cooperation work, often despite their privately wry observations on the faults of the bodies for which they work. There is at least in some circles a clear will to develop the role and competences of all three IOs of the Middle East, which can only bode well for the future, no matter what the immediate regional political environment.

2 How has this hindered their genesis, design, and agency?

Having said this though, it is clear that the number one institution of the region, sovereignty, has and will continue to play a significant role in inhibiting the ability of the organizations to develop the kind of agency seen in other international bodies. The structures of all three organizations are carefully built to maintain real power in the hands of the member states. Some of the pessimism surrounding these organizations is real because they were constructed and remain focused in real terms on promoting the sovereignty norm, despite the, at times, rather ridiculous rhetoric and over-ambitious plans that accompanied the genesis and foundation of each of the three bodies.

3 What are the main similarities and differences between the region's IOs?

The AMU and the GCC, in particular, exhibit a great many features in common being more clearly attempts at unity (at least in rhetorical form) than the Arab League, which more closely mirrors organizations such as the UN than it does regionalist projects such as the EU. In more recent years the League has attempted to move down the hybrid route taken by the African Union but has made little headway in this regard. Both the GCC and AMU therefore look structurally very similar; indeed, it seems that the AMU had learnt some lessons from the GCC and was in part inspired by the successes of the GCC over the course of the 1980s. With their simple central structures, small memberships and secretariats, and focus on economic issues, both organizations exhibit real similarities. The differences between them in reality, though, are marked: the GCC represents a much more coherent entity with greater levels of trust and interdependence between its member states, while the Maghreb region appears to be the exact opposite. This perhaps demonstrates the truth behind the realist observation of the utility of having a common external threat, something which the Maghreb states have not really had; instead the threats have been internal, which has directly affected the AMU's ability to function. The Arab League on the other hand has perhaps a worse hand than the AMU. In trying to encourage cooperation between 22 diverse states with widely differing levels of economic success, different political systems, and a whole host of external alliances, which have linked the region to wider geopolitical struggles, it has faced significant difficulties. What the Middle East has ended up with, rather unsurprisingly, is a spectrum of organizations that reflect the diversity of the region.

4 What have been the main achievements of the region's IOs?

It is all too easy at times to find fault with these institutions. There are, without doubt, significant structural, attitudinal, and regional impediments to the successful projects of cooperation and integration that have been placed under the auspices of these three bodies. Yet despite these difficulties all three organizations have made real achievements both large and small. Often these achievements are obscure, functionalist, and at times, frankly, rather dull. The information gathering and sharing, the reporting, the accounting, the meetings and conferences, the training and the monitoring; the development of technical standards, the coordination of work programs, and the liaison with other bodies—the work that makes global governance actually function—is often overlooked. All three organizations are severely understudied and often do not help themselves through the external promotion of their work but this work is extensive and important in building trust and enabling the organizations' larger successes to come to fruition. The League has made real progress through GAFTA, has done important work in dispute resolution, and has an extensive network of specialized agencies, which have produced concrete results in many fields. The GCC, easily the region's most successful organization, has created a common citizenship, eliminated tariffs, created common standards in a range of areas, and spawned a network of joint companies and technical agencies, which are drawing the region more closely together in many key areas. The very existence of the Peninsula Shield Force is an important symbol of Gulf solidarity, something the UN has not been able to achieve, for example.

However, perhaps the most important success of these bodies is that they have become fixed in the minds of the region's population. The GCC has become a clear sub-regional identity and shorthand for the region. The League is the default body for regional engagement. Even the AMU has had an ideational and constructing impact upon its sub-region's politics. All three have become important political arenas, shaping and expressing the politics of the Middle East.

5 To what extent have the region's IOs evolved and changed over time?

Even these supposedly "insubstantial ... organizations,"[2] which "slumbered on"[3] with their focus on sovereignty have all evolved and changed over time. The GCC has consistently expanded its work and added a wide range of agencies and bodies to support its programs. Likewise, the Arab League has created a wide network of agencies, panels, and coordination bodies, working with the wider industrial, financial, and social bodies of both the member states and the wider Arab Unions and Arab cooperative bodies, which have been driven by businesses and the continuing pan-Arabist sentiment in the Middle East. Sometimes this institutional expansion is a useful cover, to appear to be making progress while in fact stalling for time. While the central core—the charters of the three organizations—have not changed at all, around this all three bodies have seen real expansion in their work. The

League in particular has had to partially reinvent itself several times. This dynamism is at times genuine, though, and demonstrates that these bodies are alive and evolving—indeed, attempts at stalling for time do have a habit of taking on a life of their own. The more bodies working on inter-Arab cooperation, the more likely that there will be some fruits to be derived from these endeavors.

The framework

The four-stage framework outlined in Chapter 1 was explicitly designed to force us to examine the Middle East's three international organizations through a range of prisms in order to give us the tools to see their efforts in the round. These four broad ways of exploring these IOs have been used as background analytical tools through this volume, and rather than being an attempt at theory building they have instead served to provoke reflection, comparison, and analysis. The *regional environment* frame has been a recurring one throughout the volume. By exploring the often fraught inter-state relations of the region, the obsession with sovereignty and the history of interaction, we have seen how regional relationships, alliances, and tensions have clearly had a profound impact upon cooperation. We have also continually reflected on the way in which these regional relations have important internal dimensions within the states. Often it is these internal–external security dilemmas that either have driven or impeded the work of the region's international institutions. Remembering the early stage of state build-ing, and often even state formation, that many of the region's states were undergoing is something that can be too easily lost in some of these analyses.

Thus it seems any analysis of the IOs of the Middle East must have an eye firmly fixed on the multi-layered games that comprise the regional environment, and both realist and constructivist tools are vital in engaging in this analysis. There is a danger, though, in becoming too preoccupied with the regional dimension and losing sight of the *multiple purposes that IOs play in international relations*. Thus we have seen through the course of this volume a mixture of their use as pure instruments of the states but also their important role as an arena, not just as a stage for symbolic posturing but also as an important clearing house and place of functionalist interaction. Likewise, despite the deliberate attempts of states to maintain a tight rein on the region's IOs there have also been cases in which the IOs have been able to deploy some level of agency, however limited when compared with other IOs elsewhere in the world.

Connected to this we have been better able to see some of these interactions and processes, both in terms of agency and the arena role played by the IOs of the region, when we bore in mind some of the various *theories of international organizations*. The clear instances of functionalism, the limited but present instances of spillover effects, and the models of potential change were all helpful. While this literature is often not specifically designed to account for the development and functioning of the IOs of the Middle East, being as it is focused largely on Western processes of IO function or examining the particular dynamics of the UN, these models have still proven important in explaining some of the dynamics that have been witnessed, even if on a smaller scale than those elsewhere.

Finally, the fourth frame was that of *organizational goals and achievements*. This is critical to any examination of the region's IOs and especially important in light of the general descriptions of the Arab League, GCC, and AMU as failures. By exploring the different ways in which achievements of these IOs are recognized or ignored (often linked to the particular theoretical framework used), the way the failures are analyzed and how the organization's explicit and implicit goals are used as benchmarks, we can see an additional range of prisms which offer markedly different insights into these bodies, and which have shaped the literature on these international organizations in profound ways. It is hoped that by using these four framing devices this volume has been able to provide a more nuanced perspective on the successes and failures, the opportunities and constraints presented to the international organizations of the Middle East.

The future?

Both the Arab League and the GCC have largely emerged unscathed from the Arab Spring. Considering both the scale and the suddenness of the uprisings, as well as the surprise they caused, it would seem odd that these supposedly weak bodies survived such an unprecedented shock. This reality perhaps belies their flexibility but also their surprisingly deep roots in the region's consciousness.

In terms of the short-term impacts of the Arab Spring upon the region and its three main international organizations, after the initial shock had worn off, the picture is somewhat mixed, for while survival in itself might seem like a positive result, these organizations remain important for the Middle East on both the practical and the ideational levels. In the immediate aftermath of the main wave of uprisings in 2011 the AMU saw a slight increase in activities,[4] and the Arab

League was more active and seemed to have regained a sense of direction, if not exactly much in the way of concrete progress. It is really the GCC that was most affected by the region's turmoil and tensions, with a whole host of new initiatives being announced.

In the longer term, though, it is clear that there is much work to be done to improve economic development and to increase the quality of people's lives both in terms of the practical requirements of better infrastructure, health care, and education, but also to increase Arabs' involvement in decision making and social and political freedoms. It seems likely that something has changed in a more profound way in the Middle East than the geopolitics of the region would currently suggest,[5] and that in the longer term the region will see changes that could reinvigorate its regional institutions as increasingly democratic states seek genuine cooperation. That transition seems quite some way off at present, however, leaving the region's international organizations facing both problems and opportunities. If there is increased political will to tackle these issues then these organizations could still play an important ideational, political, and functional role in improving people's lives.[6]

Notes

1 Silvia Ferabolli, *Arab Regionalism: A Post-Structural Perspective* (London: Routledge, 2015).
2 Charles Tripp, "Regional Organizations in the Arab Middle East," in *Regionalism in World Politics: Regional Organization and International Order*, ed. Louise Fawcett and Andrew Hurrell (Oxford: Oxford University Press, 1995), 308.
3 Bill Law, "How the Arab League Embraced Revolution," *BBC News*, 2 December 2011, www.bbc.co.uk/news/world-middle-east-15948031.
4 For some examination of the AMU in the context of the Arab Spring but more on the Mediterranean and EU response, see: Peter Seeberg, "Old Dogs, New Tricks? The Role of Regional Organizations in the Mediterranean after the Arab Revolts," *Democracy and Security* 11, no. 2 (2015): 208–226.
5 Nils Butenschøn, "Arab Citizen and the Arab State: The 'Arab Spring' as a Critical Juncture in Contemporary Arab Politics," *Democracy and Security* 11, no. 2 (2015): 111–128.
6 Khalid Sekkat, "Inter-State Tensions and Regional Integration: Could the Arab Spring Initiate a Virtuous Circle?" *Contemporary Arab Affairs* 7, no. 3 (2014): 363–379.

Select bibliography

L. Fawcett and A. Hurrell (eds), *Regionalism in World Politics: Regional Organization and International Order* (Oxford: Oxford University Press, 1996). An excellent introductory volume to regionalism with a useful chapter on the Middle East, with good coverage, a good example of a more pessimistic viewpoint on the regional IOs of the Middle East.

Silvia Ferabolli, *Arab Regionalism: A Post-Structural Perspective* (London: Routledge, 2015). A fascinating recent re-examination of the regionalism of the Middle East. The volume is not focused entirely upon the region's IOs but on the material and mental spaces of Arabism and their ongoing importance in shaping the region. The book is highly critical of existing accounts in the literature.

A.M. Gomaa, *Foundations of the League of Arab States* (Upper Saddle River, N.J.: Prentice Hall, 1977). An important examination of the politics and history surrounding the foundation of the League in 1945. Vital for understanding the diplomacy and regional environment that shaped the body's inception.

Michael Hudson, *The Middle East Dilemma: The Politics and Economics of Arab Integration* (New York: Columbia University Press, 1999). A very useful series of essays which explore all three regional IOs and beyond. Somewhat dated in parts now, this remains an essential volume.

Badr El Din A. Ibrahim, *Economic Cooperation in the Gulf: Issues in the Arab Gulf Co-operation Council States* (London: Routledge, 2007). A good, recent overview of elements of economic cooperation and integration in the Gulf States, and the successes, failures, and challenges facing the GCC in this crucial sphere.

Matteo Legrenzi, *The GCC and the International Relations of the Gulf: Diplomacy, Security and Economic Coordination in a Changing Middle East* (London: I.B. Tauris, 2011). An excellent book which is essential reading for those seeking to understand the GCC. It mixes history and IR theory, along with useful interviews to provide a theory-driven examination of the GCC.

Matteo Legrenzi and Cilja Harders, *Beyond Regionalism?: Regional Cooperation, Regionalism and Regionalization in the Middle East* (Farnham: Ashgate, 2008). This is an excellent edited volume with a diverse and thought-
provoking mix of theoretically and empirically driven analysis (and some
useful comparative studies) of the diverse range of attempts at cooperation
across the region.

Robert Macdonald, *The League of Arab States: A Study in the Dynamics of
Regional Organization* (Princeton, N.J.: Princeton University Press, 1965).
Perhaps the best existing volume on the League, very much outdated today
of course, but it provides an essential and very valuable viewpoint on the
League's problems at the height of the Arab Nationalist era.

Emilie Rutledge, *Monetary Union in the Gulf: Prospects for a Single Currency
in the Arabian Peninsula* (London: Routledge, 2008). A fascinating and brief
study of the problems facing the proposals for the creation of a single currency within the GCC. Somewhat more driven by economics than politics, it
is a very useful specific study of one (extreme) form of integration which
somehow demonstrates resonance for understanding a range of other
challenges.

Mark Zacher, *International Conflicts and Collective Security, 1946–77: United
Nations, Organization of American States, Organization of African Unity and
Arab League* (Westport, Conn.: Praeger, 1979). This is a useful overview of
how a range of IOs have attempted to manage issues of tension and conflict
between their member states. It is especially useful to compare the League's
performance with that of other regional bodies and the UN itself.

Index

Printed in Great Britain
by Amazon

23628238R00119